本书为：

2016年度教育部人文社会科学研究专项任务项目（项目编号：16JDSZ1010）

浙江省哲学社会科学重点研究基地"浙江省社会科学院浙学研究中心"2019重点课题阶段性成果（项目编号：19ZXZD03）

浙江省"文化育人"示范载体"阳明学堂—中华文化传播与体验基地"建设成果

用声音叙事：我是阳明青年

浙江大学宁波理工学院2016—2017年度"用声音叙事"活动调研报告

2016—2017年度"用声音叙事"活动指导委员会

主　　任　费英勤

副 主 任　梅乐和　黄光杰

主任委员（以姓氏拼音为序）　陈立明　谌晓煜　王小潞　杨祥龙　周树红

策　　划　蔡　亮

执　　行　韩晶晶　芦美丽　阮　征　王碧颖

编委与指导教师（以姓氏拼音为序）

蔡　亮　曹雅娟　韩晶晶　李　炜　芦美丽

Terry Needham (爱尔兰) Paula S. Robb (美国)

阮　征　王碧颖　王雪芹　徐志敏　张静燕

2016年度教育部人文社会科学研究专项任务项目
（项目编号：16JDSZ1010）
浙江省哲学社会科学重点研究基地"浙江省社会科学
院浙学研究中心" 2019重点课题阶段性成果
（项目编号：19ZXZD03）

用声音叙事：我是阳明青年
Beyond the Voices:
I'm a Practitioner of
Yangming Culture

名誉主编◎王小潞 陈立明
主　　编◎蔡　亮
副 主 编◎王碧颖 阮　征
英文校对◎Paula S. Robb（美国）　Terry Needham（爱尔兰）

ZHEJIANG UNIVERSITY PRESS
浙江大学出版社

有一种"思想"叫"行动"

An Idea for Action

蔡 亮

Cai Liang

近百年来，西方学者从未放弃以自家理论来解释中华大地上所经历的风雨或辉煌，然而，"不可预知性"让他们不断地陷入新的困惑和迷茫；四十年来，中国的改革开放在一往无前的探索中砥砺前行，然而，外部世界的质疑与唱衰之声始终如影相随。在新的历史起点，中国的和平崛起和民族复兴大业蓄势待发，然而，国际社会上一些更为复杂的"陷阱"和危局预言已如期而至。那个横亘于历史长河的命题再一次响起：什么样的内生动力可以让一个民族不断地在危急关头找到突围的方向？有人将之归因于东西方文明冲突中的调整和适应，有人将之归因于人类行为的意外后果，然而，他们却忽略了一个不争的事实：中华文化本身所具备的生命力、包容力、凝聚力、变革力和创造力。拥抱过游牧文明和海洋文明的农耕文明渗透着更具亲和、勇健和灵动的气质；衍生于这片沃土的儒家文化在兼容并蓄中既学会了否定和抛弃，也学会了守望和回归。我们将这种塑造民族魂魄的力量称为精神传承，这个民族在长期历史发展中形成的精神足以支撑起中华儿女向着未知领域的不懈探索。

中国历史发展的宏大叙事因为那些洋溢着民族"精气神"的群体更加鲜活，他们倔强而骄傲地用这种精神书写着历史，这就是一代代先辈孜孜以求的圣贤之学、君子之学、天下之学、亲民之学、身心之学、精一之学、明伦之学、经世之学、致用之学、格物之学、致知之学、力行之学、实干之学。有一种"思想"叫"行动"，这种精神，即学即道，即要即旨，承尧舜，接孔孟，继程朱，传陆王；千古圣圣，一以贯之。五百年前出生于宁绍大地的哲人王阳明将之归纳为良知之学，此良知二字可去除私欲之蔽，贯通天理人心。致良知，"即心即理，即知即行"，于物为发现规律本质，"天地感而万物生，实理流行也"；于人为完善道德意识，"是理也，发之于亲，则为孝，发之为君，则为忠，发之于友，则为信"。衍生于儒家传统的阳明精神或者阳明文化代表着一种思想与行动高度统一的世界观和方法论，其理论可以运用到广阔的人类实践领域，诸如治国理政、教书育人、商贾经营、百工技艺、科学探索等。于是，在现代语言的诠释之下，不同场域中的阳明精神便转化为科学精神、公益精神、企业家精神、工匠精神、公务员精神等。

阳明文化是中华优秀传统文化的重要组成部分，是中华民族向心力、凝聚力的重要源泉。习近平总书记高度赞扬阳明文化，2015 年 3 月全国"两会"期间，他指出："王阳明的心学正是中国传统文化中的精华，也是增强中国人文化自信的切入点之一。"宁波是王阳明的故乡，王阳明先生"致良知""知行合一"和"万物一体之仁"的思想是宁波贡献给世界的精神财富。深入挖掘和研究王阳明思想的现代启示，尤其是阳明文化在社会实践中的应用是高校弘扬和传播传统文化的重要举措。2008 年至今，浙江大学宁波理工学院外国语学院"用声音叙事"活动弘扬阳明先生"知行合一"和"良知体验美学"精神，以"行学至善"的理念指导专业实践教学活动，该模式主张语言学习者实施真实行动计划，服务社区群体需求，师生先后共同创作和完成书稿六部。2011 年"用声音叙事"活动创设"公益汉语课堂"，2013 年升级为"阳明学堂"，成为宁波市中华文化体验与传播基地。2015 年活动创立"阳明乐咖啡"公益品牌，项目与灵山慈善基金会合作，由听力残障人士与大学生团队共同运营。2016 年 2 月，"阳明学堂：行学至善、文以化人"获得宁波市宣传文化创新奖。

有一种"思想"叫"行动"，正如习近平总书记在谈及阳明思想时所指出的："知是基础、是前提，行是重点、是关键，必须以知促行、以行促知，做到知行合一。"2016 年 7 月，"用声音叙事"团队以"探索阳明文化海外传播"为主题开展专业实践和社会实践项目，团队成员走访了二十多位企业家、公益活动者、知名学者、非遗工艺传承人等，力求向大众介绍奋斗在不同领域的阳明文化传播者和践行者。通过探访践行民族精神的社会群体，青年学子聚焦宏大叙事中的个体参与，关注伟大时代中群体的精神世界，领悟中国社会发展中的文化自觉。青年人，作为伟大时代的见证者和参与者，当他们面对发展的反复和困境，面对外界的质疑和批判，面对不可知和不确定的时候，可以有先贤的精神、学人的风骨，以"任他宝马绝尘去，我自孜孜乐孔颜"的态度拥抱未来。

（蔡亮 副教授，浙江大学宁波理工学院外国语学院 副院长、副书记）

目 录

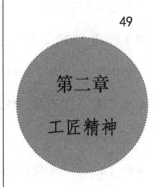

219

第五章

公益精神

Table of Contents

Chapter One

Scientific Spirit

Chapter Two

Craftsmanship

Chapter Five

Public Service
Spirit

Postscript　"The Unity of Knowledge and Action" Makes It Possible　Wang Jiexin

Appendix

第一章　Chapter One　Scientific Spirit

科 学 精 神

Introduction

西方的物理学等自然学科在早期译介到中国的时候被统称为"格物之学"。"格"有"穷究"之意,格物意为探究事物的道理。格物本为儒家认识论和方法论的重要命题,是儒家倡导的提升个人道德修养八个步骤的基石。阳明先生有言:"言格物,则必兼举致知、诚意、正心,而后其功始备而密。"其意在于强调以本体功夫实现思维世界与客观世界的贯通。

阳明思想对科学精神的启示首先在于启蒙。科学精神孕育着宝贵的启蒙思想,即认同科学知识,弘扬理性思维,尊重客观事实,不被愚弄蒙蔽。这种启蒙包含着启迪智慧、开发智力、锻炼能力、解决问题的意蕴,王阳明在《训蒙大意》一文中指出对儿童的启蒙要"栽培涵养之方",目的在于"发其志意""肃其威仪""开其知觉"。知识启蒙应该重视个体价值观的塑造和认识客观事物的能力培养,二者是同等重要的。科学思想的启蒙会激发个体主观能动性的发挥,所以能"趋向鼓舞,中心喜悦,则其进,自不能已"。有了高远的人生发展志向,严谨的职业道德修养,独立解决问题的能力素养,人就会创造自我的价值、科学的价值和社会的价值。

其次,阳明思想对科学精神的启示在于求是。他认为:"君子之学,岂有心乎同异,惟其是而已。"这种"求是"的精神就是以不妥协、不迎合、不媚俗的态度治学做人,追求真理,探索和改造客观世界。王阳明说:"夫学贵得之心,求之于心而非也,虽其言之出于孔子,不敢以为是也,而况其未及孔子者乎!求之于心而是也,虽其言之出于庸常,不敢以为非也,而况其出于孔子者乎!"受其影响,竺可桢先生更将科学精神概括为"只问是非,不计利害",鼓励青年追求真理要"不以孔子的是非为是非"。1938年浙江大学西迁路上,竺可桢以《王阳明先生与大学生的典范》寄语青年,后形成浙江大学"求是"校训。

（蔡 亮 撰写）

●吴光：我自孜孜究阳明

Wu Guang: My Life Study of Wang Yangming

　　吴光，曾任浙江省社会科学院哲学研究所所长、浙江国际阳明学研究中心主任；现任中国孔子基金会副会长、浙江省文史研究馆馆员、黔浙文化合作论坛阳明学中心主任等。他主持完成了《黄宗羲全集》《王阳明全集》《马一浮全集》等共计两千多万字的大型古籍整理、编辑、点校，撰著出版了《儒家哲学片论》《吴光说儒》等十多部专著、文集。先后应邀在新加坡东亚哲学研究所、日本九州大学、韩国中央大学、中国浙江大学等三十多个研究所和院校作了两百余场学术演讲。一位"知良知，行良知"的儒者，以"惟求其是"的精神，一步步地深思和探索阳明文化，并将阳明精神融入心中，是当之无愧的阳明文化的践行者和传播者。

　　Wu Guang was the former director of the Institute of Philosophy, Zhejiang Academy of Social Sciences, and the director of Zhejiang International Research Center of Wang Yangming. He is currently the vice president of the Confucius Foundation in China, professor of the Zhejiang Provincial Museum of Culture and History, and the director of the Yangming Center in the Guizhou-Zhejiang Cultural Cooperation Forum. He presided over the completion of several large-scale ancient books, including *The Complete Works of Huang Zongxi*, *The Complete Works of Wang Yangming*, *The Complete Works of Ma Yifu*, and so on, which amounts to a total of more than 20 million words. He also published his own writings, more than 10 monographs and collected works including *A Fragment of Confucian Philosophy*, *Wu Guang's Interpretation of Confucianism*, and so on. He has been invited to deliver more than 200 lectures in more than 30 institutions like Institute of Southeast Asian Studies in Singapore, Kyushu University in Japan, Chung-Ang University in R. O. Korea, and Zhejiang University in China. He is a conscientious Confucian and he personifies the spirit of "seeking truth". He has devoted his whole life to thinking about and exploring Yangming culture and instilling the Yangming spirit into his heart. Therefore, he is a well-renowned Yangming culture practitioner and communicator.

我自孜孜究阳明

口述：吴 光
整理：王洁心
指导教师：蔡 亮 王碧颖

引 子

君子之学，岂有心乎同异？惟其是而已。

——摘自《王阳明全集》

初识阳明，为伊消得人憔悴

我从初识阳明，到深入了解并开始传播阳明学的过程，是漫长而又艰辛的。

我最初接触到阳明学是通过读《中国哲学史》《中国思想通史》这两本书。那个时候，阳明学尚未被许多人所知或接受，甚至有些人是批判、反对它的。在20世纪80年代的思想解放运动中，我开始对哲学思想中关于哲学历史的问题，即唯心主义和唯物主义两大阵营对垒的历史产生了怀疑。从这以后许多人对王阳明也开始重新反思，他们逐渐认同王阳明的一些思想，特别是阳明的"知行合一""明德亲民"思想对群众的影响最大，人们开始怀念王阳明，认为王阳明对经济发展、社会发展、文教事业的发展有功。浙江、江西、贵州等地逐渐出现许多纪念王阳明的文物景点，例如：浙江的余姚有王阳明故居，绍兴有王阳明墓；江西的南昌有阳明路，大余县青龙铺有王阳明纪念碑，崇义县有阳明祠；贵州的修文有龙场驿阳明洞与王文成公祠等。而我于20世纪80年代末首先发起了对王阳明遗著的整理。那时候条件困难，而且颇多曲折，但是我靠着"肯坐冷板凳"的精神与"学术乃天下之公器"的信念坚持了下来。我主持整理的《王阳明全集》最早的一版是1992年出版的，到现在一共有繁体、简体、精装、平装四个版本。我就这样通过对古籍的整理编写对阳明学越来越了解，最终定型于逐步深入地研究阳明学理论，从形而上的哲学思考到综合性的价值思考。

虽然这个过程令我备尝艰苦，但我很欣慰自己当初对阳明学的探索和坚持铸成的书籍能为如今想学阳明精神的人们提供帮助。我想，这是我身为一个儒者尽自己力量所能做到的最好的事情了吧。

整理阳明遗著，艰如逆水行舟

对阳明古籍的整理，可以说是我真正开始思考、探索阳明学的起点。

古籍整理是一门大学问，需要整理人员非常的谨慎，甚至可能是十年磨一剑。在主持整理《王阳明全集》之前，我先是主持整理了《黄宗羲全集》，为后来王阳明遗著的整理打下了基础。但是整理古籍，不仅需要你对历史事实有准确的把握，也要对各方面的学术知识均有涉猎，因为整理古籍不是一项单纯的、简单的工作，而是需要对每个标点做出正确判断，这就需要你的知识面足够广阔全面。但无论怎样细致，我们的标点断句还是存在谬误，因而受到别人的质疑和批评。我们十分欢迎外界的批评，因为这样可以让古籍整理工作不断提高质量。我们先后整理出版了四个版本的《王阳明全集》。

采访吴光教授

　　我个人非常喜欢读书、写书，但是我花了很多时间整理古籍，所以使我少写了几本思想研究专著。然而我却不后悔，因为我的古籍整理成果给学术界提供了基础性的原始资料，可以供更多的人学习探讨。

阳明学的科学精神，吾将上下而求索

　　"知是基础、是前提，行是重点、是关键，必须以知促行、以行促知，做到'知行合一'。"[1] 这是习近平总书记对王阳明"知行合一"论的阐发。

　　阳明心学由四大部分构成：一是"良知即天理"的良知本体论，二是"致良知"的修养方法论，三是"知行合一"的力行实践论，四是"明德亲民"的民本政治论。那么，阳明心学的科学精神是什么？

　　我将阳明学精神概括为四大方面，即道德自觉、人文关怀、多元兼容、力行

---

1 朱康有. 从知行合一的角度要求自己[N]. 人民日报，2019-05-14(9).

实践。而其核心是"知行合一"。四大精神皆由"知行合一"所贯穿，靠"知行合一"去实现。科学发展是目前高速发展的中国所重视的领域之一，我认为在科学研究领域完全能够体现并运用阳明精神的核心"知行合一"。首先，科学强调主体性，而在阳明学中有着"身之主宰便是心"的理论，就是指从事科学研究的人员要发挥主观能动性。其次，科学强调创新思维，而王阳明的思想理论相比于程朱理学就有更多创造性突破。我们常说的科学精神中，还包括敢于质疑、怀疑精神，而阳明精神在《传习录》中就体现了突破以往教条的怀疑精神，强调的是"求异"。独立的思考，是一种科学的求是精神。最后，我认为科学的最高宗旨就是以民为本，以符合全人类利益为最高追求：民之所好好之，民之所恶恶之；亲亲而仁民，仁民而爱物；明德亲民与修己以安百姓，要求科学必须体现爱民、亲民、安民的根本宗旨。而民本宗旨在《传习录》中就体现为阳明的"亲民"思想，如"民之所好好之，民之所恶恶之，此之谓民之父母"。

吴光教授展示四版《王阳明全集》

科学和真理的探索，应该充分发扬"知行合一"的阳明精神。马克思主义是一种重实践的哲学，马克思说过："以往的哲学只是解释世界，而问题在于改造世界。""解释世界"是"知"，改造世界就是"行"，而重点就在于"行"。对科学和真理的探索也必须落实到改造世界的实践活动，才是真知。王阳明"知行合一"说的重点也是归结于"行"。如他所说，"知者行之始，行者知之成"；"圣学只一个功夫"，这个功夫就是"致良知"。黄宗羲解说王阳明"致良知"学说时说："良知为知""致良知为行""致字即是行字""必以力行为功夫"。这样理解，王阳明的"致良知"就成了"行良知"，即良知的实践了。

科学精神和阳明精神是一致的，科学的发展也离不开阳明精神，而阳明精神的传扬也离不开科学理性的态度。

吴光教授与队员讨论问题

以冷静态度看待成为显学的阳明学

如今的学术研究条件越来越好了，阳明学研究成为显学，迎来了自身发展的鼎盛时期，但是，我们应该秉持科学冷静的态度，不要头脑发热，也无须言必称阳明。

阳明良知心学是孔孟仁学的继承与发展，王阳明是宋明心学的集大成者；阳明心学是儒学发展的新阶段、新高峰，也是当代儒学发展的强劲动力。有人说，21 世纪是王阳明的世纪，我不同意这种独断妄说。我认为只能说，21 世纪将是阳明良知心学发扬光大的时期。如今由于习近平总书记的推崇，阳明学研究成为显学。这是中国社会从改革开放到和平崛起新阶段干部官德教育和全民道德教育的需要，是儒学发展的大好时机。

习近平提出要"学习、敬重王阳明"、提倡"共产党人的心学"，是要求广大共产党人和干部群众要修身立德，真正做到"知行合一"，践行良知，为实现中华民族伟大复兴的中国梦而努力奋斗，而不是要大家关门修炼，"狠斗私字一闪念"，念念不忘"存天理，去人欲"，否则就可能把阳明心学当作新教条，重新堕入"道德万能""精神万能"的桎梏，阻碍科学与社会的发展。

阳明文化"火起来"是好事，但要薪火相传，而非心急火燎的功利主义和随心所欲的胡编乱造。大家学习王阳明，应该真正做到"知行合一"。做学术研究呢，不能够盲目跟风、人云亦云。这是一个严肃的科学研究，应该保持一个科学冷静的头脑，理性地学习研究王阳明与阳明学。

传承阳明文化，寄厚望于阳明新青年

立志勤学，知行合一。

中国上下五千年有许许多多珍贵的文化与先辈的精神值得现在的年轻人学习和传承，并且可以把中国特有的文化传播到海外。习近平总书记2011年5月在贵州大学的讲话中谈到王阳明时指出，不仅中国人敬仰他、学习他，而且心学传播到东北亚地区，影响日韩。由此可见，阳明学在海外传播的力度是很大的。我于1987年应日本阳明学家冈田武彦先生之邀访问了日本九州、京都、名古屋、东京的七八所大学，与多位阳明学研究专家会谈交流，后来又三赴日本访问、研究、出席学术会议。又自1988年以来多次应邀至新加坡、韩国与中国台湾、中国香港访问、研究与讲学，接触了不少名家大儒，开展关于儒学、新儒学、阳明学的学术文化交流，取得了一些成就。但现在老了，精力渐衰，需要年轻一代薪火相传。你们年轻人如果要为阳明学的海外传播贡献力量，这需要基本的素质与知识的积累：首先，应该抱着对王阳明和阳明学的崇敬态度，对王阳明及其学说有最基本的了解，也应该精通外语和古汉语，这样才能更好地向外国友人展示中国文化的风采。至于传播的方法，就要考验大家的创新力和传播力了，可以挑选自己有兴趣且能理解的王阳明代表作进行翻译，例如翻译《传习录》《阳明先生年谱》就很有必要。但不能急于求成，一定要慢慢深入学习才能做得更好。大家作为阳明新青年，应该将阳明精神融入自己的心中，做到知良知、行良知。

吴光教授为本次活动写寄语卡

我只是一个景仰王阳明、传播阳明学的儒者，无非尽了自己作为儒者为人为学为道的微薄力量。一介儒生，一生求索，我自孜孜究阳明，知行合一致良知也。

吴光教授与队员合照

My Life Study of Wang Yangming

Narrator: Wu Guang

Compiled by: Wang Jiexin

Supervised by: Cai Liang, Wang Biying

Let Plato be your friend, and Aristotle, but more let your friend be Truth.

—English Translation for the Motto of Harvard University

First Acquaintance with Yangming, Growing Haggard for It

From the beginning with my initial knowledge of Yangming to gaining a deeper understanding and starting the process of spreading Yangming was a long and arduous journey.

I first came into contact with the Yangming school when I began to read the *History of Chinese Philosophy* and *An Intellectual General History of China*. At that time, Yangming had not been widely known or accepted by many people and some people were highly critical of it. During the ideological emancipation period of the 1980s, I began to question the history of philosophy and the history of idealism and materialism. Since then many people have begun to rethink Wang Yangming. They gradually came to agree with some of Wang Yangming's ideas, especially Yangming's thinking of "the unity of knowledge and action" and "to enlighten the brilliant virtue and make intimate association with people". People began to recall Wang Yangming, and to think of the merits Yangming could bring to economic, social, cultural and educational development. Zhejiang, Jiangxi, Guizhou and other places gradually began to commemorate Wang Yangming and treasure his cultural relics, such as his former residence in Yuyao (Zhejiang), the Wang Yangming Tomb in Shaoxing (Zhejiang), the Yangming Road in Nanchang (Jiangxi), the Qinglongpu Wang Yangming Monument in Dayu County (Jiangxi), the Yangming Temple in Chongyi County (Jiangxi), the Longchang Yi Yangming Hole in Xiuwen (Guizhou), Wang Wencheng Temple (Guizhou) and so on. In the late eighties of the 20th century, for the first time I initiated the compiling of the works left by Wang Yangming. At that time, the conditions were difficult and there were many twists and turns, but I relied on being "willing to sit on the bench" and the faith of perseverance. I presided over the finishing of *The Complete*

Works of Wang Yangming and the first edition was published in 1992. So far, there are a total of four versions—traditional, simplified, hardcover, and paperback. Through the compilation of ancient books on Yangming, I gained more and more understanding and ultimately a gradual in-depth study of Yangming theory, from metaphysical philosophical thinking to the comprehensive value of thinking.

Although this process presented many difficulties, I am very pleased that my original study of Yangming and my persistence with the books can now help people who want to learn the spirit of Yangming. I think this is the best thing that I have done as a Confucian scholar trying to do my part.

Compiling the Yangming Works, Rowing against the Current

The point at which I really began thinking about and exploring Yangming was during the collation of the Yangming ancient books.

The collation of ancient books is a great science; it is necessary for the collating staff to be very careful in finishing, and it may even take a decade of grinding the sword. Before the collation of *The Complete Works of Wang Yangming*, I presided over *The Complete Works of Huang Zongxi*, gaining some experiences for my further work. For the collation of ancient books, it is not only necessary to have an accurate grasp of historical facts, it also requires you to have covered all areas of academic knowledge, because the editing of ancient books is not a straightforward or simple task, but demands that the right judgment be made for each punctuation mark, which requires your knowledge to be broad and comprehensive. But no matter how meticulous, our punctuation may still be wrong sometimes, and thus we are questioned and criticized by others. We are very welcome to criticism because these suggestions can help us continue to improve the quality of the work on ancient books. We have compiled and published four versions of *The Complete Works of Wang Yangming*.

I personally like to read books and write books, but I spent a lot of time on editing of ancient books, so I researched and wrote only a few monographs on the study of thought. However, I do not regret this, because the ancient books I collated provide a basic source of information for the academic community and for more people to learn and explore.

The Scientific Spirit of the Yangming School, Search from Top to Bottom

"Knowledge is the foundation and the premise, the action is the focus and the key. We must learn to use knowledge to promote the action, to use action to promote knowledge, so as to practice 'the unity of knowledge and action'." This is the analysis of General Secretary Xi Jinping on Wang Yangming's "the unity of knowledge and action" theory.

Yangming's Mind Studies are composed of four major parts: The first is the conscience ontology—conscience is heaven; the second is the self-cultivation method of "the conscience"; the third is "the unity of knowledge and action"; the fourth is the people-oriented politics of "the doctrine of enlightening the brilliant virtue and making intimate association with people". So, what is the scientific spirit of Yangming's Mind Studies?

I will sum up the spirit of Yangming in four themes, namely moral consciousness, humane care, compatibility, and practice. And its core is "the unity of knowledge and action". The four major themes are carried through the theory of "the unity of knowledge and action". The development of science is one field that China attaches great importance to at present, and I think the field of scientific research can fully reflect and use the core of the Yangming spirit, "the unity of knowledge and action". First of all, science emphasizes subjectivity, and in Yangming school there is a theory that "the master of the body is the heart", that is, the personnel engaged in scientific research should take initiative. Secondly, science emphasizes innovative thinking, and Wang Yangming's theory of thought has more creative breakthroughs compared to Neo-Confucianism. We often say that the scientific spirit also includes the courage to question and doubt, and the spirit of Yangming in *Instructions for Practical Living* broke through the past dogmatic spirit of suspicion, emphasizing "seeking differences". Independent thinking leads to a kind of scientific spirit of seeking truth. Finally, I think the highest purpose of science is people-oriented, in line with the interests of all mankind as the highest pursuit. And the people of this purpose in *Instructions for Practical Living* is embodied in the "pro-people" thought of Yangming, for example, "the people of the good, the people of evil, this is the parents of the people," which fully embodies the Wang Yangming thought of the people first.

The exploration of science and truth should give full play to the Yangming spirit of "the unity of knowledge and action". Marxism is a practical philosophy, so Marx said that "the philosophy of the past is only to explain the world, and the problem lies in the transformation of the world". "Interpretation of the world" is "knowledge", and "transformation of the world" is "action", which is the focus. The exploration of science and truth must also be carried out to the practical end of transforming the world, which is the real knowledge. In Yangming's "unity of knowledge and action", the focus is also attributed to "action". As he said, "Knowledge is the beginning of the action, and action is the completion of knowledge", Confucianism only need one thing, which is the "conscience". Huang Zongxi explained Wang Yangming's theory of "conscience" as "the conscience is knowledge", "the conscience is the action", "the achievement is the action". In this understanding, Wang Yangming's "conscience" has become an "action with conscience", that is, the practice of conscience.

The scientific spirit and the Yangming spirit are consistent; scientific development is inseparable from the spirit of Yangming, and the spread of the Yangming spirit is also inseparable from a scientific and rational attitude.

Maintain a Sensible Attitude when Spreading the Yangming Culture

Now the academic research conditions are getting better and better, and the study of Yangming has become a famous school and ushered in the heyday of its development, but we should hold to a scientific and rational attitude, and do not become hysterical.

Yangming's Mind Studies (conscience) is the inheritance and development of Confucius and Mencius, Wang Yangming is the master of the conscience of the Song and Ming dynasties. Yangming's Mind Studies was a new stage of Confucian development, a new peak, and also a strong driving force for the development of contemporary Confucianism. Some people say that the 21st century is the century of Wang Yangming; I do not agree with this arbitrary judgment. I think it can only be said that the 21st century will be the period of Yangming's Mind Studies, that is to say, Confucianism. Today, thanks to the General Secretary Xi Jinping, Yangming studies have become a popular subject. This is the need of Chinese society from the reform and opening-up to the peaceful rise of the new stage of cadres and moral education, which marks a good time for the development of Confucianism.

Xi Jinping proposed to "learn and respect Wang Yangming" and promoted "the Mind Studies of Communists". This is to ask the majority of Communists and cadres to cultivate virtue and truly practice "the unity of knowledge and action", to carry out conscience and work hard and achieve a great rejuvenation of the Chinese nation and the Chinese dream; but not to cultivate virtue behind the doors, to "severely criticize yourself immediately when selfishness appeared in a flash", to be obsessed with "uphold justice, annihilate desire". Otherwise it may refall into the phenomena of being "moral omnipotent", "spiritual omnipotent" when treating Yangming's theory as a new dogma, which may instead hinder the development of science and society.

The popularization of Yangming culture is a good thing. Passing it down to the next generation needs to be done hand in hand, which involves time and patience but not anxious utilitarianism or reckless invention. When we learn Wang Yangming, we should really put into practice "the unity of knowledge and action". So to the academic research, it cannot blindly follow with the trend, or just repeat other's words like a parrot. Since this is a serious scientific study, we should maintain a scientific and sensible mind, and rationally study Wang Yangming and Yangming learning.

Yangming Cultural Heritage Sends Great Hope to New Yangming Youth

Once determined to study, try to achieve "the unity of knowledge and action".

China has five thousand years of precious culture and the ancestral spirit worthy of being inherited by the youth of today, and this unique culture of China can be spread overseas. In his speech at Guizhou University in May 2011, General Secretary Xi Jinping said, "Not only the Chinese people admire him (Wang Yangming) and learn from him, but this admiration is also spread to the northeast region of Asia, affecting Japan and R. O. Korea." This shows that there is a great Yangming influence overseas. In 1987, I visited several universities in Kyushu, Kyoto, Nagoya and Tokyo at the invitation of Mr. Okada Takehiko, a Japanese Yangming scholar, and exchanged views with a number of Yangming experts, and afterwards I went to Japan to visit, research, and attend academic conferences in succession. Since 1988 I have been invited to Singapore, R. O. Korea, and other regions of Asia, as well as Taiwan and Hong Kong of China to visit, carry out research and give lectures, make contact with a lot of famous Confucian scholars, and to carry out Confucian, Neo-Confucian, and Yangming academic and cultural exchanges, and I made some achievements. But now, getting older, my energy is declining and there is need for a younger generation of enthusiasts. It is for you young people to contribute to the spread of Yangming overseas. This requires the basic quality and accumulation of knowledge: First of all, you should respect Wang Yangming and study his philosophy with reverence, have a basic understanding of Wang Yangming and his theory, be proficient in foreign languages and ancient Chinese, so as to better share the Chinese culture with foreign friends. And as for the method of spreading his ideas, it is based on everyone's innovation and communication skills, and you can choose your favorite parts of his writings to translate, such as the translation of *Instructions for Practical Living*, *Chronicle of Mr. Wang Yangming*. But one cannot be anxious, rather it takes slow in-depth study to do better. As new Yangming youth, you should integrate the Yangming spirit into your hearts to know your conscience and practice the conscience.

I am just an admirer of Wang Yangming who is spreading Yangming's theory and Confucian thought. For a Confucian scholar, life is a quest of searching. I diligently study Yangming and strive to practice "the unity of knowledge and action".

谦谦儒者，从心而歌

王洁心

指导教师：王碧颖　蔡　亮

在采访吴光先生之前，我了解到先生编写整理了《王阳明全集》等多种优秀的古籍，撰写了多部学术专著，他是国内阳明学研究的翘楚，受邀在全国及世界各地进行学术演讲，是当之无愧的阳明文化的践行者和传播者。面对这样一位阳明学的大家，我的心情激动而又忐忑不安，可当这位慈眉善目、温和敦厚的儒者与我开始一番攀谈时，我觉得吴光先生没有大家的孤傲自许、目无下尘，有的是传道授业、平易近人的师者风范。

《明儒言行录》中记载着王阳明这样一个故事：有人曾当面评论王阳明说："以先生的文章、政事、勋业足盖一世，若除却讲学一事，便是完人。"王阳明却笑着回答道："我宁愿从事讲学，不愿其他。"王阳明一生集事功、文章、道德于一身，但是最令他本人自豪的还是创立学说，从事教育。他不仅是个伟大的思想家，同时也是一个热心从事于教育事业的教育家。他曾经在贵州讲学于龙冈书院，在江西修建濂溪书院，在绍兴、余姚开辟稽山书院、姚江书院，无论是宦海沉浮、戎马倥偬，或赋闲在家，几乎无处不讲学，无时不弘道……我眼中的吴光先生就是一位谦谦儒者，他研究阳明学说，提炼阳明精神，传播阳明文化，更让人感动的是，他"知行合一"，将阳明先生的教育理念潜移默化地融入与后学的交往中。

作为一名普通大学生，我没有专业采访者所配备的器材，甚至缺乏专业的采访和摄影技巧，但是面对如此不专业的我，吴光先生没有丝毫的不耐烦，而是热情地为我讲述他与阳明学研究的那些传奇故事，用他的专业知识一步一步地引导身为初学者的我了解阳明、深入学习阳明学知识。走进吴光先生古色古香的书房，我仿佛置身于书的海洋之中，成堆的书籍因书柜放不下而堆积在桌子上、地板上，我羡慕着吴光先生散发着兰香的治学生活，也佩服吴光先生编写如此之多书籍的坚持不懈。翻开我从学校的阳明学堂带来的《王阳明全集》，吴光先生细致地为我讲解了古籍编写最重要的标点断句问题："这不仅需要你对历史事实有一定的把握，也要求你对各方面的学术知识广有涉猎，因为整理古籍不是一个单纯的、简单的工作，而是要细致到每个标点的定断，这就需要你的知识面足够广博。"先生向一头雾水的我耐心地解释着标点在古文中的重要性，为了更形象生动地让我理解，他更是不厌其烦地举了许多例证使我茅塞顿开。我刹那间明白了学术精神首先要有严谨求是的科学态度，任何对于真理的探索，都应该发扬"知行合一"

的阳明精神。

吴光先生将"道德自觉、人文关怀、多元兼容、力行实践"归纳为阳明学的四大精神,其核心是"知行合一"。四大精神皆由"知行合一"所贯穿,靠"知行合一"去实现。当我询问到作为阳明新青年的我们该如何传播阳明文化时,吴光先生为业余的我们给出了他专业的意见:"青年是文化建设的生力军,想要为阳明的海外传播贡献自己力量,首先要对王阳明和他的理论有最基本的了解;其次应该学好文化知识,精通外语和古汉语,这样才能更好地向外国友人展示中国文化的风采;最后,要抱着对王阳明和阳明学崇敬的态度,才能更有积极性去传播。"这一番话让我顿时觉得阳明文化的传播之路是格外艰辛的,而先生却对我充满了信心,不断地鼓励我,敢于立志,结合专业,从点滴做起,"立志勤学,知行合一"是吴光先生在寄语卡上写下的八个浑厚有力的大字。

在采访接近尾声时,吴光先生从他的书海中挑选出几本适合我读的阳明书籍和杂志赠送给我,拿着沉甸甸的先生珍藏的书籍,我看着眼前和蔼可亲的吴光先生,真诚地说了一声"老师,谢谢您"。笔墨无言写春秋,我想这就是一位全身心践行阳明精神的儒者,留给晚生后学的深刻印象。他淡泊名利,平易近人;他甘当人梯,身体力行;他保持着一颗对人类知识的童心,坚守着一颗对科学精神的初心,怀着一颗对中国文化的责任心,致力于阳明精神的实践与传播,又无私地培育着一拨又一拨的"阳明新青年"。

团队成员:胡 双 王洁心

A Modest Scholar, Studying Yangming from the Heart

Wang Jiexin

Supervised by: Wang Biying, Cai Liang

Before interviewing Mr. Wu Guang, I learned that he had compiled *The Complete Works of Wang Yangming* and many other excellent ancient books and written a number of academic monographs. He is a leader of domestic Yangming scholarship and is invited to give academic lectures throughout the country and around the world. He is a well-renowned practitioner and communicator of Yangming culture. Faced with such a learned Yangming person, I felt excited and uneasy. But when the kindly, gentle and honest Confucian and I began our interview, I found Mr. Wu Guang was levelheaded, not aloof, with a preaching, approachable teaching style.

In *The Recorded Account of Wang Yangming by Ming Confucian Scholars*, there is a story that someone criticized Wang Yangming face to face, "Your writings, political performance and social achievements are really profound; if we do not take your teaching into account, you are perfect." Wang Yangming replied with a smile, "I would rather engage in teaching, and I do not want to do other things." Wang Yangming's life was dedicated to his work, writings, morality, but he was most proud of his own creation of theory and devotion to education. He was not only a great thinker, but also an educator who was enthusiastic about education. He once lectured in Longgang College in Guizhou, built Lianxi College in Jiangxi, opened Jishan College and Yaojiang College in Shaoxing, Yuyao. With imperial ups and downs, during wartime or when unemployed at home, he was teaching wherever he was. In my eyes, Mr. Wu Guang is a modest Confucian scholar, a researcher of Yangming's theory, a refiner of the spirit of Yangming, a spreader of Yangming culture, and most importantly, a practitioner of "the unity of knowledge and action".

As an ordinary college student, I am not a well-equipped professional interviewer, and even lack professional interview and photography skills, but in the face of my unprofessional manner, Mr. Wu Guang did not have the slightest impatience, instead he enthusiastically told me about the legendary stories of Yangming, with his expertise guiding me step by step to understand Yangming and in-depth study of Yangming knowledge. In Mr. Wu Guang's traditional Chinese-style study, I seem to be placed in an ocean of books, piles of books arranged in the bookcase and many stacked up on the table and the floor. I envy Mr. Wu Guang's scholarly life, and also admire Mr. Wu Guang's perseverance in compiling so many books. Opening up a volume I brought from the Yangming Academy, *The Complete Works of Wang Yangming*, Mr. Wu Guang carefully explained to me the problems in preparing of ancient books—the most important of which is the punctuation. "This requires you not only to have a certain grasp of historical facts, but also requires you to have a wide range of academic knowledge, because the collation of ancient books is not a pure, simple task, but it is necessary to pay careful attention to each detail of punctuation, which requires that your knowledge is broad enough." Mr. Wu Guang patiently explained the importance of punctuation in the ancient Chinese language; in order to help me understand more accurately, he took the trouble to give a lot of examples to enlighten me. I suddenly understood that the academic spirit must first have a rigorous scientific attitude; any exploration of the truth should promote the Yangming spirit of "the unity of knowledge and action".

Mr. Wu Guang summarized "moral consciousness, humane care, compatibility, and practice" as the four major spirits of Yangming, its core is "the unity of knowledge and action". The four major spirits are carried through the theory of "the unity of knowledge and action". When I asked how new Yangming youth should spread Yangming culture, Mr. Wu Guang gave his professional advice for the amateur: "Youth is the new force of cultural construction, wanting to spread Yangming overseas. To contribute their own strength, first of all have the most basic understanding of Wang Yangming and his theory; secondly, learn cultural knowledge, and be proficient in foreign languages and ancient Chinese, so as to better share Chinese culture with foreign friends; finally, embrace Wang Yangming and the Yangming school with an attitude of reverence, in order to be more motivated to spread the culture." This remark makes me feel that the road of Yangming culture is extremely difficult, but Mr. Wu was full of confidence in me, and constantly encouraged me to dare to aspire, to start from the bottom with the combination of my major. "Be determined to be diligent, put knowledge into action" is what Mr. Wu Guang wrote on the message card in eight vigorous and powerful characters.

At the end of the interview, Mr. Wu Guang from his sea of books picked out a few books and magazines for me to read about Yangming and presented them to me. Holding the heavy collection of books, I looked at the face of the amiable Mr. Wu Guang, and sincerely said, "Thank you, Mr. Wu." The pen and ink are silent but they record history. I think he is a Confucian of the spirit of Yangming, leaving a deep impression on the younger generation. He is indifferent to fame and fortune; he offers his help to everyone without hesitation; he holds childlike innocence for human knowledge and adheres to the original conscience of the scientific spirit, with a sense of responsibility for Chinese culture, committed to the practice and dissemination of the Yangming spirit, and the selfless cultivation of another wave of "new Yangming youth".

Team members: Hu Shuang, Wang Jiexin

钱冠连：动心养性之余，恍若有悟

Qian Guanlian: Cultivating Nature Helps Comprehend Truth

钱冠连，著名语言学家，外语界西方语言哲学领航者，是我国最早在国外语用学刊物上发表文章的学者之一、国际语用学会中心访问研究员。现任广东外语外贸大学语言学及应用语言学研究中心专职研究员、二级教授、博士生导师。在国内外发表语言学、语用学论文七十九篇，主要著作有《汉语文化语用学》《美学语言学》《语言全息论》《语言——人类最后的家园》。其中《汉语文化语用学》获 1999 年广东省优秀社科著作奖（后被当时的国家教委选入研究生推荐书目），《美学语言学》获中国第七届城市出版社优秀图书一等奖。另有文艺评论、散文、翻译作品共二十万字。他的学术活动对中国语言学界产生了广泛而深入的影响。

Qian Guanlian, a famous linguist, a navigator in western language and philosophy studies, a visiting researcher of International Pragmatics Association (IPrA), is one of the earliest scholars who published works in foreign journals of pragmatics. He is now, as being a second-grade professor and a PhD supervisor, still working as a full-time researcher in Foreign Studies Research Center for Linguistics and Applied Linguistics in Guangdong University of Foreign Studies. His 79 linguistic and pragmatic theses were published in the world, including *Pragmatics in Chinese Culture*, *Aesthetic Linguistics*, and *Language—Human's Last Homeland*. *Pragmatics in Chinese Culture* won the award for excellent social science works of the Guangdong Province, 1999. And *Aesthetic Linguistics* won the first prize for the 7th excellent Chinese books from the China City Press. He has written 200 thousand characters of literary criticism, essays and translated works, and more. His academic activities have had a profound and widespread influence in Chinese linguistics circles.

动心养性之余，恍若有悟

口述：钱冠连

整理：钱　昊

指导教师：王碧颖

引　子

> 大人者，以天地万物为一体者也，其视天下如一家，中国犹一人焉。
>
> ——王阳明

不忘初心，方得始终

宇宙观与世界观成就了一个人的追求方向。我在年轻时并没有特意投身语言学研究。我的青壮年时期，时逢"文化大革命"，那时候有"不学 ABC，照样干革命"的说法。我在教授外语的同时也在教授汉语与音乐。很多同事、朋友曾劝我改行，说外语没有人学了。我问自己："难道没有人学就一定意味着外语没有用吗？"而且我当时的学生们一来上课就完全忘记了"外语没有用"这个说法，发疯似的跟着我在课堂上进行各种各样的活动。他们的热情使我下定决心，抛却杂念，潜心研究外语。

我的研究方向是不断变化的，先是英美文学，然后变成了理论语言学，又变成了语用学，不久又变成了分析哲学，最后又开始了我的后语言哲学，到最近这几年又研究起来了人生哲学。退休以后我没有闲着，在不断地写文章，做研究，每天看两条《牛津哲学辞典》里的词。要知道研究方向改变意味着我要更换自己研读的书目，也就是说我的参考书目要全部换掉，同时也意味着我又要换一批不同种类的单词。别人会说我这不是为难自己吗？但是我坚持过来了。

在我眼中，现在的大学生、知识分子、学者很浮躁，不那么安静。都说大学改变命运，大学决定其饭碗，其实这话把大学降格了。大学是构建人的宇宙观、世界观和人生观的，是建立一个人的哲学眼光的，是给一个人的知识打基础的，是学术传承的重镇。所以说，我是在确立好自己的宇宙观、世界观和人生观后才能保持对语言学的研究与追求。

我在年轻之时就接触到了王阳明先生的心学思想。当年在鄂西时我正在研究唯物主义，王阳明先生则成了当时人们认为的唯心主义的代表人物。我对他的思想非常感兴趣，可惜限于当时条件，没能比较系统地去研究他的思想，直到最近几年才有了深入的了解。但他的事迹，"知行合一"的思想一直给予我在今后的为人处世当中，以及语言及语言哲学研究方面很大的启发。当年王阳明被打了 40 廷杖后就被皇帝贬到贵州龙场，那个地方是少数民族聚居的边远高山地区，但是，它也是很安静的地方。一个人在痛苦的时候，找一个亲近自然的地方是最好的选择。王阳明认为悟性是人人都有的。"圣人之道，吾性自足，向之求理于事物者误尔"，他是针对朱熹的"格物致知"来说的。

不忘初心，方得始终

志趣虽不同，自古惺惺惜

在"文革"期间，我恰巧也有与王阳明先生相似的经历。那十年客观来说是国家的一个大动荡，但我想到朱光潜曾经说过王阳明被贬到贵州龙场是一个机会，所以我把它当成了一个机会，也悟通了很多人生的道理。比如当时我就想："我要不要放弃对知识的追求呢？"当时我被当作"靠边站"的人，但我就想哪一个时代、民族、国家可以不要知识呢？因此求知永远也不会有错的，我就不相信现阶段自己的祖国的文明，乃至祖国以后的文明不要知识了。那个时候我也在研读恩格斯的《自然辩证法》和《反杜林论》，毛泽东的《实践论》和《矛盾论》，读得非常仔细。我还读过《澳大利亚先锋报》的英文版，并通过它学习了很多英文，而且我还看了很多有毛泽东著作的英文版本。那个时候，我还想学德语，因为德国出了很多大哲学家。但是，因为物质条件太差，我被迫终止了。所以说，王阳明先生有个"龙场思索"，我也有个对"文革"的思索，完成了对人生哲理的领悟。

学问不惧多，关键在运用

后来在我的语言哲学研究的过程当中，王阳明先生的"知行合一"思想也给予了我在研究语言与科学的过程当中诸多启发。所谓的"知行合一"，就是理论和实践要合二为一，不可过分偏重一方。所以我用语言外的功夫解决语言内的问题。我的百科知识结构比较全面，从小学开始，到初中、高中、大学时，我都不止学习一类知识。物理、化学、生物、历史、地理，我统统喜欢。语言表达思想，但它同时又是人的心智的创造物。语言与科学，这两个看似毫无干系的事物实际上密不可分。毫无疑问科学是要以经验作基础的，所谓的经验就是"格物致知"，但这与科学走向语言哲学有何关系？我通过我所学的知识研究人类用语言交流中所蕴含的美学，了解到声音是一种物质性的东西，因此我所著的关于语言研究的书的前半部基本上是科学性的研究方式，后面的结论则完全是抽象性的。最后的结论是为什么语言是美的，就是因为宇宙的结构是美的，所以它和宇宙同构。正如西方的哲学思想感兴趣的是外在的存在物，注重系统性，比如宇宙结构、世界结构，第一阶段是存有论，第二阶段是知识论，第三阶段是语言性转向。它尽管有三个阶段，可是它的核心问题只有一个，就是存在论。虽然是方法变了，对象没有变，注重系统性。说到中国哲学的核心问题，成中英教授曾说中国哲学的问题以一元一体三结构，即易经、儒家、道家，悟自然之道和人性之道。我在语言研究方面所追求的东西实际上是悟觉自然之道和人性之德，我的语言研究其实最后都要到哲学那边去报到，有时你觉得与这不相关的知识或思想反而有一定的联系，那就得去了解，去探究。不能只为了研究语言学而去研究语言学。这一点就与我之前所提到的王阳明先生的思想不谋而合了。简单说来，我研究语言学，就是为了探究其中所蕴含的关于宇宙及人生的价值规律，然而这个规律需要去学习其他很多学科的知识才能领悟到。

"求是"是作为学者的立身之本

我对语言学的研究其实就是我对"求是"精神的追求体现。有一个奇怪的现象：一个事物越普通，就越被人们视而不见。作为一个民族、一个国家的语言，是要被天天使用的，但是它的价值人们不屑于研究。其实语言是非常重要的：第一，语言是日常交际的工具，没有它就不成社会了。第二，语言是使存在物出场的东西，西方哲学就是研究 to be。第三，语言形成了一切朴实价值的词语，没有语言，宇宙世界人生那些价值规律就无法固定下来。第四，语言本身就是一个存在物。第五，语言是人类文明精神传承的载体。如果没有语言，可以说现在整个世界都是黑暗的，很多人看不出它的价值就是因为它太普遍了。并且外语对真理的探索是非常有意义的，因为它能把国外先进的知识引进来。多学一门外语就等于多打开了一扇通向世界的窗口：窗口越多，视角就越多；视角越多，解决事情就越顺利。所以我的结论是研究语言，以及研究其中所包含的价值规律是非常吸引人的。

研究学问，如果仅仅为个人的利害，顾面子，就不应该选择学问，受不住清贫、宁静，就也不该做学问。一心不能二用。"动心养性之余，恍若有悟"，一个人惟有在宁静深致之时，才能悟到真正的智慧。

Cultivating Nature Helps Comprehend Truth

Narrator: Qian Guanlian

Compiled by: Qian Hao

Supervised by: Wang Biying

The great man regards Heaven, Earth, and the myriad things as one body. He regards the world as one family and the country as one person.

—Wang Yangming

The Original Mind Itself Is the Most Accomplished Mind of True Enlightenment

The cosmology and world view of a person have an influence on what he will pursue. I didn't deliberately throw myself into linguistics when I was young. During my youth, there was the "Cultural Revolution", and a general view of people at that time was: "It's no use to learn ABC (a foreign language)!" And other than teaching English, I also taught Chinese Language and Music. Many colleagues and friends of mine advised me to change my profession—they explained that nobody in China studies English. I asked myself: "Is English useless just because nobody studies it?" My students at that time solved my confusion: They engaged in various activities in English class with such enthusiasm, it was as if they totally forgot the view that "A foreign language is useless". Their enthusiasm made me determined to give up such thoughts and to carry on my research of English.

My research direction is constantly changing. My first research was British and American Literature, then it changed into Theoretical Linguistics, after that it changed to Pragmatics and soon turned to Analytical Philosophy, and finally I began to research Post Linguistic Philosophy, until in recent years I started researching the Philosophy of Life. It's never too late to learn, so I kept myself busy after retirement, and I never stopped writing and researching. Each day I read two lists of English words in the *Oxford Dictionary of Philosophy*. Changing research means I have to change all my research books, which means all my references and jargon must be changed. Others may say I was hard on myself. But I made it.

In my eyes, college students, scholars and people who have knowledge are more fickle than in the past: They can't get down to work. There is a saying that university is a place where people can change their fate and decide their career; actually this view lessens the status of the university. The university is a field where people establish their cosmology, world view and their view of life; it also helps people to develop their philosophical and interpretative insight and establishes their foundation of knowledge; it is also a place where learning can be passed on. So I could keep pursuing linguistics research after establishing my own cosmology, world view and view of life.

I have known Wang Yangming's Mind Studies since I was young, and when I was researching materialism in western Hubei, Wang Yangming was thought to be a representative of idealism. I was very interested in his ideas but I couldn't research his theory systematically until recent years because of the material conditions of that time. But his story and the idea of "the unity of knowledge and action" have been enlightening my individual behavior and research of linguistics as well as research of the philosophy of language. According to historical accounts, after being punished with 40 lashes, Yangming was demoted by the emperor and exiled to Longchang, Guizhou Province. Longchang was a place inhabited by ethnic minorities in a remote mountainous region, but it was also a very quiet place. Finding a quiet place close to nature was thought to be the best option when a person was in pain. So Yangming thought every person has the ability to understand nature. "It is enough to understand the wisdom of Tao by myself, it's not right to seek truth by outward thing." These words of his were aimed at Zhu Xi's "investigation of things and extension of knowledge".

Different Interest and Inspiration, Still Appreciate Each Other

I happened to have a similar experience to Wang Yangming during the "Cultural Revolution". Well, objectively speaking, those ten years were our country's turbulent period, but Zhu Guangqian once said that it was an opportunity for Wang Yangming when he was exiled to Longchang, so I also regarded it as an opportunity for me to understand many truths of life. For example, I asked myself, "Should I give up the pursuit of knowledge?" At that time, I was regarded as a person who was "marginalized", but I wondered how could an era, a nation, or a country abandon knowledge? So pursuing knowledge is always right, and I didn't believe that our nation's culture could develop from the present into the future without knowledge. In western Hubei, I was also carefully researching Engels' "Dialectics of Nature", and "Anti-Duhring", as well as Mao Zedong's essays "On Practice", and "On Contradiction". I even read the English versions of The Vanguard and Mao Zedong's books, and I learned a lot of English words from these writings. Because there were many great philosophers in Germany, German was the second foreign language that I would have liked to learn, but I was forced to stop because of poor material conditions. So, just as Wang Yangming did a lot of thinking in Longchang, I also had my thinking years during the time of the "Cultural Revolution" to bring to light many of the truths in life.

It Is Applying Value, Not Number That Makes Knowledge Worthy

Wang Yangming's "unity of knowledge and action" inspired me with my research of language and science. The so-called "unity of knowledge and action" is the combination of theory and practice, but without too much emphasis on one side. So I often use knowledge that goes beyond the mere linguistics to solve questions within language. I have studied more than one type of knowledge from primary school through to university, and because I have studied not only language, but also physics, chemistry, biology, history, geography, and so on, my broad base of knowledge is much more comprehensive. Language expresses thought, but it is also the creation of the human mind. It seems that language and science have no connection, but actually, they are inseparable. There is no doubt that science is based on experience, which is the study of the nature of things. Some people may be wondering how science relates to the philosophy of language. According my knowledge of aesthetics in human language communication that I have researched, I know that sound is a material thing, so the research for the first half of my book about language was basically taking a scientific approach; the rest of it was completely abstract conclusions. The final conclusion is that the reason why language has beauty is that the structure of the universe contains beauty, so language is isomorphic to the universe. Just as Western philosophy is interested in external existence, focusing on systematicness such as the structure of the universe and the structure of the world, its first stage is the theory of being; its second stage, the theory of knowledge; the third stage, linguistic transformation. Although it has three stages, the core problem is only one, that is, the theory of being. So it is the method that has changed, not the object, and the focus is on the systematicness of philosophy. When talking about the core of Chinese philosophy, Prof. Cheng Zhongying believes that the main questions of Chinese philosophy are made by "one unit, one body, three structures" which contains *The Book of Changes*, Confucianism, Taoism, truth of nature and humanity. Actually what I am pursuing in language research is understanding the truth of nature and the virtue of humanity, so my research of language is always related to philosophy. Generally, you sometimes feel unrelated to the knowledge or ideas, but there is always a certain connection, and it is necessary to understand, to explore. Linguistics cannot simply be studied solely for its own sake, for the sake of studying linguistics. This coincides with the thought of Wang Yangming, as I mentioned earlier. In simple terms, I study linguistics in order to explore the implications of the universe and the value of life, but to understand these laws it is necessary to learn other subjects.

"Seeking Truth" Is the Soul of the Scholar

My research of linguistics embodies my pursuit of the spirit of "seeking truth". There is a strange phenomenon that the more common a thing is, the more people are blind to it. The language of a country and a nation is used every day, but few people research its value. In fact, language is very important. Firstly, language is a tool of daily communication, without which society could not be built. Secondly, language can express the meaning of existence and Western philosophy studies "To Be". Thirdly, language creates words of universal value; without language, the values and laws of the universe, the world and life cannot be fixed. Fourthly, the language itself is a matter of existence. Fifthly, language is the carrier of the spiritual heritage of human civilization. The whole world would be chaotic without language; many people cannot see its value because it is too common. What's more, learning a foreign language is very helpful to pursuing the truth, because it can introduce advanced knowledge from foreign lands; learning a foreign language is like opening a window to the world: The more windows, the more perspectives; the more perspectives, the more easily problems are solved. So my conclusion is that studying language and studying the value of the laws therein is very appealing.

One cannot research knowledge for personal benefit, and one cannot choose knowledge for personal honor and treasure. One cannot run after two horses at the same time. Cultivate original nature to help comprehend truth. One can only comprehend real wisdom in a quiet and far-reaching environment.

当阳明文化遇上语言学

钱 昊

指导教师：王碧颖

几年前的畅销书《明朝那些事儿》以丰富的思想和幽默的语言描写，让许多人知道了王阳明，我也是在那时了解到了明代竟有那么伟大的一位思想家。作为一名外语专业的学生，我深信阳明文化也一样适用于语言学术方面的学习与探究，就这样我联系上了钱冠连教授——一位毕生都在学习、研究语言的学者。在这之前，我还怀疑一位身在广东、年过七旬、知识渊博的学者恐怕不会那么轻易地答应我这么一个在浙江的无名小辈的采访。没想到钱教授在电话里得知我们采访的意图以及我们学院阳明文化的背景后非常高兴，他表达了自己强烈的意愿：作为学者，他有义务来帮助我们年轻一代学子更好地了解与传承阳明文化。

所谓阳明文化，即以陆九渊、王阳明命题的"心即理"的哲学理论为主体的心学思想，强调"致良知"与"知行合一"。在采访过程当中，钱教授用过硬的专业知识，加之以丰富的人生经历为我们详细讲解了他所理解的阳明文化，以及他是如何将阳明精神与自己的语言学研究结合起来的。虽然我在采访的过程中对钱教授所谈论的阳明文化理论理解得不大深刻，比如"求是"精神在研究语言方面的运用，东西方哲学思想的核心问题等，甚至觉得有些地方过于深奥，但这些内容是很值得我此后去细细咀嚼，品味一生的。我想这也正是我采访钱老先生的巨大收获之一。采访中可以看出钱教授对我们的采访问题做了相当充分的准备，每一个问题钱教授都回答得相当有深度，并时时做出点评。正如我之前所了解到的一样，钱教授在讲学时是全身心投入且富有激情的，本次采访钱教授也不例外，他不仅把自己所理解的阳明精神一一解释给我们听，而且专门写了王阳明先生的心学四诀"无善无恶心之体，有善有恶意之动；知善知恶是良知，为善去恶是格物"给我们，可见钱教授对阳明学的喜爱和对我们此次活动的关注之深。

作为一名英语专业的学生，所谓语言，我之前对它的理解就是一项交流的工具，或者是一项用以在社会上谋生的工具，也是开阔眼界的窗口。经过这次对钱冠连教授这位国内语言学界领航人的采访，我对语言这门学问有了新的认识:语言是探索真理的途径。正如钱教授所说:"年轻人写书、做学问不求多，但求创造与深刻。你们不要指望我在课堂上讲的句句都是正确的，有一两句话能启发出你们的智慧来，我的任务就尽到了。"正所谓"弟子不必不如师，师不必贤于弟子，闻道有先后，术业有专攻"，仅仅这一句话我就感受到了钱教授在履行"求是"精神上所达到的境界之高，即放弃一种固执的愚蠢，就是朝智慧更进了一步。

"语言与科学"是我本次采访的主题。在采访当中钱教授将语言与科学的关系分析得头头是道，并指出语言即是一种形式的科学，语言方面的很多问题需要用科学知识来解决，并最终走向哲学。钱冠连教授对物理、化学、生物等理科方面的知识也有相当深厚的造诣，这对于他形成科学的人生观和世界观都有巨大助益。人们可能会疑惑，掌握了理科方面的知识再去研究王阳明哲学不会产生学术研究上的冲突吗？想到王阳明先生既是大思想家，也是杰出的军事家，以上疑问也就不足为奇了。正如爱因斯坦是伟大的科学家，也是小提琴拉得极好的艺术家；达·芬奇是伟大的艺术家，但也因为用绘画的技术来研究生物结构与发明工具而被誉为科学家。这样看来语言与科学又有什么矛盾之处呢？所以钱教授在语言与科学的"知行合一"的造诣上与上述伟人的造诣本质上是相同的。

"多学一门外语，就多打开了一扇世界的窗口，多了一扇窗口，就多了一份对真理的探索。"这是钱冠连教授在采访结束之余，给我们大学生学习外语提出的建议。对于阳明心学，我的真实感受是我大可以鹦鹉学舌般地说出"知行合一"这四字真言，但以我现在的知识水平以及阅历来看，要真正理解其含义，实现自己内心的"知行合一"是远远不够的。这就是所谓的"知道得越多，反而就明白知道得越少"吧！我明白我在学习英语的道路上要走的路依然漫长，但我坚信我这条路的方向是正确的，即学英语，传播中华文化。我曾经听过一位前辈劝学英语的话：如果学了英语而不用于交流，将来怎么在国际上传播我们中华民族的文化？如果我们不传播自己民族的文化，别人又怎么会了解我们？所以说既然学了外语，就得学以致用，凡事只要做久了，其中的真理自会明朗。正所谓实践出真知，只有亲力亲为，才能够获得真理，贯彻"知行合一"精神。

听君一席话，胜读十年书。采访钱冠连教授给我的就是这样的感觉，毕竟与一位学识渊博、人生经历丰富的学者促膝长谈的机会实属难得。采访也使我感受到了一位年近耄耋的长者对真理的不懈追求，也感受到了阳明文化在华夏大地上的蓬勃生命力，历久弥新。我现在对阳明文化的理解也是"只见树木，不见森林"，要真正理解阳明文化，还须自己行动起来，亲自去体会。也正因为如此，强烈的使命感提醒我应把这些宝贵的民族文化遗产继续传承下去，为阳明文化的传播与发扬贡献出我自己的力量。

团队成员：贺　芸　谢雨诗　钱　昊

When Yangming Culture Meets Linguistics

Qian Hao

Supervised by: Wang Biying

Several years ago, a popular book named *The Ups and Downs of the Ming Dynasty* introduced Wang Yangming to many people. I didn't know the Ming Dynasty had such a great philosopher until I read that book. As a foreign language major student, I believe that the philosophy of Wang Yangming can also be used to the study and research of language. That is why I got in touch with Professor Qian Guanlian, a scholar who devotes himself to studying and researching linguistics. Before the interview, I had been worried that Professor Qian, an old, erudite scholar who lives in the Guangdong Province would not readily accept an interview request from an unknown junior from the Zhejiang Province. However, after learning our purpose and the background of our university's Yangming school, Professor Qian was very glad to accept our request and express his strong willingness as a scholar that he has responsibility to help the younger generation of students to better understand and inherit Yangming culture.

"The Mind Is Principle" makes what is called the culture of Wang Yangming (Yangming culture), and it emphasizes "the extension of innate knowledge" and "the unity of knowledge and action". During the interview, Professor Qian used his excellent professional knowledge and abundant life experiences to teach us his own understanding of Yangming culture and how he combined it with his research of linguistics. I felt it a little difficult to understand Professor Qian's theory of Yangming culture like the application of "seeking truth" to language research, the main questions between Western and Eastern philosophy and I even thought some of it too profound, but these theories are worth reading over and over again. I think it in particular is one of the most important benefits I got from Professor Qian. Professor Qian had reviewed our questions in advance of the interview, and during it, he was well prepared for each of our questions, and each answer he gave was insightful. As I had learned before, Professor Qian was passionate and immersed himself when giving lectures, so in this interview, he not only explained each part of the philosophy of Wang Yangming to us, but also wrote Yangming's four aphorisms for us. It can easily be seen that Professor

Qian loves Yangming school through the great attentiveness he gave to our activity.

As an English major student, I previously thought that language is a tool used to communicate or a tool for managing in society and also a window to broaden one's horizons. However, after interviewing Professor Qian, the navigator of philosophy of language in Chinese, I have new understanding of language. Language is a way to explore the truth. Just as Professor Qian said, "In writing books or acquiring knowledge, young people should pursue quality (be creative and profound) instead of quantity. Don't wish that each word I spoke in the classroom was right; if one or two of them inspire you, my mission is accomplished." Like Confucius said, "Pupils are not necessarily inferior to their teachers, and teachers are not necessary better than their pupils; one might have learned the theory earlier than the other, or might be a master in his own specialized field." From just this one sentence of Professor Qian, I felt the high level that he had reached to carry out "seeking truth": For the spirit to attain the higher realms, giving up excessive stubbornness can help a person to get one step closer to real knowledge.

"Language and Science" was the theme of my interview. Professor Qian analyzed the relationship between language and science very well and pointed out that language is one form of science, and many questions of linguistics need to be solved by knowledge of science, and all of these will finally be related to philosophy. It is hard to believe that Professor Qian had such an amazing knowledge of physics, biology, chemistry, and so on, which helped him to build his world view and perspective on life. People may wonder whether mastering the science of knowledge in studying Wang Yangming philosophy will produce a conflict in academic research. It is not surprising that Wang Yangming was not only a great thinker but also an outstanding strategist, just as Albert Einstein was a great scientist and an excellent violinist, and Leonardo da Vinci was famous as an artist but was also hailed as a scientist, using his artistic skills to study biological structures and invent tools. So is there a contradiction between language and science? The essence of Professor Qian's achievement in the attainment of "the unity of knowledge and action", which is reflected in his research of language and science was no different from that of Einstein or da Vinci.

"The more foreign languages you learn, the more windows that lead to the world are opened. More windows mean more ways to pursue the truth." This is the advice given by Professor Qian as the interview came to the end. My own feeling towards Yangming's Mind Studies is that I can speak the words "the unity of knowledge and action" simply like a parrot, but I can't fully understand them or realize them in my heart with my present knowledge and life experience. Such is the saying: "The more you know, the less you know." I know I still have a long way to go with learning English, but I believe that I am going in the right direction, that is, studying English can help spread Chinese culture. One predecessor once said: If we don't learn a foreign language, how then can we spread our nation's culture abroad? If we don't spread our own culture, how can others know about us? So we should learn foreign languages in order to practice, and the truth will be there if we persist with it. Experience is the best teacher. Only doing something by ourselves can we obtain truth and carry out the principle of "the unity of knowledge and action".

A single conversation across the table with a wise man is worth a month of studying books. I got this same feeling from the interview with Professor Qian; it is, after all, rare to have the chance to talk with a knowledgeable, experienced scholar. From this interview, I also felt Professor Qian's vigorous pursuit of truth and the vigorous life of Yangming culture in China. Now my understanding of Yangming culture is also "not seeing the forest for the trees". If I want to go a step further, I need to learn by myself. Therefore, the strong sense of purpose reminds me that I should embrace this valuable national cultural heritage and help to spread Yangming culture.

Team members: He Yun, Xie Yushi, Qian Hao

赵新华：人机融合，用良知求是

Zhao Xinhua: The Integration of Man and Machine, Conscientiously Seeking the Truth

赵新华，剑桥大学博士，现任浙江省余姚市机器换人中心主任，中国机电一体化技术应用协会智能工厂分会秘书长。

Mr. Zhao Xinhua is a PhD of University of Cambridge, director of the Center for Machine Substitutions in Yuyao, Zhejiang Province, and secretary-general of the Intelligent Factory Branch of the China Association for Mechatronics Technology and Application.

人机融合，用良知求是

口述：赵新华
整理：施　懿
指导教师：王碧颖

引子
志不立，天下无可成之事。

——王阳明

自从进入清华大学机械工程与自动化专业之后，我就与机器人产业结下了深厚的缘分。到后来考入英国剑桥大学继续攻读机械专业，我这辈子和机械就分不开了。

中国几代人的梦——智能工厂

改革开放后虽然"中国制造"已经在全球制造业中扮演重要角色，但一直不能摆脱"低端"的标签，这是目前中国制造业的现状。因此实现智能工厂在中国的跨越式普及已经是非常必要了。智能工厂其实就是工业 4.0，简单来说就是让外行的人能够以最快的速度管理并且能不断提升自我。针对目前中国制造业的现状，智能工厂体现了国家的意志，体现了很多深入一线的企业家的梦想，同时也体现了未来 20 年中国能够在世界占有一席之地的重要程度。就像我们很多人都不进入农田所以我们不知道自己多依赖于农业。同理，因为我们都不进入工厂，所以不知道中国经济有多大程度依赖于我们父辈严谨的科学精神以及几十年如一日的工匠精神。智能工厂是中国一代人甚至几代人的梦想，值得去奋斗，但它绝对不是简单的事情，不是一蹴而就的。英国工业革命一百多年以来涌现出了很多诺贝尔奖获得者，很多聪明的科学家都在拼命地做事，可是即使到了 2025 年英国人也不敢说自己能够达到工业 4.0 的水平。所以对于工业基础相当薄弱的我们国家来讲，实现智能工厂的跨越式普及更是一项任重道远的工程。我们的国家也认识到了这一点，制订了"中国制造2025"计划来实现这个目标。我有幸能参与这个计划，目前就任中国机电一体化技术应用协会智能工厂分会的秘书长。

中国制造之殇——标准缺失互通难

中国机电一体化技术应用协会智能工厂分会的主要任务之一就是组织智能工厂领域的国际技术合作、交流活动，举办国内及国际展览业务，为企业开拓国内外市场创造条件。在开展国际交流过程中我们协会也遇到了很多困难，其中最大的困难就是国内标准的缺失。这个标准的缺失，造成了中国十几亿人口的市场、几千万人的自动化领域的从业人员在某些点上不能形成合力，然后导致了彼此的技术标准和设备之间不能互联互通。比如说苹果的手机不能用安卓的程序，手机上一些相当好的程序不能用到 PC 机上。再比如中国的某家企业开发出了一套程序，另一家企业也开发出了一套程序，可是相互之间的数据格式、数据标准不同，造成其在投标过程中有微弱优势，但是一旦想做一个更大的格局的时候就会面临很大的问题。我们用这种零散的方式去做国际合作的话，很容易被国际厂商所淘汰，只能被迫遵循他们的标准。这个问题在未来五年至十年都还是中国制造的一个最难克服的问题。

赵新华老师与采访团队合影

科学精神与王阳明

2016 年 6 月份在余姚举办的第三届中国机器人峰会开幕式的一个亮点就是以王阳明先生为原型的写字机器人惊艳亮相，机器人还为大会题写了"知行合一"四个字。我自己也有幸参与到了阳明机器人的评审工作中，也非常认同王阳明先生的"知行合一""致良知"在我所从事的科学领域上所体现的科学精神。不断追求真理,让科学为人类服务,让人类的生活更加便利就是我所理解的科学精神。人拥有良知。如何将良知体现在机器人当中,就是"致良知"。人机融合实际上就是"知行合一"。现在对于人工智能大家讨论得最热的一件事情不是如何去做这件事情,而是为什么做这件事情以及将来有一天人工智能会不会把人类打败。人机融合,就是在告诉所有机器人的从业者你在做机器人的时候必须要带着一种"知行合一"和"致良知"的精神,带着一种人机融合的思维,把人对社会的良知用一种方法灌输到机器人里面去。我们把王阳明机器人作为我们第一台高仿真机器人,其实其中也蕴含了我们的一个目标,就是希望将来的机器人不仅拥有超过人类的能力,也拥有能与人类共生的智慧,让机器人也拥有人类社会的良知。当未来机器人产业越来越发达的时候,不可避免地就会出现不利于人类社会发展的战争机器人,但我们希望所有机器人的从业者能够领会人机融合的精神。

宁波余姚市智能研究院内景

用良知创新,从"心"到"芯"

如果中国的 90 后认为"颠覆"世界还需要几年甚至十几年的时间的话,那说明你们 90 后还在用 60 后的思维考虑事情。机器人行业也不例外。我认为五年之后机器人产品的价格会低到五万元以下，能处理简单家务活。十年之后，能完成跟人的交互。特别是在养老行业，它能满足中国老龄化社会对服务机器人巨大的需求量。我们研究院肯定就是这个重任的承担者，我们秉承着"人机融合"和"致良知"的精神，发扬严谨的科学精神，把我们对社会的良知灌输给机器人，让科学更好地为人类社会的发展服务。"人机融合，让机器人更智能"的目标任重道远，吾辈将上下求索！

The Integration of Man and Machine, Conscientiously Seeking the Truth

Narrator: Zhao Xinhua

Compiled by: Shi Yi

Supervised by: Wang Biying

That nothing reaches completion is all an outcome of the fact that the determination has not been fixed.

—Wang Yangming

Since entering the mechanical engineering and automation major of Tsinghua University, I've been destined to have a future in the robotics industry. Later admitted to the University of Cambridge to further study mechanical engineering, my life and machinery could not be separated.

The Dream of Generations in China—Intelligent Factory

Since the reform and opening-up, "made in China" has played an important role in the global manufacturing industry, but it has been unable to get rid of the "low end" label which is the current state of the manufacturing industry in China. Therefore, it is necessary to rapidly make known and popularize the intelligent factory in China. In fact, the intelligent factory is the Industry 4.0; in simple terms, it is a factory that allows people to be able to use the fastest operation speed and allows continuous improvement. In view of the present situation of the manufacturing industry in China, the intelligent factory embodies the will of the country and the dream of many dedicated entrepreneurs, and also reflects the importance of China's position in the world in the next 20 years. Just as many of us don't go onto farmland and therefore don't know how much we depend on agriculture, similarly, because we do not enter the factory, we do not know how much the Chinese economy depends on the rigorous scientific spirit of our parents as well as decades of the craftsman's spirit. The intelligent factory is the dream of a generation or even generations of people. It is worth fighting for, but it is definitely not a simple thing to achieve and will not happen overnight. A lot of Nobel laureates have sprung up in Britain since the Industrial Revolution over a century ago, and many clever scientists are doing their best, but even by 2025 the British people will not say that they have reached the level of Industry 4.0. Therefore, since the industrial base is quite weak in our country, the widespread realization of the intelligent factory is a long way off and will be a difficult task to achieve. Our country is aware of this and has formulated a "Made in China 2025" plan to achieve this goal. I am fortunate to be able to participate in this project, currently as the secretary-general of the Intelligent Factory branch of the China Association for Mechatronics Technology and Application.

The Pain of Chinese Manufacturing—The Incompatibility of Industrial Products

One of the main tasks of the Intelligent Factory branch of the Association is to organize the international technical cooperation and exchange activities in the field of the intelligent factory, to hold domestic and international business exhibitions, and to create conditions for enterprises to open up domestic and international markets. In the process of international exchanges, our association has encountered many difficulties, the biggest one being the lack of domestic standards. Due to the lack of the standards, China's market of over a billion people, and tens of millions of workers in the field of automation cannot cooperate with each other, which results in their technological standards and products not being compatible. Apple's mobile phones, for example, cannot use Android's programs, and some pretty good programs on the phone cannot be used on PCs. Another example is that a company in China has developed a program, in the meantime another enterprise also has a similar program, but when they compete in a bidding process, one company may enjoy the advantages on a small scale. If this company wants to have a bigger market, it will face many problems because of its limited data and format. When we use this fragmented approach in international cooperation, we can easily be eliminated by international manufacturers and forced to follow their standards. The problem is one of the most difficult to be overcome in China manufacturing in the next 5 to 10 years.

The Scientific Spirit and Wang Yangming

A highlight of the opening ceremony of the Third China Robotics Summit, held in Yuyao in June 2016, was the stunning debut of the *Calligraphy* robot with Wang Yangming as a prototype, which inscribed the four Chinese characters "知行合一" for "the unity of knowledge and action" on the scene. I have also been fortunate enough to participate in the evaluation work of the Yangming robot, and also very much agreed with Wang Yangming's "unity of knowledge and action" and "conscience" in the scientific field I engaged in, which embodies the scientific spirit. The continuous pursuit of truth, to make science serve humanity and make human life more convenient, is the scientific spirit I understand. People have a conscience. How to embody it in a robot—the integration of man and machine, is actually "the unity of knowledge and action". Now the most popular question about artificial intelligence is not how to make it, but why and whether there will be a day in the future when artificial intelligence will defeat humans. With human-computer fusion, it is necessary to tell all the robot makers that when you are making a robot, you must have knowledge of unity and the spirit of conscience with a kind of man-machine integration of thinking, and we must find a way to make the conscience of society become part of the robot. We regard the Wang Yangming robot as the first of our high simulation robots; in fact, it also contains one of our goals, which is to hope that the future robots not only have more than human capabilities, but also have the wisdom to coexist with mankind, so that robots also have a human social conscience. When the future robotics industry is more highly developed, there will inevitably appear war robots that are not conducive to the development of human society, but we hope that all robot makers can understand the integration of man and machine.

Innovation with Conscience, from "Heart" to "Core"

If the millennial generation of China think that it will take several years or even more than a decade to change the world, it means they are still thinking with the mind of the generation of the 1960s. The robotics industry is no exception. I think in five years' time, the price of robot products will be less than 50,000 yuan, and the robots can manage families' simple household chores, and in ten years' time robots can successfully interact with people. Especially in the old-age industry, it can meet the huge demand for service robots in China's aging society. Our institute definitely undertakes the responsibility of this commitment; we uphold the man-machine integration and the spirit of conscience, and carry forward the rigorous scientific spirit, with our social conscience instilled in the robot so that science can better serve the development of human society. Human-computer fusion, with the aim of making the robot more intelligent, has a long way to go. We will continue to strive!

用心，创芯

施 懿

指导教师：王碧颖

"如果你们90后认为'颠覆'世界还需要几年甚至十几年的时间的话，那说明你们90后还在用60后的思维考虑事情。当然机器人行业也不例外。"

创新应是90后之魂

赵新华老师的这句话让我感触颇深。机器人，即所谓的机械自动化装置，对于我一个日语专业的学生来讲，真的陌生到我只知道这个词在日语中怎么说，其他的便一概不知。但是，与赵老师短短的五十分钟的交流让我对这个领域有了一定的了解和兴趣，甚至让我对机器人产业的普及充满期待。我2015年寒假去日本短期游学后，发现日本的家庭和公司里到处都有服务机器人的身影，这也成为我想咨询赵老师的问题来由。中国什么时候也能像日本这样让机器人产业走进百姓的生活生产中呢？这时赵老师反问我："你认为需要多久？""说实话我认为需要很久，"我笑着答道。这便有了文章开头赵老师的答语。试想，在十年后中国大多数家庭中都出现了服务机器人的身影，能把人类从繁杂的家务活中解放出来，也能在年轻人工作繁忙时照料老年人的生活起居，这是多伟大的产业创新啊！

机器人产业创新之后

在准备采访稿的时候，我通过网络恶补了很多有关机器人的知识，看到网上有报道说，用于家庭打扫的机器人由于家务繁重竟然采取"自燃"的方式进行自毁，感到心有余悸。随着机器人产业不断创新发展，机器人变得越来越"聪明"，那么"将来有一天人类真的会被机器人打败吗？"后来在采访的过程中发现这个问题竟然也成为我准备的这一系列问题中的核心问题。因为每个从事机器人研发的工程师都是在用良知创新，工程师不仅自己内心拥有良知，还把自己的良知用科学技术灌输到机器人的芯片当中去，这是一个"知行合一"的过程，一个从"心"到"芯"的过程。这是每一个机器人从业者都一直秉持的良知。我想，我们可能无须再过分担心这个问题，因为每一个有良知的机器人工程师不仅仅是通过自己掌握的科学技术进行机器人的创新，更是用自己的良知塑造机器人。

外语人的创新

外语专业在外行人眼里貌似就是背单词背单词背单词，和创新、用脑一点都搭不上边。可是我却认为，外语专业与赵老师从事的机器自动化行业也是有相通之处的，也是需要用脑，也是需要创新的。学外语是需要背记大量的单词，但是如何运用王阳明先生的"知行合一"思想智慧地背单词就是每个外语人的创新之处了。采访过后我更加确信了创新这个理念的正确性，靠自己理性的判断结合实际来创新才能更好地服务于我的专业和生活。

团队成员：施 懿　朱嘉平　高志海

Innovation from Heart to Core

Shi Yi

Supervised by: Wang Biying

"If you, the millennial generation, think that it will take several years or even more than a decade to change the world, then it shows that your way of thinking is like the generation of the 1960s. Of course, the robotics industry is no exception."

Innovation Should Be the Soul of the Millennial Generation

Zhao Xinhua's words made me think more deeply. For me, a Japanese language major, the so-called robot is a mechanical automation device; it is really strange to me to only know how to say the word in Japanese, but not to know anything more about it. After the short 50-minute interview with Mr. Zhao, however, I had a certain understanding and interest in the field and I was even filled with expectation given the popularity of the robotics industry. During a winter vacation trip to Japan in 2015, I discovered that families and companies everywhere have service robots; I wanted to ask Mr. Zhao's opinion as to when in China, like Japan, the robot industry's products will become a part of people's lives? Then Mr. Zhao asked me, "How long do you think it will take?" "To be honest," I replied with a smile, "I think it will take a long time." Just imagine, in ten years there will be service robots in most families in China; it could free people from a variety of household tasks and could also help busy young people with daily life care for the elderly. This would be a great industrial innovation!

After the Innovation of the Robotics Industry

When preparing for the interview, by gathering a lot of information about robots from the Internet, I saw an online report that a robot used for household cleaning, due to the heavy household work-load, spontaneously combusted as a way to self-destruct. The fear is that, as the robot industry continues to innovate and develop, the robots will become more and more "intelligent", and then "Will mankind be defeated by robots one day in the future?" Later, in the course of the interview, I found that this problem had become the core issue of my series of questions. Because robotics research and development engineers use conscientious innovation, they not only use their own conscience, but also use science and technology to instill their conscience into the robotics chip, which is "the unity of knowledge and action", a "heart" to "core" process. This is the conscience that every robotics practitioner has always upheld. I think that we may not have to worry too much about this problem, because every conscientious engineer is not only using his own science and technology to effect robot innovation, but is also using his own conscience to shape the robot.

Innovation of Foreign Language Learners

Foreign language majors in some layman's eyes seem only to memorize words, which is not relevant to innovation and does not require much use of the brain. But I think, the machine automation industry Mr. Zhao engaged in and the foreign language profession have similarities: They both need the brain and innovation. Learning a foreign language involves memorizing a lot of words, but how to wisely put Wang Yangming's principle of "the unity of knowledge and action" into practice is the innovation of the people speaking each foreign language. After the interview, I am more convinced that the concept of innovation is correct, as I rely on my own rational judgment combined with innovation to better serve my profession and life.

Team members: Shi Yi, Zhu Jiaping, Gao Zhihai

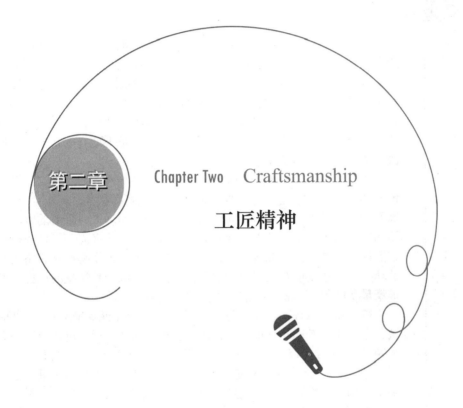

第二章

Chapter Two　　Craftsmanship

工匠精神

导言

Introduction

《道德经》有言：大道至简，一以贯之。世间真理简之又简，奥秘所在，只一个"一"字了得，即一心一意、从一而终。阳明先生曰："一者天理，主一是一心在天理上。"人心与天理相通，实现了一如既往就求得了真理。心，有所属而无旁骛。阳明先生曰："如读书便一心在读书上，接事便一心在接事上。"有事是一，无事也是一；闲时修心是一，忙时修身也是一。不被外物左右，不受虚无纠结。一是不动心的状态，更是不改变的功夫，所谓工匠精神：技艺之道，惟精惟一。

"惟精惟一"是如何用功？阳明先生曰："惟一是惟精主意，惟精是惟一功夫，非惟精之外复有惟一也。"不解此间真意者，恍如身处云端。殊不知，一是事物的本质、问题的关键、为学的功夫、求道的方法。春簸筛拣有农夫惟精的功夫，纯然洁白达米粒惟一的境界；不舍昼夜有老妇磨杵惟精的功夫，细致光滑有刺针惟一的境界；摸爬滚打有路人惟精的功夫，飞檐走壁有侠客惟一的境界。惟精到惟一是蜕变的过程，没有惟精量变的积累，就没有惟一质变的成就。

曾有诗人点评一位生不逢时却又终其一生行善乡里的老人："抱一诚、守一德、专一经、执一艺，修之于身，化之于行，自壮至老，不改其操。"令闻者动容，唏嘘不已，这怎又是一个"一"字了得！阳明先生曰："要晓得圣人之学，只是一诚。"抱一诚是一片丹心的诚意；守一德是始终如一的修为；专一经是一往情深的追随；执一艺是一生不舍的依偎。"只因为在人群中多看了你一眼，再也没能忘掉你的容颜。"于是别人笑我太疯癫，我笑他人看不穿！承诺是一，坚守是一，固执是一，倔强是一；小而美是一，大而全是一，少而精是一，广而博是一。

一生二、二生三、三生万物。这"一"的精神，是天得一则清，地得一则宁，人得一则生。对于匠人，或者制造业从业者，工匠精神就是固本培元。本即生存的根本和支撑力，元是发展的元气和生命力。秋山师承有"守、破、离"三法则，这是匠人求得一技之长的不二心法，也是匠人由术入道的终极升华，安身立命在前，兼济天下在后。工匠精神就是一种沉着稳健、精益求精的心性，是对心性长久磨砺之后形成的此心廓然的气质。

（蔡 亮 撰写）

张晞：心纯则色翠

Zhang Xi: Purity Makes Perfect

　　张晞，1972 年出生于浙江省龙泉市宝溪乡制瓷世家。1988 年，他辍学从艺，拜龙泉青瓷民间杰出老艺人张高岳先生为师。经过二十几载的磨炼，他精通龙泉青瓷传统烧制技艺的各项工序，擅长手拉坯，精于雕刻，继承传统，推陈出新。2010 年 7 月，他被授予"浙江省工艺美术大师"称号。青瓷古法柴烧技艺践行者，"跟我一起烧一窑青瓷"众筹项目发起者。

　　Zhang Xi was born in 1972 to a family of celadon masters in Baoxi Village, Longquan City, Zhejiang Province. In 1988, he dropped out of school for art, and served an apprenticeship to the outstanding folk artist, Zhang Gaoyue, who was a marvelous master in Longquan celadon. After more than 20 years of trials and tribulations, he is greatly proficient in the traditional sintering workmanship of Longquan celadon. In July 2010, he was honored with the title of "Master of Industrial Arts in Zhejiang Province". He is a practitioner of the traditional firing technology for Longquan celadon, as well as the organizer of the crowdfunding of "fire a kiln of celadon with me".

心纯则色翠

口述：张　晞
整理：叶珈妤
指导教师：王雪芹

引　子

惟一是惟精主意，惟精是惟一功夫，非惟精之外复有惟一也。

——王阳明

采访张晞先生

心到了，你就知道了

我出生在龙泉青瓷的发源地——龙泉宝溪，这里也是让我有真正接触到制瓷的感觉的地方。爷爷在清末民初的时候是民间青瓷艺人的杰出代表，他对瓷器十分热爱，对手艺一直有一种坚守。在当时，制瓷的设备没有现在发达，爷爷都是在家自己研究。为了能够全面地掌握制作的技艺，他要求自己的每件作品都做到精益求精。小时候在我的印象中，爷爷就是魔术师，能够控制炉火的大小和温度的高低。一句"温度到了"，就预示着一批柴烧的问世。我曾无数次问过爷爷掌握火候的秘诀，爷爷总是淡淡说："心到了，你就知道了。"

在家乡这样一个大背景下，在爷爷的影响下，我十七岁就开始跟着爷爷学青瓷的制作技艺。在那个年代，没有想过要把瓷器发展到什么程度，纯粹就是想做一个匠人，有以此为生的想法。回想最开始随同爷爷到山上找矿土，用石磨手工磨细矿石。龙泉青瓷的风格以造型见长，以釉取胜，以浅浮雕饰为优势。其釉色细腻滑润，似玉非玉，看起来很通透，所以磨制时要十分用心。如有一道工序不符合标准，最终出来的瓷器将是次品。爷爷悉心教导我，告诉我要"以勤补拙"，他希望我能像他一样比较全面地掌握技艺。勤学苦练两年后，我学会了仿古青瓷的整套工艺。爷爷的严格要求让我有了很扎实的基本功，精通龙泉青瓷传统烧制技艺的各项工序，擅长手拉坯与雕刻。

心和瓷连在一起的快乐

我从事了二十多年的制瓷，大大小小的称号也获得了很多，但我心里有很清醒的认识，很多是政府认为你对陶瓷事业做出了一定的贡献而给予的认可。我认为自己还没有达到所谓大师的水平，我还认为我们匠人不应该痴迷于这些称呼，应该要更加投入到瓷器的制作中，始终要对得起自己的作品，对它们中的每一件负责。那种身心和瓷器连在一起的快乐只有自己体会得到。每每有灵感的出现，会立刻去研究制作，很多时候从想法到成品的出现要磨合很长时间。但是难免也会有成品做不出来或是没达到预计效果的时候，会有一段消极的时间，但是脑子里那些好的想法始终不忍心放弃，我会重新调整，一遍遍去尝试，直到满意为止。

我从开始制瓷到 2007 年主要是制作仿古青瓷。龙泉青瓷的鼎盛时期是在南宋，釉色和造型都达到高峰，仿古可以让沉淀几千年的东西在现代继续展现出来。这种古代样式的瓷器在消费群中是很受欢迎的。

但是仿古仿得再好，它始终是赝品，它缺少了我自己的想法，没有理念附加在其中。而在大家对手艺人越来越尊重这样一个社会背景下，我想在现有的技艺下突破自己。2007 年之后我开始转型做艺术瓷。我有此前多年的经验，再依托自身比较扎实的基本功，以及对瓷器从古到今清晰脉络的掌握，所以，在掺杂了很多龙泉窑文化的基础上，我的作品里蕴含着这么多年自己对瓷器的理解。可以说，这是在传统的瓷器上加入个人认知进行的创新，而这种创新离不开龙泉窑文化这个庞大的系统。说到龙泉窑，你可能会想到造型、釉色和雕饰，它没有一个明确的载体。我对于龙泉窑的传承主要就是它简约的整体、厚重的釉色、大写意。我从这些文化里汲取了很多养分。

仅有传统的青瓷文化及个人的理解还是不够的，我常常去意会其他手艺人对瓷器的理解，多次去苏州大学等处进修，与一些全国顶尖的手艺人在一起相互学习。这些经历让我得到很多知识，大家相互学习但又不丢弃自己独有的想法。更值得一说的是，有些对青瓷特别有兴趣的朋友会从自己的角度表达对青瓷创作上的看法，尽管他们并非专业的人士，但他们往往更能找到与众不同的突破口，让制作出来的青瓷更富有情感和生命力。

心纯了，色就翠了

龙泉青瓷烧制技艺在 2009 年的时候被评为人类非物质文化遗产，这种烧制技艺就是龙窑的烧制技艺，这是老祖宗给我们留下来的传统烧制技艺。筹备一次古法柴烧青瓷一般需要四个月时间，且烧瓷时间选在秋季最为理想。烧制一次需要三十个小时，要由二十多个窑工一起完成，什么时候添柴，什么时候出炉，都很有讲究。柴烧就是用心烧，不容有半点马虎、半点杂念。心纯了，色就翠了。正是因为这些"苛刻"条件，从 20 世纪 90 年代开始，这个手艺渐渐被液化气窑取代。新的东西有好的一面，它把青瓷做得更加完美，更加符合大众的审美。不足的一面就是它缺少了一种古朴的美、精细和更加贴近大自然的厚重感和古朴。龙窑可以真正体现出青瓷的美。制瓷人对于自己的作品是可以发挥一百分的心思，投入一百分的力。但是这往往还是要经受火的考验，很多制作出来的成品是会和我们想象的有着天差地别，但是这种巨大的差别又会让我们遇到难以想象的独一无二的作品，所以这种柴烧的技艺很值得我们去传承。我认为这种技艺是不能因为时间而流逝的。虽然前两年这一方面也得到了政府的一些资助，继续去传承这个手艺，但是我们的精力也还是有限的。我就想，作为一个手艺人我应该为此尽一点绵薄之力。

目前，龙泉在从事青瓷制作的手艺人有千余户，而古法柴烧却渐渐被人们淡忘，这门手艺的传承人也越来越少，我想在古瓷之乡恢复古法柴烧技艺。有媒体朋友想到现在一种比较流行的方式——众筹。希望通过这种实践，让古法柴烧青瓷这门古老的手艺得到保护和传承，让更多的人看到"青如天、明如镜、声如磬"的龙泉柴烧青瓷。经过设计和准备，"众筹"项目得以推出，大家的反响比较热烈。我们在"众筹"平台上发出了"跟我一起烧一窑青瓷"的倡议，短短半个月时间就吸引了四百多人"认筹"。"众筹"款从 200 元到 3 万元不等，分为七个档次，最终共筹集 40 万元。"认筹"人来自全国各地，远至新疆、广西，近至江苏、上海，虽然大部分人对古法柴烧青瓷技艺并不了解，但是我感受到了他们对传统文化的热爱。当我和窑工们打开窑门，取出一件件如玉般清澈明丽的青瓷时，"认筹人"和游客们一拥而上，激动不已，纷纷用手机和相机记录下期盼已久的瞬间。

我刚开始还是比较担忧的，认为现在的年轻人对于这种传统的东西兴趣不大，对于古法的烧制也是很担忧的。那次众筹给我很深的感受，感觉到这种传统烧制技艺的前途会因有那么多人的喜爱而光明。这让我更有理由、更有责任将古法柴烧很好地继承下去。我会用更多的方式让对这门技艺有兴趣的人更深地了解和接触到它。

对于徒弟们，我像爷爷曾经教我时那般严格，因为这门技艺的传承需要他们静下心来，用心地、全方位地学。我们要把瓷器制作到自己最满意的程度。我相信龙泉青瓷的未来必定是美好的，优秀的会越来越优秀，几千年的文化不会在这代消逝，而是薪火相传，留传它最纯粹的青色。

Purity Makes Perfect

Narrator: Zhang Xi
Compiled by: Ye Jiayu
Supervised by: Wang Xueqin

Singleness is the goal of refinement and refinement is the effort to achieve singleness. It is not that outside of refinement there is another thing called singleness.

—Wang Yangming

Your Mind Is Here, and Then You Know

I was born in Baoxi Village, the birthplace of Longquan celadon. It was in Baoxi that I came into real contact with porcelain making. My grandfather was an outstanding folk celadon artist in the late Qing Dynasty and the early period of the Republic. He loved the art of celadon so much that he never thought about giving up on the craft. At that time, the equipment of porcelain making was not as advanced as it is now; he carefully studied the process and strived for perfection in every piece of celadon. In my childhood memory, my grandfather was a magician capable of perfectly controlling the fire and the temperature of the kiln. His saying, "the temperature is just fine" announced the completion of each new celadon. I asked my grandfather many times about the secret of mastering kiln, but grandpa always lightly told me, "When your mind is here, then you will know."

Under the influence of my grandfather as well as the celadon-making atmosphere in my hometown, I began to learn the technique of celadon making at age 17. In those days, I never had a deep thought about how far I could go on the road of developing the technique; I only wanted to be a craftsman who could earn a living by making celadon. Looking back at that time when my grandfather and I went into the mountains, we continually searched for fine-grained natural rocks or soil material, and then ground the rocks by hand into finer ores with stone mills. Longquan celadon is famed for its shape, glaze and decoration in low relief; the glazed celadon pieces look like jade—smooth, bright and pure. Consequently, the process of grinding needs to be carried out very carefully. If one process doesn't meet the standard, the porcelain will finally be defective. Grandpa gave me careful instructions and kept telling me that "practice makes perfect." He hoped I could fully master the skills as he did. After two years of hard work and practice, I learned the entire process of antique celadon making. My grandpa's strict requirements equipped me with a very solid mastery of basic skills, making me proficient in the traditional technique of Longquan celadon, such as molding and sculpturing.

The Happiness of My Devotion to Celadon

Having engaged in celadon making for more than 20 years, I was granted a great many diverse titles. I have a very clear understanding, knowing that most of these titles embody our government's recognition of my contribution in celadon production. I deeply believe that I am not a real master yet, and we craftsmen are not supposed to be obsessive about these forms of address. Instead, we need to be more involved in the production of porcelain, being more responsible for each piece of work. It is only ourselves who can truly feel the happiness of devotion to celadon. Whenever inspiration flashes, I will immediately go to my study. Usually it takes a long period of time to bring your ideas into practice. It is inevitable for you to feel depressed and frustrated for an even longer time, since the finished product is not successful nor has it achieved the expected results. However, I will not give up these good ideas in my mind; thus I will readjust and retry again and again, until I find satisfaction.

From the time I started making celadon to the year 2007, I mainly made antique celadon. The golden age of Longquan celadon was during the Southern Song Dynasty when its glaze and shape both achieved a peak in history. Antiquing can let things that have been accumulated over thousands of years continue to show in modern times. This kind of ancient celadon is popular to consumers.

However, antique celadon is not real antique after all, no matter how excellent it is; what's more, it lacks my own original ideas and concepts. In our society, there is a growing respect for craftsmanship, thus I would like to make significant breakthroughs based on current technology. After 2007, I began to make a transition to art porcelain production. Years of experience and my own solid basic skills, as well as the clear understanding of celadon culture, made it possible for me to bring forth my own innovation and improvement. It can be said that such innovation and improvement of traditional porcelain is inseparable from the Longquan celadon culture. Speaking of the Longquan celadon, you might think of shape, glaze and decoration, but it does not have a specific carrier. I mainly carry on its simplicity, jade-like glaze, and freehand decoration. Fortunately, I have absorbed a lot of values from these cultures.

Familiarity with the traditional celadon culture and personal interpretation leave much to be desired. Therefore I often try to feel other artisans' understanding of china. I have been to Suzhou University and other places for further study from time to time, learning together with top artisans by exchanging views, which helps me to accumulate a lot of knowledge and experience. We learn from each other but do not lose our own ideas. It is worth mentioning that some friends with keen interest in celadon expressed unique and original ideas, though non-professional, which could enable me to find a breakthrough. All these can help empower celadon to be more alive and emotional.

Purity Makes Perfect

Sintering technology of Longquan celadon was inscribed on the list of the Intangible Cultural Heritage of Humanity in 2009; such celadon firing using woods as fuel is called the Longquan Kiln firing technique, inherited from our ancestors. Preparation for adopting an ancient method to produce celadon normally takes 4 months, and burning in autumn is the best. The burning process takes 30 hours, and it needs to be completed by more than 20 workers. When to add wood, when to take out of kiln—all this needs carefulness, without any sloppiness or distraction. As long as you make effort, you concentrate, and you devote yourself, it will be made perfect. The color of the celadon will be emerald. New technology came and it was replaced by liquefied gas kilns in the 1990s. The positive aspect is that liquefied gas kilns produce finer porcelain, meeting the aesthetic needs of the masses. The negative aspect is that it lacks a kind of ancient beauty, delicacy, and purity. Longquan Kilns can truly reflect the beauty of celadon. Every craftsman will exert all his effort in his work. But the final work has to be tested by fire; therefore, many products prove to be greatly different from our expectations. This huge difference will lead to incredible works, so this artistry is worthy of our inheritance. This artistry will not die away as time goes by. Two years ago, our government sponsored us to continue to inherit this skill, but it is still limited. As a craftsman, I am responsible for making more effort.

At present, there are more than one thousand households engaging in Longquan celadon production. The old firing method is gradually being forgotten. The ancient way of using wood as fuel is no longer used by people, and fewer and fewer artisans are willing to inherit this technique. I want to restore the old technology of using wood as fuel in Longquan. Some of my media friends have thought of a more popular way—"crowdfunding". It is hoped that through this practice, the ancient craft can get an inheritance and protection, helping more people see Longquan wood fired celadon which is "green as the sky, bright as a mirror, and sounds like a chime stone". After careful design and preparation, crowdfunding has elicited positive responses. We issued a call of "fire a kiln of celadon with me" on the crowdfunding platform. After half a month, more than 400 people supported the proposal. The funding ranged from 200 yuan to 30,000 yuan, which could be divided into 7 levels. Eventually, we raised a total of 400,000 yuan. The individuals who supported the proposal came from all over the country, as far as Xinjiang, Guangxi, and as close as Jiangsu and Shanghai. Although most of them had no idea about using woods as fuel to burn celadon, their love for traditional culture was beyond all doubt. When we opened the kiln door and took out the jade-like celadon, all those present rushed forward, excited and anxious. They all couldn't wait to record the long-awaited moment with their mobile phones and cameras.

At the very beginning, I was rather worried, assuming that nowadays young people have little interest in these traditions, as well as being anxious about the inheritance of the ancient method of firing. The crowdfunding impressed me profoundly, which made me believe the future of the traditional firing technique will be brighter since so many people love it. This gives me more reasons and more responsibility to inherit the ancient technology. I will adopt more diverse ways to help those interested to have more access to a deeper understanding of Longquan Kiln firing technique.

I treat my apprentices as strictly as my grandfather taught me, because the inheritance of this skill needs them to be calm and devoted. We shall make most satisfactory products. I truly believe that Longquan celadon possesses a bright future and its influence will increasingly be widespread. Thousands of years of culture and cultivation will not die away in this generation; celadon kilns in Longquan will successively pass on the purity and emerald dream in future generations.

看我扁舟望翠微

叶珈妤

指导教师：王雪芹

2016 年"用声音叙事"活动的主题是：我是阳明青年——探索阳明精神的传播者和践行者。对于王阳明的陌生感并没有因为集训而消除殆尽，我想跳出高中课本中那个被定格的历史人物，从另外一个角度去思考这个神一样的男子。我的思绪不断地被几个关键的字眼所打断，"心即理""致良知""知行合一"。我无法迅速地厘清其间的逻辑，更无法准确地定位何为阳明精神，直到在讲座中听到："阳明文化的精髓就是把个人对事业和美的追求结合在一起，落在具体的事情上，落到具体的人上，延伸到企业家身上就是企业家精神，到慈善家身上就是公益精神，到工匠身上就是工匠精神。"于是阳明在我心里突然间就鲜活起来了，他首先是一个纯粹的人。

工匠精神对我而言，就像是雕琢一块木头。起初，你只是想把它打磨得平滑一些，看起来顺眼一些。后来，你觉得给它弄出个形状会更有意思。到这里你不再只是把它当木头看，你开始不满足它的不完美，因此不断地改造着它。你作为一个塑造它的人在不断追求着实在而美的视觉，然后在不自觉中已经把自己融入其中，你不甘于它和自己的普通。工匠手中的那些作品在普通人眼里只是精美，对他自己而言这代表着严谨、付出，甚至折射着自己的影子。

寻找符合主题的采访对象是一个艰难的过程，我几次都从准备放弃的念头中爬出来，那个工匠到底在哪里？网络、身边的同学、亲朋好友，不放过任何可能有用的信息。一封封发出去的邮件就好像落入深渊，没有一点回复的动静……直到偶然看见几件精美的龙泉青瓷作品，纯净的翠绿带着些厚重感，它们给我一种平静而美妙的感觉。我开始从网上找它们的作者，初步了解了青瓷的制作以及以往的故事。目标明确了，事情就开始顺利起来，我通过朋友联系到了这位大师。那些作品的灵动，让我觉得它们是附有人的感情的，我坚信这就是那位纯纯粹粹地追求着美、在坚守中创作美的人。这样的人，才是我所理解的具有工匠精神的阳明文化的传播者和践行者。

我采访的人是一位制作龙泉青瓷的省级工艺美术大师——张晞。采访当天我们来到他的青瓷作坊，在办公室等待。没过多久衣着简朴的他匆匆赶来了，看样子是刚忙活完青瓷的制作。张晞先生从小就随爷爷接触到这门手艺，如今小有名气却没有一点架子。开始采访时，我感觉对面坐着的只是一位亲切的长辈在向我们讲述他经历的一些事情。如果没有这次采访的机会，我可能不会去了解那些精美的瓷器，更不会知道随着时代变迁，一些传统的精粹正在慢慢流失。张晞先生从小在爷爷的严格要求下全方面学习制瓷，虽然刚开始谈不上有着伟大的志向，但是渐渐地对这门技艺有了感情，也取得了一定的成果，便觉得应该让龙泉青瓷在自己的努力下有新的发展。从仿古到艺术瓷，再到最近的传统古法烧制的回归，每一步都是对工艺的发展，对美的追求和对传统的继承与发扬。我们认为的工匠精神是一种严谨的态度，是一种对美的追求。张晞先生20多年来从事制瓷工作也正坚守着这种精神，始终对得起自己的本心，对自己的作品负责。从他的言语和坚定的眼神中，我感受到的是他对自己手艺的自信，对龙泉青瓷的自豪感以及对传统青瓷文化的那份执着。当现代工艺慢慢替代古法的时候，他依旧坚信，传统的、优秀的烧制技艺不会流失，因为他正用自己的方法为之努力着。关于这些经历，或许他自身从没想过这就是对于阳明精神的实践。纯粹只是为了制造出好的瓷器，不断摸索学习，一直跟随着自己的心，制作出对得起自己、对得起龙泉青瓷文化的作品。当传统的东西在流逝时，他仍没放下传统的那份责任，依旧追求更有质感的青瓷。

　　我从最开始了解阳明文化，到采访阳明文化的践行者，把原本觉得陌生又乏味的知识变为我感兴趣的部分并存储在脑子里，并且从一个人身上一点点得到印证，也更加明了了阳明文化向我们传递了些什么。"致良知""知行合一""事上磨"等等并不是表面那几个字可以解释清楚的，只有当你投入实践中，才会有深刻体会。看我扁舟望翠微，我观望着、探寻着阳明精神，悠悠荡荡，正被其中的奥义深深折服的时候，我发现它正投射着光芒照开我的心路。一条我从没走过的"路"。我现在所感悟到的只是浅显的部分，在以后它或许能给我带来更多不简单的感受。

团队成员：叶珈妤　董　路　项金龙　李　铭

Pursue Purity, Enjoy Beauty

Ye Jiayu

Supervised by: Wang Xueqin

The theme of "Beyond the Voices" in the year 2016 is "I'm a Young Practitioner of Yangming Philosophy". The strange opinion of Wang Yangming has not been eliminated by training. I want to get rid of the fixed image of Wang Yangming in high school textbooks, trying to think of him from another angle besides a godlike man. My mind was wholly taken up with several key words—"mind is principle", "the extension of innate knowledge", "the unity of knowledge and action". I could not quickly clear my mind, nor be able to fully comprehend the spirit of Yangming, until I heard one sentence in a lecture: "The essence of Yangming culture is putting the pursuit of career and beauty together, and falls on specific things and people. To an entrepreneur, it is the entrepreneurial spirit; to a philanthropist, it is the spirit of public service; to a craftsman, it is the spirit of craftsmanship." So Yangming in my heart suddenly becomes alive; he first is a pure person.

The spirit of craftsmanship for me is like carving a piece of wood. At first you just want to polish it smoother, so it looks more pleasing to the eyes, and then you think it would be more interesting to come up with a shape. You no longer consider it just a piece of wood, but instead, you constantly transform it, since you cannot stand its imperfection. You, as a craftsman, are in constant pursuit of the real beauty of the work, unconsciously putting yourself into the product, which you demand to be extraordinary. The work piece of the craftsmen is splendid in the eyes of ordinary people, however, for himself, it represents exactness and effort, even a reflection of himself.

It was a difficult process to find an interview subject, and I was almost on the verge of giving up. Where was the craftsman I was searching for? I collected information from the Internet, classmates, friends and relatives, but it seemed to be in vain. A lot of emails were sent out and it was as if they fell into an abyss, without any reply… until I encountered some delicate Longquan celadon which was pure green and quite heavy, giving me a calm and wonderful feeling. I began to look for the creator on the Internet, getting a primary understanding of his production of celadon as well as the previous story. Things began to go more smoothly, and I managed to get into contact with this master via one friend. The inspiration of those works made me feel that they were attached with feelings and emotions; I believe that he is a person who purely pursues beauty and sticks to creating beauty. Such a person is one of the communicators and practitioners of Yangming's spirit in my understanding.

The person I interviewed, Zhang Xi, is a master of arts and crafts at provincial level, engaging in Longquan celadon production. On the day of the interview, we arrived at his celadon workshop and waited in his office. Soon he came in a hurry, simply dressed, just having finished his work on hand. We knew he had learned the trade from his grandfather since he was very young. Being a celebrity in this field, he did not put on any airs or graces. During the interview, I felt somewhat that he was like an intimate elder who was pleasantly telling us his experience. Without this interview, I would never have been concerned about those fine porcelain, not to mention that with the changing times, some traditions are slowly dying out. Mr. Zhang mastered the sintering technology of Longquan celadon from an early age under the strict instruction of his grandfather. Although he had no great ambitions at the very beginning, he developed a strong attachment to celadon production and attained great achievements. He hopes Longquan celadon will have a new trend of development through his efforts. From antique porcelain to artistic porcelain and then to the recent return of the traditional methods of firing, all of them reflect the development of the trade, the pursuit of beauty and the inheritance and development of the tradition. We believe the spirit of craftsmanship is rigorous, and is a pursuit of beauty. Mr. Zhang adhered to this spirit for more than 20 years, following his heart and being responsible for his products. His words and the steadiness in his eyes demonstrate his self-confidence in his handicrafts, his pride in Longquan celadon, and his commitment to the traditional celadon culture. When the ancient technique is gradually replaced by modern technology, he is still convinced that the excellent traditional firing technique will not be lost, because he spares no effort to carry it on. He probably never thought that his experience is a Yangming spiritual practice. Simply trying to produce better celadon, he follows his heart and continually improves himself, being responsible for himself and his products. While traditions are dying out, he refuses to abdicate his responsibility for carrying on these traditions, and he will never give up his pursuit of precious jade-like celadon.

Looking back to the time when I started to be familiar with Yangming culture, I realize the interview of the practitioner of Yangming culture makes book knowledge interesting and vivid in my mind. It makes me aware of the connotation of Yangming culture. "The extension of innate knowledge", "the unity of knowledge and action", "matter of dedication" and so on could not be comprehended easily and clearly. Only when you put these into practice, will you deeply understand. I am on my way to explore Yangming's spirit, greatly impressed by its richness and profoundness. It projects light to my heart, opening a brand-new door for me. What I have realized now is just a tip of the iceberg; in the future, it might bring me more meaningful feelings and understandings.

Team members: Ye Jiayu, Dong Lu, Xiang Jinlong, Li Ming

徐瑞鸿：以匠人之心，琢一世瓷事

Xu Ruihong: Never Regret Getting into Porcelain

徐瑞鸿，1965 年出生于台北，是台湾著名陶艺家、东海堂三陶轩陶瓷艺术公司总监。他从十四岁起接触陶艺，师从台北故宫博物院前研究员刘良佑教授研制汝窑系统，师从台湾陶艺之父林葆家教授研习釉药。2001 年他来到景德镇，创办东海堂陶瓷艺术有限公司和三陶轩陶艺工作室，专攻五大名窑之首的汝窑。徐瑞鸿倡导陶瓷的淑世民用，致力于把陶瓷带进人们的日常生活。其作品以优雅精致著称，体现了他的个人品格和美学修养。

Born in 1965 in Taipei, Xu Ruihong is a famous ceramist in Taiwan and the director of Donghai Tang Santao Xuan Ceramic Art Company. At the age of 14, he began to learn about pottery. When he was young, he learned Ru Kiln from his teacher Liu Liangyou, who used to be the researcher of the Taipei Palace Museum. He also learned the development of glaze from Professor Lin Baojia, who is the father of pottery in Taiwan. In 2001, he came to Jingdezhen and founded Donghai Tang Ceramic Art Company and Santao Xuan Pottery Studio, specializing in Ru Kiln which ranks first in five famous kilns. He advocated that pottery should be used in our daily life. His work is known for its refinement and elegance, reflecting his personal qualities and aesthetic accomplishments.

以匠人之心，琢一世瓷事

口述：徐瑞鸿
整理：郑秀媛
指导教师：王雪芹

引 子

虽百工技艺，未有不本于志者。

——王阳明

初"碰"瓷：少年励志，十四岁初识瓷器

台湾的孩子从小就开始打工，自力更生。十四岁那年的暑假，我在一家陶瓷厂打工，那是我第一次接触瓷器，从此就和陶瓷结下了不解之缘。陶瓷最主要的元素是泥土，刚开始，我以为泥土加上自己的双手就可以做出陶瓷，但是慢慢地，我发现陶瓷需要用火去灼烧，需要釉药，需要掌控温度。渐渐地，整个工艺过程变得越来越清晰。对我来说，这是陶艺兴趣的养成。但是，陶瓷的美感真正打动我的时刻，是在一次台北故宫博物院的官窑特展上，那时我才十二岁出头。

每个人在成长的过程中都会对文化有一定的关注，只是不自知罢了。我从小就喜欢画画，特别是画一些有中国传统色彩的水墨画，比如龙、凤等。那时候就已经开始关注一些有中国元素的事物了，只是当时的我并不懂得那是中国文化。而且在那个年代，当时台湾能看到传统的具备中国色彩的往往只有青花，但那时的我并不觉得青花能够代表中国文化传统的运用。直到有一天，隔着台北故宫博物院的玻璃，我第一次看见宋代青瓷。青瓷那份与世无争的恬静美深深地震撼了我。看到它之后，我才知道世界上竟然有这么美的瓷器，那份单纯的美感打动了我。情不知所起，一往而深。从那时候起，我心里懵懵懂懂地开始有了喜欢的瓷器，陶瓷对我来说已经是一个很重要的文化材料，但当时的我还是不懂得什么叫陶瓷，什么叫陶艺。为此，我放下了台北的生活只身来到大陆，开始了我的寻根之旅。

在继承和发展传统文化与社会文明方面，台湾的成就有目共睹，但是大陆更胜一筹。台湾的文化类似于一件爸爸留给我的衣服，但我心里觉得还是要有一个穿衣服的肉体，而这个肉体就在大陆。我想了解大陆的泥土、山川和其他自然资源，我想去了解蝉怎样长大，它怎么在树上成长。这才是我理想中应该有的陶艺面貌，而不是去研究、琢磨爸爸留给我的衣服，然后按照它的款式去做另外一件

新的衣服。所以，我来到了大陆。

坐着火车，我一边享受着祖国大陆的山川美景，一边体会着文化脉络在地理上给我的感受。之后我到了景德镇。景德镇以瓷都之称闻名于世界，有传统的陶瓷面貌，制瓷工艺也传承得很好，于是我在景德镇落了户。但是，渐渐我发现景德镇的文化氛围已经很淡薄，景德镇更像是一位没落的贵族，保留着千年留下来的招牌，但他的陶瓷面貌再没有变化和创新，原料的使用和很多工艺的发展都已停滞。景德镇的陶瓷工艺水平还停留在清代。他们还在用手工去表示这个器物的价值，也就是工艺的价值很高但是人的价值很低。我在景德镇当了几十年的老师教他们怎么把泥土变成泥浆，教他们什么是陶瓷的观念。陶瓷一定要是手工制作才是工艺品吗？答案当然是否定的。之后我离开景德镇，来到了浙江衢州。

常常有人问我浙江的泥土能不能做成陶瓷。有这种疑问的最主要的原因是对陶艺的不理解，事实上只要是泥土就能做成陶瓷。所以，我在浙江的一个工作重点就是要把踩着的泥土变成我喜欢的陶瓷。真正的陶艺家必须面对材料，把它变成你喜欢的东西甚至是合适的东西。我们花了几年的时间研究如何使用本地原料烧造青瓷，以及合理的温度范围和呈色效果，希望能以本地原料为基础构建一套新的青瓷体系。这就是陶艺，我把它建立在生活文化上。我认为陶艺必须与生活有关系，它是实用艺术里面最重要的一种文化现象，这就是我喜欢的陶艺。

识瓷难：人到中年，方识制瓷真谛

每天，从早晨 7 点开始，起床遛狗，接着揉泥、拉坯、配釉、写釉式、修坯……这就是我的幸福生活。还记得，刚开始学习陶艺制作的时候是日复一日的失败。在工艺上我没有老师，因此我需要自己摸索。所以，我现在做工艺传承的目的就是希望我的学生不会像我一样花二三十年的时间来完善一套工艺。我们都认为大陆的工艺已经断了，但是台湾的工艺其实早就断掉了。这个是社会发展的一个过程。而我现在要把工艺真正地、完整地拿回来，就必须身体力行地再做一遍古人做过的事，然后去判断什么是真的，什么是假的，什么是被需要的，什么是合适的。

对我来说，工艺的价值非常重要，但是我更注重的是人的价值。心到然后手到，意志到了你才会看到。我觉得心学还是要架构在行上，工艺的价值才会变成人的价值，也就是我们说的"知行合一"。做陶瓷当然也需要"知行合一"。不管是工艺还是思想，"知行合一"都是最重要的。相较于"陶艺家"的称号，我更喜欢称自己为"陶人"。我花了二十年的时间才知道我为什么喜欢青瓷，青瓷应该做成什么面貌。我在追求一种真实陶人的面貌，同样地，我追了找了二十年才知道什么叫作陶人。

我有两个老师，林葆家老师和刘良佑老师。林葆家老师帮我打开了釉药研究的大门，刘良佑老师则让我对陶艺的整个面貌有一个心到的学习方式。我是属于比较幸运的人，因为我先学的心才学的手，我的心到了那里我的手再跟上。两个老师都对我有很深的影响。如果我当时跟着林老师一辈子在工艺这一块活动，那我现在可能还搞不清自己到底在做什么。同样地，如果我跟着刘老师只在心这一块不断琢磨，那我现在可能只会有一些不切实际的想法。传承最大的一个目的就是可以少走弯路，如果没有我的两个老师那我在思维上的弯路就会走得更多。

致匠心：器物有魂魄，匠人自用心

我在想，我们社会工匠精神的提出是受到日本的影响。日本的工匠精神是以认真两个字作为基础的。他们认真地做好一个人应该做好的每一件事。我觉得我们应该学习的不是工匠精神，是认真。我们可以谈工匠精神，但是要更深入，它只是一个基础，不会是文化发展的最终目的。

工匠精神还有重要的一点就是美感，对美的追求。别人把我做的东西叫汝瓷，但是我从来都没有想过要去复制汝窑。汝窑难做的说法是从清代开始的，但他们不是因为技术困难而是因为没有美感，也就是，心没到，所以他们的手一辈子都到不了。我能做到的原因是我知道什么是美，而不是知道什么是汝窑。事实上，美感怎么确定，我也是花了快二十年的时间才知道的。对我来说，美不是创造出来的而是积累出来的。神秀大师讲的"身是菩提树，心如明镜台，时时勤拂拭，莫使惹尘埃"和慧能大师讲的"菩提本无树，明镜亦非台，本来无一物，何处惹尘埃"是相反的方式。慧能大师是天才，我不是，我宁可像神秀大师一样找到我自己的心然后把它保持好。我不是天才，我只不过是善于积累和观察，善于学习，把我喜欢的真实的东西发掘出来。这就是我要的美。我的每一个线条都是经过非常多的失败产生出来的。

中国的陶瓷语言最重要的一部分就是实用思想，也就是王阳明先生提出的"亲民"思想。任何工具都具备淑世思想，都会产生人的价值。我想要把瓷器变成实用的器具，如果只是做一个放在橱柜展览的花瓶，那么，这个不是陶艺，只是一种陶瓷生产的方式。陶艺必须是创作者身体力行，跟釉药、泥土和火发生碰撞，而只有从创作者的手中传递到使用者的手里，才算完成一次真正意义上的陶艺行为。所以，我把我的工作室命名为三陶轩，这三陶指的就是"轻微修身，温文养人，淑世民用"。一件瓷器，摆在那里供人参观，只是一件死物，惟有融入日常生活，它才能真正"活"起来。我很喜欢陶瓷，更喜欢烧瓷，喜欢到可以用一生去探索，更加愿意把陶瓷烧制的手艺世代传承下去。

Never Regret Getting into Porcelain

Narrator: Xu Ruihong

Compiled by: Zheng Xiuyuan

Supervised by: Wang Xueqin

Though there are a hundred different professionals, there is not a single one but depends upon the determination.

—Wang Yangming

The First Time I Became Attached to China

Children in Taiwan started to find part-time jobs in their youth. When I was 14, I worked in a ceramics factory during my summer vacation, bringing me into contact with ceramics and making me irrevocably committed to it. The main part of porcelain is clay. At the very beginning, I thought that making ceramics just needed clay and my hands. However, as time went by, I found that I needed to master fire, glaze and temperatures to transform clay into porcelain. Gradually, the whole process became more apparent, and for me, it developed my interest to a great extent. But when porcelain really impressed me was the time that I joined a porcelain exhibition in the Taipei "Palace Museum" at the age of about 12.

Everyone would show concern for culture while growing up, but sometimes we were just unaware of it. I loved painting when I was a child, and I especially liked painting ink paintings of the dragon and phoenix with culturally traditional Chinese colors. At that time, I began to concentrate on traditional elements but I didn't know it was culturally Chinese. In that period, only blue-and-white porcelain representing Chinese tradition could be seen in Taiwan. But I didn't agree that the porcelain could represent the application of Chinese cultural tradition until one day, I saw a piece of Song Dynasty porcelain in the Taipei "Palace Museum". I could see it clearly through the glass. Its beauty shocked me deeply. After that, I fully realized that there is such beautiful porcelain in the world. Its pure beauty touched my heart. Love is blind; I never know where love comes from while I am passionately devoted to ceramics. From then on, I began to love porcelain. For me, porcelain is of vast cultural significance, even though I was unable to thoroughly understand what ceramics were and what the ceramic craft really was. So I came to the Mainland by myself and started my root-searching trip.

Taiwan contributes greatly to the inheritance and development of traditional culture and social civilization, but the traditional culture and social civilization in the Mainland are profoundly richer. The culture in Taiwan is like a suit of clothes left by my father, but I still needed to search for the flesh and blood, the real incarnation, inside the suit, which was definitely in the Mainland. I was eager to know the land, the mountains, the rivers and other natural resources, and eager to see how the cicadas grew in the trees. This was the ceramic craft that I expected: I was not supposed to make a brand-new one according to the style of my father's suit; instead, I need to know more and experience more. That's why I came to the Mainland.

Along the railway, I enjoyed the splendid views of the mountains and the rivers, feeling the abundance of the geographic character and the cultural venation. Then I arrived at Jingdezhen, a place immersed in ceramic culture. Known around the world as the City of Porcelain, it had a traditional ceramic culture and inherited the ceramic process and technology, making me determined to stay there. However, gradually, I recognized that the cultural atmosphere of ceramics here was very weak. The ceramic process and technology in Jingdezhen was more like a declined aristocracy, without any improvement or innovation since the Qing Dynasty. It still used handwork to represent the value of the artifacts, which meant that the value of the process was high while the human's value was low. I taught them how to transform the clay from mud and how to truly comprehend the value of ceramics for dozens of years. Must ceramic crafts be handmade? Definitely not. Then I left for Quzhou, Zhejiang Province.

All too often, people ask me whether the clay in Zhejiang could be made into ceramics. Such doubt comes from the fact that they don't thoroughly understand pottery. The truth is any clay can be made into ceramics. One of my major works in Zhejiang is processing the earth under our feet into delightful ceramics. Real potters must look for the available materials and turn them into their favorite piece of work or a suitable product. We have spent a couple of years researching the celadon sintering process with the local clay as raw material, the reasonable temperature range, as well as the color generation, hoping to built a new system of celadon making with local raw material. This is the essence of ceramic crafts, in my mind, based on daily life. I am convinced that pottery must be closely related to life, an indispensible part in applied art. That is my understanding of ceramics, a kind of work of practical and artistic nature.

Having Insights into Porcelain at Middle Age

Every day, from seven in the morning, I get up and walk my dog, then I return and rub the mud, shape the clay, prepare the glaze, write the glaze formula, shape the base, etc. This is my happy life. I still remember my numerous failures when I began to learn pottery. Because I didn't have a teacher in handicrafts, I needed to find my own way. Therefore, now I am concerned with the inheritance of technique and craftsmanship because I don't want my students to spend many years perfecting the whole process. We all thought that the craftsmanship in the Mainland was not passed down, but in reality, it was not passed down in Taiwan. That was a process of social development and now I want to get the whole process back, so I have to undergo what our ancestors have done. Then I can know whether it is real or not, what is needed and what is feasible.

For me, the value of craftsmanship is of supreme importance, but the value of people is especially focused; in other words, it has to do with your mind and your hands. Where there is a will, there is a way. I am convinced that the Philosophy of Mind should be based on act and then the value of technology would become human value. That is what we call "the unity of knowledge and action". It is also needed when creating ceramics. No matter it is handicraft or thought, "the unity of knowledge and action" is the most important. Compared to the title of "pottery artist", I prefer to call myself a potter. In fact, I spent twenty years to know why I love porcelain and what look it should possess. I was in pursuit of real pottery; in the same way, I spent twenty years to learn what it's like to be a potter.

I had two teachers, Lin Baojia and Liu Liangyou. Mr. Lin helped to open the door of glaze research to me and Mr. Liu helped me become devoted and insightful in pottery. I was lucky because I grasped the knowledge first and then I put my knowledge into practice. Both of them had a deep impact on me. If I had followed Mr. Lin all my life, I might not know what I should do nowadays. Similarly, if I had followed teacher Liu, I might just have an unrealistic dream. Without them, I would have experienced many detours.

The True Meaning of Craftsmanship

I believe that in our society the proposing of the spirit of craftsmanship has been influenced by Japan. In Japan, the spirit of the craftsman is based on the word—conscientiousness. They seriously and earnestly do what a person should do. What we should learn is not the craftsman's spirit, but conscientiousness. We can talk about the craftsman's spirit, but we should go much deeper. It's just a basis and it cannot be the final goal of the cultural development.

Another very essential element in the spirit of craftsmanship is aesthetics and the pursuit of aesthetics. Some people call my products Ru Kiln, but actually, I have never thought of re-producing Ru Kiln. Since the Qing Dynasty, people thought that it was difficult to make Ru Kiln. The reason why they couldn't make it is not their lack of technology but their lack of aesthetics, which means that they didn't grasp the knowledge first and couldn't put knowledge into practice. I can make it because I know the essence of beauty instead of understanding what Ru Kiln is. In fact, I spent twenty years finding what beauty is. As far as I'm concerned, beauty can't be created but should be accumulated. Master Shenxiu once said, "The body is a Bodhi tree, the mind a bright standing mirror. At all times polish it diligently, and let no dust alight." Master Huineng said, "Bodhi is fundamentally without any tree, and the bright mirror is also not a stand. Fundamentally there is not a single thing, where could any dust be attracted?" The meanings are opposite. Master Huineng is a genius but I am not, so I choose to listen to my inner voices as Master Shenxiu did and let them guide me. I'm not a genius; I'm just good at accumulating, observing and learning, exploring my interest and potential. That's what I want. I can't create beauty, but I can accumulate it. Every single line is produced by a lot of failures.

The most important part in Chinese ceramic languages is pragmatism, which is equal to Wang Yangming's thought of people first. Everything has human value and can be used in daily life. I'd like to turn ceramics into useful appliances. If I just make a vase that is placed in the cabinet for exhibition, then it's just a ceramic production method instead of pottery. Pottery must carry a close connection with the creator who sparks it with fire, glaze and clay. Its real meaning lies in being passed from hand to hand. My studio is named Santao Xuan, which means cultivation, devotion and practical use. If porcelain is just displayed in the cabinet, it's useless and lifeless. Only when it is put into daily life, is it truly alive and valuable. I love ceramics, and I prefer to fire porcelain. I could spend my lifetime in exploration and I'm willing to pass down the craftsmanship from generation to generation.

精于工，匠于心

郑秀媛

指导教师：王雪芹

2016 年"用声音叙事"活动的主题是：我是阳明青年——探索阳明精神的传播者和践行者。阳明文化博大精深，匠人精神更是细节里的心学。以前的我认为，工匠精神就是十年磨一剑的坚强和忍耐。但是在采访徐瑞鸿之后，我慢慢地发现，工匠精神还是用心活，用心干，用心经营，把自己的手艺当成是这个世界呼吸吐纳的入口，不论这手艺是什么。匠人精神是一种沉静务实、淡泊名利、格高致远的精神，是擅于发自内心的自我欣赏和在不断完善工作过程中品味成就感所带来的一种自我激励。一流的匠人，肯定是人品比技术重要。一个人首先要淬炼心性，养成自己，唤醒体内的一流精神，才能达到一流的技术。从他身上，我看到了工匠的另一面。

十四岁开始他第一次接触陶瓷，从此一发而不可收。从舞勺之年到如今的知天命，四十余载的光阴他都致力于对文化的追寻和对美的追求。对于徐瑞鸿来说，他追寻的不是汝窑，与其说是试图找回那失落的技艺，不如说他在追逐的是一抹气韵，一种情怀。在我看来，他很好地诠释了什么是真正的陶艺文化。

陶艺家对于土地似乎有着一种别样的感情。徐瑞鸿想要把踩着的土地变成他喜欢的陶瓷，把陶瓷建立在生活文化上。这也是他的工作室三陶轩中的其中一陶。对三陶，他的定义是"引轻微以为修身，引温文以为养人，引淑世以为民用"，这其中有青瓷之美，有器物的服务之心，也有陶人淡泊的心性。我非常赞同徐瑞鸿先生所倡导的观点——让陶瓷走向生活。古往今来，陶瓷都是在被文人雅士观赏的领域，并没有走向人们的日常生活。但是，徐瑞鸿先生所倡导的"淑世民用"真正地把陶瓷融入进了人们的日常生活，这和王阳明先生倡导的亲民思想不谋而合。陶艺是泥土和火的艺术，他必须通过创作者的身体力行，从创作者手中传递到使用者手里才算完成一次真正的陶艺行为。陶瓷艺术和陶艺艺术最大的不同点在于：年轻的陶艺家才有办法通过自己的身体力行把分享的这个概念完整化。对于徐瑞鸿来说，一件器物惟有融入生活，它才能真正活起来。徐瑞鸿想用生活来诠释陶艺，用陶艺来美化生活。这是他喜欢的，我相信这也是社会今下陶艺发展的方向。

之所以说徐瑞鸿先生是一位诗人是因为他有一种文人风骨，这在他的作品上也有一定的体现。在采访过程中，他也多次提到"做陶瓷不是我人生的全部"。陶艺家需要钱可是不爱钱,所以他才能做出自己喜欢的东西而不是别人喜欢的东西。对于他来说,陶瓷只是一个载体,是他行走的工具,而他真正追逐的是中华文化,是美。他花了大半辈子的时间才知道什么是美什么是陶瓷,这种坚持和觉悟又有多少人能够做到?

诗性的人生大抵都是如此。

徐瑞鸿先生曾经谈到过他最理想的状态是:"有几棵大树在工作室窗外,有阳光和雨露,有鸟鸣,有树影。路过的车子不断呼啸而过,而树叶静止如同老僧禅定。待夜幕降临时,我开灯,放音乐,开始一天的陶艺生活。写釉式、调和釉药、制坯、烧窑,日子一天一天地到来,我一天一天地去面对,假如坚持不住了,那就明天再继续想办法坚持,那树那鸟天天守着我,而我守着我的满室陶瓷。"如今,他做到了,过得精致,像青瓷一样生活。日出而作,日落而息,凿井而饮,耕田而食,不操心,不糟心。从明天起,做一个幸福的人,制坯烧瓷、烹茶饮酒,不必周游世界也很美好。这种生活状态不是每个人都能做到的,但徐瑞鸿先生那种享受人生、对生活认真的态度非常值得我们思考。

用手劳作,用心感受。请存一颗工匠般的心去做事,去生活。

团队成员:郑秀媛　沈旭桐　车晚静

Proficient in Work: A Craftsman's Heart

Zheng Xiuyuan

Supervised by: Wang Xueqin

In 2016, the theme of "Beyond the Voices" is "I'm a Young Practitioner of Yangming Philosophy". Yangming culture is broad and profound, whereas the spirit of the craftsman is the core of the Philosophy of Mind. I used to think craftsmanship was persistence and patience, like taking ten years to sharpen a sword. But after this interview, I realize that craftsmanship is putting one's mind into living and working. Their handicrafts are the access to the world, no matter what their handicrafts are. The spirit of craftsmanship is placidity, pragmatism, indifference to fame and fortune, and high-minded and ambitious. It's a self-appreciation from the heart and a sense of self-motivation in constant improvement and achievement. For first-class craftsmen, certainly moral qualities are superior to techniques. In order to achieve first-class techniques, a person first needs to purify his mind, perfect his nature and awake his potential. From him, I saw the other side of the craftsman.

His first contact with ceramics was at the age of 14. From then on, he persisted for many years and would never give up. From 14 to 50, several decades, he devoted himself to the pursuit of culture and beauty. For Xu Ruihong, what he has been pursuing is not Ru Kiln, but passion, artistic conception and spiritual resonance. From my perspective, he offered a good interpretation of real pottery culture.

Potters seem to have a different kind of affection for the land. Mr. Xu Ruihong wants to transfer the earth under our feet into ceramics, believing that pottery must be based on life's cultures. This is embodied in his studio name. His studio is named Santao Xuan, which means cultivation, devotion and practical use. The beauty and practical use of porcelain as well as his devotion and dedication without worldly desires are clearly demonstrated. I can't agree more with Mr. Xu Ruihong's viewpoint that pottery should be used in real life. Throughout the ages, ceramics have been appreciated by literati, but seldom integrated into our daily lives. It has the same ideals as Wang Yangming's—they both advocate people first. Ceramics is an art of clay and fire; the art of ceramics is wholly complete only after the pottery is passed from the creator to the user. The biggest difference between ceramic art and clay art is that young potters can invite more people to partake in the appreciation of the artwork. For Mr. Xu Ruihong, only when the porcelain is put into daily use, is it truly alive and valuable. He uses daily life to interpret ceramic art while using pottery to decorate and beautify daily life. This is what Mr. Xu likes and I believe this is also the direction of pottery development.

The reason why I say Mr. Xu Ruihong is a poet is that he is urbane and artistic, which is embodied in some of his works. During the interview, he mentioned that ceramics were not all his life several times. Potters need money but they do not love money, so they can create what they love rather than just meeting others' satisfaction. For Mr. Xu, ceramics are just a tool that can help him go further. What he really has been chasing is Chinese culture and beauty. He has spent most of his life learning what porcelain is and what beauty is. How many people could have made it like he has?

Poetic life is probably like that.

Mr. Xu Ruihong once described his ideal life: "Outside the studio stand some trees, with rain and sunshine, some birds and shadows of trees here and there. Cars roar and leaves do not rustle. While the night falls, I turn on the light and music to begin my work. Writing a glaze formula, mixing the glaze, blanking and firing, days go by and I persist. If I can't hold onto it, I will put it down and wait till tomorrow; I will continue to think of ways to persist. Birds and trees accompany me every day and I am affectionately attached to my room full of pottery." Now, he has made it, leading an exquisite life as elegant as porcelain, beginning at sunrise and ending at sunset. He does things all by himself, without worries. From tomorrow on, he will be a man full of happiness, blanking and firing, brewing tea and drinking wine: Life would also be beautiful and wonderful without travelling around the world. Most of us can't lead such a rosy and cozy life like him, but we can learn from his attitude towards life, earnestly enjoying our life.

Labor with your hands, and feel with your heart. Please keep a craftsman-like mind to become a decent person and lead an exquisite life.

Team members: Zheng Xiuyuan, Shen Xutong, Che Wanjing

周正武：三尺龙泉剑，百淬始提出

Zhou Zhengwu: A Three-Feet-Long Longquan Sword Was Made Out of Hundreds of Forging Attempts

周正武，1968 年出生于浙江省龙泉市铸剑世家，是高级工艺美术师、龙泉市刀剑行业协会会长、龙泉正武刀剑文化研究院院长。他擅长于研究制作传统手工精品刀剑与恢复古代刀剑铸造技术，曾获得 2003 年中国工艺美术协会银奖、浙江省工艺美术协会金奖，2005 年参加澳门艺术博物馆"国际铸刀（剑）大师作品展"并被列入国际大师名录。他是第一位参加世界级铸剑大师展的中国刀工，奠定了中国精品刀剑在国际上的地位，为中国刀剑在国际上的发扬光大做出重大贡献。

Zhou Zhengwu was born in 1968 to a family of sword makers in Longquan City, Zhejiang Province. As a senior arts and crafts artist, he is the president of Longquan Sword Industry Association as well as the director of Zhengwu Sword Culture Research Institute in Longquan. He specializes in the study and making of traditional handicraft sword forging and the restoration of ancient sword-casting technology. He has been awarded the silver medal at the 2003 Chinese Arts and Crafts Association and the gold medal at the Zhejiang Arts and Crafts Association. In 2005, he was selected as the master of the International Sword Exhibition by the Macao Art Museum and listed in the International Master Catalog. He is also the first Chinese swordsmith to participate in the International Master Swordsmith Exhibition. All his contributions provided a profound foundation for promoting Chinese sword culture and establishing its international status.

三尺龙泉剑，百淬始提出

口述：周正武
整理：项金龙
指导教师：王雪芹

引 子

要得此米纯然洁白，便是惟一意。然非加舂簸筛拣惟精之工，则不能纯然洁白也。

——王阳明

初识器：良工锻炼凡几年

我是从小在炼炉边看着大人打剑长大的。那个时候，龙泉所有的刀剑厂都在生产一种被称为"铁条"的宝剑。为什么称作"铁条"呢？其实就是把现成的钢板通过轧床冲压成形，粗粗打磨一番后，再配上廉价刀鞘和金属装饰，一把"龙泉宝剑"就算完工。当时，我的家族剑铺也不例外，和所有铸剑师一样，我的父亲和伯父日复一日地守着轧床，搜罗那些半成品到车间，打造所谓的"宝剑"。

采访周正武先生

从父辈们的日常讲述中，我清楚地认识到，真正的龙泉宝剑绝不是这样的"铁条"。许多男孩心中都有一个英雄梦，当时的我，就有一个宝剑梦——打造一柄自己的"龙泉宝剑"。

　　正武堂前身为龙泉市武术器械厂，是我父亲周家强所创；正如其名，器械厂生产的都是些粗制滥造的武术器械。我十六岁时初中毕业，父亲寄望于我，希望我能继续读书，改变周家辛苦的手艺人的命运，但我自知不适合读书，也到了分担家庭压力的年纪，于是我决定拜父为师，学习铸剑手艺，从学徒做起。其实铸剑跟打铁的原理一样，想成为一名优秀的铸剑师，首先要成为一名优秀的打铁匠。起初我跟着伯父打了两年铁，之后的十年时间里我学了一些工艺剑的锻造方法，但我认识到，这些粗制滥造的剑只是一件件样子货，并不是古时候百炼成钢的龙泉剑，更不是真正的中国传统刀剑；这样的剑，不过是龙泉商家为了经济利益而制造的铁片！

　　那时，龙泉的制剑产业无不是这种情况；想要有所突破，周家的剑就要有所创新。但最大的难题是，那些锻造传统龙泉剑的口传心授的古法在中国近代百年的战乱以及近现代冷兵器的逐渐没落的情况下早已失传。况且，那时的我技艺有限，只是个合格的打铁匠而已，又如何能靠自己的技艺来恢复传统剑技法，这一度困扰着我。后来经过努力我在剑厂里坐到了管理人员的位置，与刀剑爱好者们的交流也增加了；我发现，许多收藏刀剑的爱好者们为在中国买不到传统刀剑而发愁，这确实也是比较尴尬的。当时的龙泉只生产低端刀剑，这些刀剑都是用机器锤锻打并用砂轮机研磨的，不仅质量不好，经济效益也是问题。刀剑收藏者们只能去台湾等地收购所谓的"传统刀剑"来收藏。我意识到现代中国在古刀剑这方面还是一个空白，所以我萌发了这么个想法，要将中国的传统刀剑锻造技法重新恢复起来，打破这个空白。网上的各大刀剑论坛交流让我接触到很多中国港台地区和日本、美国、澳大利亚等地的刀剑爱好者和收藏者们，他们丰富的刀剑理论知识以及相关的古籍收藏都给了我很大的帮助。龙泉剑在清末就已经失传了，一直到 20 世纪 90 年代都是采用比较简单的不经人工复合的纯钢铸剑，可以说龙泉剑的锻造技法空白了一百多年。但 1986 年的一天，事情出现了转机，我在路过龙泉的时候，在一家农户柴房堆里看到一把锈迹斑斑的古剑，剑刃完好，剑身属复合锻造，我当时就认定这把剑是非同寻常之物。农户告诉我，这是他几年前在山上破庙捡来的，顺手拿来砍柴用，我当时一阵窃喜，就拿一把柴刀、一把短剑和五元钱来与他交换，农户立马答应了。回到家后，我磨光了剑身的锈迹，发现此剑钢火结构罕见，的确是稀世珍宝。于是，对此剑深入研究后，我重新查找和整理龙泉剑的资料，开始点炉、抢锤，进行一次次锻打、淬火尝试。2002 年，在攻克宝剑材质、材质比例、锻打炉温、淬火剑温、炉温等难题后，第一把传统工艺制作的龙泉剑终于诞生，我将其取名为"光复"。此剑光复的不仅是刀剑的锻造工艺，更是我们失传已久的传统。此后，我又相继成功复原出秦、汉、唐、宋、清等各时期的龙泉刀剑，使龙泉宝剑重回世界名刃的行列，在龙泉宝剑的发展上也逐渐找到了方向。

识真钢：百淬百炼名龙剑

剑身锻造、剑鞘制作和装具配置是制成一把龙泉宝剑必不可缺的三道工艺，涉及磨工、木工、漆工和金工等多种工艺，每道工艺又可细分出十几道程序，加起来有上百道工序。一把龙泉剑在成型前，需要进行普通锻打和折叠锻打，这是锻造龙泉剑最艰难也是最艰苦的环节。铸剑的技术要传承，打铁的艰辛和枯燥也要传承。把数种不同的钢铁熔锻复合，反复折叠锻打至三万两千余层，在不断折叠锻打中去除杂质，增加剑身的强度和韧性，这就是所谓的"千锤百炼"。也正是这三万两千余层的叠压，剑身的表面最终会形成一层奇异的花纹。当你选择了做一件事情，你就得耐着性子把它完成，享受过程中所经历的，就像原本就不平坦的人生，当它被完完全全呈现出来时，一切又都是值得的。

在铸剑过程中，"淬火"是铸剑过程中最为关键的一步，也是赋予一把剑灵魂的时刻。剑坯燃烧到750～800摄氏度，便可淬火。这是事关成败的一步，此前与此后，可以经历数万次的反复锻打与磨砺；惟独这一步，却只有电光火石的一次机会。瞬息之中，便可决断一切。一招不慎，就前功尽弃。铸剑师与打铁匠的差别就在此一刹那。

剑在中国文化中已经被赋予了很多的神秘色彩，而事实上，剑的传统铸造方式，从原料到成品，要经过锻、铲、锉、刻、淬、磨等28道主要工序，所谓"十年磨一剑"，指的就是铸剑的艰辛，这也是对一个铸剑师耐心的考量。一柄躺在匣中的龙泉剑，只要轻轻一带手腕，涌出的凌厉寒光与色彩沉闷的刀鞘形成鲜明的反差，无论多么外行的观者，心头都会为之一凛。我始终认为铸剑人的剑应当透露着"重义、守节、利他、从文、尚武"的士族精神。

致良知：绝知此事要躬行

在我的带动下，龙泉其他刀剑厂家也逐步开始研发多层锻打的花纹钢刀剑。目前我也有了一些相关的头衔，也在尽力宣传龙泉宝剑，弘扬龙泉宝剑文化，尽到推动龙泉宝剑产业发展的社会职责。我尽可能地参加全国、世界各类具有行业影响力的刀剑铸造竞赛和展览，作品受到了国内外刀剑铸造师和收藏爱好者的一致肯定，这更坚定了我的信念，要为龙泉刀剑在强手如云的中国刀剑、世界刀剑界争得一席之地。

龙泉剑，现如今早已失去了作为兵刃的实用功能，但它作为一种手工艺术品，依然以其丰富的历史文化内涵和精湛的工艺被人们所喜爱和珍藏。目前，我正朝着不断研究制作传统手工精品刀剑和挖掘恢复失传刀剑锻制技法而不断前行。

　　近年来社会上"工匠精神"这个词日渐流行，几乎每行每业都标榜自己的"工匠精神"，但我以为在类似于我这样的匠人或者说是工艺家的前提下，"工匠精神"并不值得夸耀；对于一个匠人来说，"手艺"跟"匠心"都是安身立命之根本，想成为行业里的大师，必须要将自身定位为艺术家，那才是我真正需要去做的。现在社会上最爱推崇"工匠精神"的那些人，他们一定是外行。在我的视角所看到的"工匠精神"，即是以古扬今，突破自己的技艺。而对于现代中国来说，从宏观层面来讲，特别是企业，更需要这样的工匠精神，例如世界五百强的华为，是我最为敬佩的企业，倘若每个中国企业能将自身定位到华为这样的层次，那么现在谈及"工匠精神"人们首推日本、德国的局面也许能够改变，"中国制造"真正能以高姿态走向世界，中国的强大也能指日可待。

A Three-Feet-Long Longquan Sword Was Made Out of Hundreds of Forging Attempts

Narrator: Zhou Zhengwu

Compiled by: Xiang Jinlong

Supervised by: Wang Xueqin

Singleness means having the rice absolutely pure and white. However, this state cannot be achieved without the work of refining, such as winnowing, sifting, and grinding. These are the work of refining, but their purpose is no more than to make rice absolutely pure and white, that is all.

—Wang Yangming

Recognizing the Sword for the First Time: Years of Forging Contributed to a Skillful Technique

Since my childhood, I had been watching my elders forging swords from beside the melting furnace. At that time, all the local sword producers in Longquan were producing swords nicknamed "steel bars". Why were they called "steel bars"? The steel was rolled out into plates and bars, and then the blacksmith would coarsely grind them and accessorize them with cheap scabbards and other metal ornaments. After this process, they thought a "Longquan Sword" was completed. My father's sword shop was no exception. Like all other swordsmiths, my father and uncle just stuck to the old ways by collecting these semi-finished products and making these so-called Longquan Swords in their workshop day after day.

From my elders' daily conversations about the traditional Longquan Sword, I clearly recognized that the real Longquan Sword was definitely not the sword like those steel bars. Perhaps every little boy has a heroic dream, and I was no exception. Having heard so many Longquan Sword stories in my childhood, I also had a dream—to forge a real traditional Longquan Sword on my own.

Zhengwu Tang grew out of the Longquan Martial Arts Equipment Factory founded by my father; the factory mainly produced rough martial arts equipment. I left school at the age of sixteen; my father hoped I would to continue my study and change our family's destiny of being a craftsman, but I knew I had no talent for study.

84

Believing that I had reached the age of sharing family responsibility, I decided to be an apprentice to my father to learn forging in the sword-casting factory. Forging a sword is similar to forging iron; being an excellent swordsmith requires one to first be an excellent blacksmith. So I forged iron with my uncle for two years, and in the following decade, I learned some forging methods for crafting swords. However, I recognized that these shoddy craft swords were neither real Longquan Swords nor the traditional Chinese swords—they were just the products of the local businessmen's pursuit of economic profit.

Examining the whole system of the Longquan Sword industry made me aware of the fact that every workshop was the same, engaging in the production of shoddy craft swords instead of real Longquan Swords. Innovation needed to be carried out for breakthrough to occur. The greatest challenge was that the traditional method of forging the Longquan Sword was lost due to hundreds of years of war and the gradual decline of modern cold weapons. Besides, I was then only an eligible blacksmith and was not well-skilled. How could I restore the traditional forging of the Longquan Sword all by myself? These thoughts obsessed me. Later I worked my way to the top of the sword factory, and I got more chances to communicate with traditional sword fans all over the country. They were worried about being unable to buy traditional Chinese swords. It was actually embarrassing for all swordsmiths in Longquan, because we were only able to produce low-end swords at that time. These low-end swords were forged by steam hammers and ground by rotary sanders, not only of poor quality but also with poor economic profits. Therefore, many sword collectors had no other way out but to go to Taiwan or other places to buy so-called "traditional swords" for their own personal collections. I realized that there was a gap in traditional swords in modern China, so I came up with the idea of recovering traditional Chinese swords and filling this gap. The communication and exchange on the sword forums helped me come into contact with a great many sword lovers and collectors from Hong Kong and Taiwan of China as well as Japan, America, Australia and other places whose rich sword theories and precious collections of ancient sword books offered enormous help in learning about traditional Chinese swords. Actually, the method of manufacturing traditional Longquan Swords had already been lost during the Qing Dynasty. Swordsmiths in Longquan used pure steel without duplex forging in the 1990s, which meant the gap in traditional Longquan Swords had existed more than one hundred years. However, things turned for the better one day in 1986. When passing through Longquan, I saw a rusty sword in a farm room, whose blade was in good condition and was definitely duplex forged. I firmly believed that the sword must be unusual. The farmer told me that he took this sword from a monastery on a hill a few years ago, and mainly used it for chopping wood. I chuckled to myself and offered to barter a chopper, a dagger and five yuan for the sword and he accepted the offer immediately. On my return home, I polished the rusty blade, finding the rare structure of this sword. I was very excited to find such a rare treasure. After deep research, I reorganized the related data and came back to the sword-forging factory to prepare for forging. Firing, hammering, quenching and tempering, I tried again and again. After I worked out the difficult problems like the metal material, proportion of material, furnace temperature, quenching temperature of the sword and the furnace, eventually, in 2002, the first traditional handicraft Longquan Sword was born and I named it "Guangfu Sword", which literally means restoration. This sword not only meant the restoration of the traditional forging method of Longquan Sword but also demonstrated that our lost tradition of sword making has begun to recover. Since then, I recovered Longquan Swords from different dynasties like Qin, Han, Tang, Song, Ming, and Qing. Consequently, the Longquan Sword returned to the world stage and I also found the direction of sword forging on my way.

Evaluating Real Steel: Longquan Sword Was Born After Hundreds of Forging Attempts and Thoroughly Tempering

Blade forging, scabbard making and assembling are three essential techniques in making a Longquan Sword, involving multiple processes such as grinding, carpenter work, painting and metal processing. Each process can be subdivided into a dozen procedures, adding up to more than one hundred steps. The most difficult and challenging part is that Longquan Swords need to be commonly forged and then folding forged before molding. On the one hand, we need to inherit this technology and craftsmanship; on the other hand, we are expected to bear the hardships and dullness of bricking. Before its molding comes out, a Longquan Sword should be thoroughly tempered. The hardest process to join these different pieces of metal together in forging might be the folding, which means folding the steel more than thirty-two thousand times. Impurities are removed in this process, while the strength and toughness of sword is improved. Because of this process, elaborate and unique patterns will be formed on the sword. When you choose something in life, you should be patient enough to complete it with appreciation and enjoyment. It is similar to our life's journey—it is rough, but our efforts are richly rewarded.

"Quenching" is the most critical step in the process of sword production, which gives the sword its soul. When the temperature reaches 750-800 degrees Celsius, it is time to quench the sword. This process is the key to the success of a swordsmith. Before and after the quenching, it can be forged numerous times, but the quenching is the only chance to make a real sword; it could fly away in a flash. All previous efforts might be wasted if one is not careful enough. That's the difference between a blacksmith and a swordsmith.

The sword has been shrouded in mystery in Chinese culture. In fact, a sword needs to be forged, spaded, filed, carved, quenched and ground, involving twenty-eight procedures to get to its end product. The saying "it takes ten years to grind a sword" reflects the hardships and difficulties of sword forging, which definitely tests the swordsmith's patience and perseverance. Even an amateur would be shocked and astounded by its flashing radiance when he takes a Longquan Sword from box and brandishes it. I still believe that noble character traits like "loyalty, integrity, altruism, literacy, and martial arts" should be reflected on a smith's sword.

Showing Conscience: Practice Goes Deeper than Theoretic Knowledge

Currently, under my leadership, other sword factories in Longquan have begun to develop pattern steel swords through multi-forging. Since I have been honored with some titles, I try my best to undertake my social responsibility to promote the Longquan Sword and its traditional culture. I attend various national and international exhibitions and competitions of swords and knives. The fact that my works are being accepted by swordsmiths and sword collectors strengthens my belief that the Longquan Sword will find its place in China and the world.

The Longquan Sword might have lost its practical function as a weapon in this modern society, but as a handmade work of art, it is still favored and collected by people due to its rich historical, cultural connotation and exquisite technique. Now, I am on my way to promote traditional handicraft sword forging and restore ancient sword-casting technology.

In recent years, "the spirit of the craftsman" seems to have become a hot topic in society; virtually every industry and firm claim their own spirit of the craftsman. However, personally, as an artisan or a craftsman, I would never boast of the spirit of the craftsman. For a genuine craftsman, the underlying quality of craftsmanship is the premise of becoming a master or an artist. Being a master in this field needs one to position himself to be an artist first, which is what I really need to do. These must be laymen who are obsessed with the spirit of the craftsman. From my perspective, the spirit of craftsmanship is following the traditions and seeking my own breakthroughs. On a macro level, companies in today's China are in bad need of the spirit of the craftsman. For instance, Huawei, my most admired company as well as one of the World's Top 500, sets an excellent example for Chinese companies. If every company in China could position itself as superbly as Huawei, the present situation that people admire Japan and Germany when speaking of the spirit of craftsmanship would be changed, while "Made in China" would step onto the international stage and make China more powerful and influential.

着力于手，皆系于心

项金龙
指导教师：王雪芹

2016 年"用声音叙事"活动的主题是：我是阳明青年——探索阳明精神的传播者和践行者。从前期的培训学习中我逐渐体会到阳明思想涵盖天地万物，而工匠精神则是一名工匠在他的领域做到"知行合一"的体现。我萌发出一个想法，我想近距离去接触一次那些一辈子用心精雕细琢、提升自身技艺的大师。而周正武先生就是我当时第一个想起的在工匠领域非常有代表性的人物。原因很简单：我曾经在中央电视台节目中看过关于他的龙泉剑的专访，也曾见识到电视剧《新三国》里他所铸的"曹操剑"的华美锋利。所以就借这次"用声音叙事"的机会到访龙泉市正武堂，与周正武先生坐而论"工匠精神"。

我对工匠精神的初步认识就是手艺人们对自己作品独具匠心、精益求精的理想精神追求。工匠有铁匠、木匠、皮匠、钟表匠等，而铁匠则堪称最苦手艺人之一。《古剑篇》中曾有 "君不见昆吾铁冶飞炎烟，红光紫气俱赫然"的描述，体现了一个铸剑师工作环境烟火纷飞的景象。而一名铸剑师在这样高温的环境中几十年如一日地抡动锤子将自己的心血锻铁成剑，化腐朽为神奇。我想这就是一名铸剑师的工匠精神。

如果不是亲身来到龙泉市，我无法想象在这个现代化的社会中还有这么一个剑铺与青瓷店布满整个街面的地方。显然，在当地有一条非常完善的产业链，这就是中国著名的宝剑青瓷之邦——龙泉。周正武先生的正武堂目前是当地数一数二的剑铺。"让更多的人认识和了解龙泉刀剑艺术的美妙之处"，这是周正武先生的期许，而现在的他完全有能力凭借自身的社会地位与能力做得更好，而他也做到了。他在 2016 年 5 月牵头龙泉本地青瓷大师，在浙江大学举办了"青瓷宝剑文化进校园"的主题展览活动，让众多浙大学子与刀剑爱好者们领略到了龙泉宝剑与青瓷文化的独特魅力。我想这便是周先生他自己"知行合一"的处世之道，将非物质文化遗产尽早地带入未来社会中坚力量——大学生的眼前，将保护传统文化的理念早一步根植于他们心中，这是周先生的期待，因为他知道，非物质文化遗产的未来需要这群年轻人。

周正武先生用传统工艺铸造的第一柄剑取名"光复"。何谓"光复"？这三尺"光复"剑，光复的不仅仅是刀剑的锻造工艺，更是我们失传已久的传统。周正武先生认为，从这一柄剑开始，他才认可自己成为一名真正的铸剑师、真正的工匠。他说，工匠精神对于工匠不过是讨口饭吃的基本职业要求而已，手艺与匠心也只能评判你是否是一个合格的工匠。一个一辈子只会敲敲打打、不会思变的工匠，他也许是合格的，但他一定不会成为一名大师。的确，传统也并不是一成不变的，社会一直在快速地发展，有些传统的技艺也应当做出适当的创新。就如近代失传百年的龙泉剑，周正武先生能以自身对古籍、文物的钻研，以及对锻造技艺的改进来恢复传统龙泉剑的锻造技法，这就是一种创新的传统。"工匠精神"应当有着更深远的信念与理想，这样才能让人在自己的领域有所寄托，走得更远。

抡锤打铁的铸剑师龙泉有，别处也有。但周正武的独特之处并非手艺的独到，而是匠心的回归，而铸剑的材料与宝剑的雕琢跟作品价值相比实在是微不足道了。这铸剑的营生其实是信仰"知行合一"的修行境界，似着力于手，实皆系于心。

工匠精神在现代对小到个人，大到企业甚至是国家都有相当大的借鉴意义。对于个人来说，"工匠精神"实际上是一种敬业精神，对自己从事的工作锲而不舍，追求卓越。而对公司、企业来说，就如李克强总理在政府工作报告中提出的，"要培养精益求精的工匠精神"。在这个快速发展的现代社会中，公司与企业就是代表国家经济活力的各个小细胞，它们承担着社会经济发展的重任，更需要对生产和产品精益求精；精雕细琢的企业"工匠精神"，能推动我国从"制造大国"变为"制造强国"。中国要强大，需要"中国制造"；中国要强大，需要"工匠精神"。

天地之大，皆为用心之处。

Handicraft Is Tied to the Heart

Xiang Jinlong

Supervised by: Wang Xueqin

In 2016, the theme of "Beyond the Voices" is "I'm a Young Practitioner of Yangming Philosophy". From my early training, I gradually realized that Yangming culture could be applied to every field. The spirit of craftsmanship is the embodiment of a craftsman's unity of knowledge and action. The idea struck me that I wanted to have a close contact with craftsmen who have carefully and meticulously made fine works and enhanced their skills throughout their lifetime. Zhou Zhengwu was the first representative I thought of in the artisan field and the reason was simple: I had watched an exclusive interview of him and his Longquan Sword on CCTV and I knew that the sharp and haughty "Caocao Sword" in the TV series *New Three Kingdoms* was forged by him. So, I planned to use this opportunity to visit his Zhengwu Tang in Longquan city and discussed the spirit of craftsmanship with him.

My initial understanding of the spirit of craftsmanship was about the craftsmen's originality and persistence, constantly striving for perfection. We know about artisans such as blacksmiths, carpenters, cobblers, watchmakers and so on. But blacksmithing is the hardest one. The *Old Sword Psalm* recorded the vivid scene where Kun Wu's gem was made into a sword with red fire and the blade with a purple flame. But a swordsmith can forge swords in such environments of high temperatures for several decades, being devoted and dedicated with patience and perseverance. I think that this is the essence of the spirit of craftsmanship.

Had I not come to Longquan, I would never have imagined that there is a long and busy street with sword shops and porcelain shops in such a modern society. Apparently the sword and porcelain industry chain is perfect enough in this kind of local place. This is why people call Longquan China's "city of swords and porcelain". Mr. Zhou Zhengwu's Zhengwu Tang is one of the best sword shops in the locality. "Let more people know and understand the beauty of Longquan Sword art"—this is Zhou Zhengwu's expectation. Now he has the capability to do even better because of his personal ability and social status, and as expected, he has achieved it. In May, 2016, he organized the "Longquan Celadon and Sword culture on the campus" activity with other Longquan celadon masters at Zhejiang University, helping numerous students and sword lovers recognize the unique charm of the celadon and sword culture. I am convinced that this is Zhou's philosophy of life, to practice Yangming's "unity of knowledge and action". He showed the non-material cultural heritage to the backbone of future society—college students. He hopes the idea of protecting traditional culture can be rooted early in students' minds, because he knows that the future of non-material cultural heritage needs these young people.

Mr. Zhou's expectation is reflected clearly by his first traditional handicraft sword which he named the "Guangfu (Restoration) Sword". He believed this three-foot sword not only restored the traditional forging method of Longquan Sword, but also presented the restoration of our long-lost tradition. Mr. Zhou told me that after the forging of his sword, he recognized himself as a real swordsmith, a genuine craftsman. He pointed out that the spirit of the craftsman is the prerequisite of an artisan, while he wouldn't become a qualified craftsman without skills and originality. A craftsman would never be a master if he works all day without innovation. Truly, traditions would by no means be immutable and frozen; some traditional skills and techniques need to be properly innovated due to our fast-changing modern society. In my point of view, Mr. Zhou's restoration and improvement of the traditional Longquan Sword forging skills is the development and innovation of tradition. Therefore, the spirit of the craftsman needs a more profound meaning to help people go much further along their road to belief.

Swordsmithing can not only be found in Longquan, but also in other places. Zhou Zhengwu's unique feature is the returning of the artisan's heart, rather than the skilled techniques. Compared to the value of his products, the materials and the forging are not worth mentioning. The work of a swordsmith is actually a belief in "the unity of knowledge and action". It seems Mr. Zhou has put forth effort with his hands but actually, it is all tied to the heart.

The spirit of craftsmanship has a significant reference to individuals, business and even countries in modern society. For individuals, the spirit of craftsman is actually devotion and dedication, pursuing excellence with perseverance. Just as Premier Li Keqiang said in one of his government work reports, "Businesses need to cultivate a spirit of craftsmanship, striving for the best." In such a highly-developed society, companies and enterprises are like the cells in the body, representing economic vitality of the nation, shouldering the responsibility of improving economic development, thus they need to keep improving their products and production. Such companies can help drive our nation from a "big manufacturing nation" to a "powerful manufacturing nation". China needs a strong "made-in-China" artisan spirit in order to be more powerful.

Under heaven and earth, there are many fields in which we can diligently work.

李光昭：诚心诚意，方得始终

Li Guangzhao: Persistence in Achievements

　　李光昭，出生于浙江宁波，工艺美术大师。年轻时拜曹厚德为师，被曹老师称为其在泥金彩漆领域"惟一的学生"。经过多年的探究与研制，他的泥金彩漆技艺达到了很高的境界，对于泥金彩漆与美学，有自己独特的见解。他提倡"知行合一"的工匠精神，用心让每一件作品变得完美。

　　Li Guangzhao was born in Ningbo, Zhejiang. He is a master of arts and crafts. When he was young, he acknowledged Cao Houde as his teacher, and he was Mr. Cao Houde's only student in illuminated painting. After years of research and development, his illuminated painting skills reach a very high level, with unique insight and taste. He adheres to the craftsmanship spirit of "the unity of knowledge and action", trying to make each piece of work perfect and unique.

诚心诚意，方得始终

口述：李光昭
整理：董　路
指导教师：王雪芹

引 子

知之真切笃实处即是行，行之明觉精察处即是知。

——王阳明

遇泥金彩漆很幸运

20世纪60年代的中国社会，正处于计划经济时代。那时候工作都是分配下来的，几乎没有选择的余地，能找到一份工作已经算不错了。正是那个时候，我与泥金彩漆结下了不解之缘，现在想起来真是幸运。泥金彩漆是一种泥金工艺和彩漆工艺相结合的漆器工艺，它的历史可以追溯到七千多年前的河姆渡文化。我现在是宁波仅剩的几个泥金彩漆传承人之一。

曹厚德老师一开始对我考验了一番，我印象很深。他知道我学过绘画，但工艺美术的东西毕竟不同于绘画，这次考验是来摸摸我的底。他拿出一块很薄的、大概两厘米厚的玻璃，涂上膏，让我在玻璃上做出刀、枪、马的样子，合起来称为"武将"。做完之后，他看了看惊讶地问："你之前做过吗？"我告诉他我是第一次做，不过以前有学过绘画。他表扬了我一番，觉得我很有天赋。

后来一直在泥金彩漆车间工作，我发现自己真的很喜欢泥金彩漆。有一种工匠，是以谋生为主的，每天工作的时候会觉得很烦，一到退休就把"它"扔了。我与他们不同，每天的热情都很高，用心去做每一件泥金彩漆的工艺品。在每次努力之后得到回报的时候，我会很有成就感、很开心。越有成就感，我就越喜欢；越喜欢，我就越想往下钻研。我立志成为一名泥金彩漆大师。

王阳明在《教条示龙场诸生》中告诫大家要立志，志不立，天下无可成之事。而且光立志是不够的，已立志为君子，自当从事于学。凡学之不勤，必其志之尚未笃也。所以我一直努力学习与探究泥金彩漆技术，努力也终于得到了回报：1964年的秋季广交会上，我们的产品因为做工精美、具有民族特色被外国企业看重，之后一大批订单接踵而至，我感受到了成功的喜悦。

学与行，在于心

学与行，在于心。阳明先生说："知之真切笃实处即是行，行之明觉精察处即是知。"现在，很多人把知和行分作两件事去做。以为知了然后能行，待知得真了，方去做行的功夫。因此一辈子都不去行，亦一辈子不去知。在泥金彩漆车间，做的是流水线，每个人的分工不同。我是个用心的人，在空闲的时候，我老是会问别人："这些为什么要这么做？"久而久之，整个流程我都知道了。工作与生活都是如此，用心的人往往会收获更大。

工匠精神就是诚心诚意，工匠精神就是"知行合一"。比方说，每个人都会有对美的追求，每个人对美的追求不尽相同。这时候，我们需要尽自己最大的能力，尽力做好自己的作品，把自己的想法融入作品，用心让每一件作品变得完美。这么多年以来，我一直抱着尽心尽力制作好每一件作品的态度，期望自己的作品越来越出色。有时候，我也不能够做到"知行合一"，做泥金彩漆时会感到烦躁。随着时间的推移，坚持过后发现泥金彩漆已经成了我生命的一部分。慢慢地，我能够体会到阳明先生所说的"良知在人心，良知即准则"。

当今社会上有一种说法，觉得现在的年轻人大部分都是心浮气躁的，不能很好地去做一些事情。我认为，现在社会上是有很大一部分人心浮气躁，但是很多年轻人都能很好地完成一些事情。对于他们来说，不过是仰望星空的时间占得太多了，让他们不能脚踏实地地去做一些事情。对于现在的年轻人，我想说："做事，应该有一种工匠精神，一步一脚印，你要认准方向走下去，坚持到最后的人往往都是成功的。现在是多元化的时代，在十字路口要把握住机会。"

学与行，在于心。每个人都要坚持不懈地去学习。在工作中，学习更精妙的工作技巧；在生活中，学习为人处事的道理。学习不是"三天打鱼，两天晒网"，学习是长久的事儿，是一辈子的事儿。就像阳明先生说的，要做到"知行合一"。勿像一种人，懵懵懂懂地任意去做，完全不知道思考，并有轻狂妄作；勿像另一种人，茫茫荡荡，悬空去思考一样东西，全不肯着实躬行。所以知和行是分不开的，要做到"知行合一"。

想为泥金彩漆做一份贡献

其实我再干几年也不行了，现在的眼睛和年轻时比差远了，我现在只能写大的字。做泥金彩漆工艺品的时候，都是凭感觉，眼睛真的不行了。对于我自己来说，已经没有什么遗憾了，五十多年与泥金彩漆相伴，一直做着自己喜欢的工作，已经很满足了。就如阳明先生临终前说的那样："此心光明，亦复何言。"

我现在关心的是泥金彩漆的传承，在这方面，如果我不做点事情，泥金彩漆在我们这一代消失了，我们岂不是成了历史的罪人。做一件泥金彩漆产品，要经过箍桶、批灰、上底漆、描图、倒漆泥、堆塑、贴金等二十余道工序，全靠手工一步一步完成。通常，做一件小型作品也需要几天时间，如果做大型作品则需要几个月甚至半年时间。学这项手艺，耐不住寂寞可不行。我曾经看到宁波聋哑学校学生们的漆画作品，很感兴趣，就把这些学生请到自己的工作室，并产生了从聋哑人中寻找泥金彩漆传承人的念头。后来，我去聋哑学校授课时收了几名聋哑学生为徒。

泥金彩漆在古时候之所以深受推崇，是因为拥有考究精致的工艺。几十年来，我一直保留着传统的纯手工工艺。原料上，漆胎以木片为主，也有少部分产品以竹编为胎。很多人做工艺品用省钱的化学漆，我一直坚持用造价高、操作难的天然漆。因为中国漆的稳定性更强，时间久了也不会掉漆。以前泥金彩漆的工艺品都是出口的，尽管在宁波生产，真正了解的当地人却不多，我希望泥金彩漆能被更多人熟知。这些年不少人慕名而来，请我与他们合作生产泥金彩漆。泥金彩漆的商业化能让该项工艺普及，但是找上门的商人大多追求利益最大化。由于对工艺、原料高要求的那份坚持，合作往往最后都不了了之。

我还会在周末空余的时间教外国友人制作泥金彩漆，让他们领略中华文化。其他国家的人甚至展现出了更强的兴趣感，他们觉得这是具有我们中国特色的东西。我也一直觉得，民族的东西就是国家的东西，我们要保护好泥金彩漆等具有鲜明民族特色的非物质文化遗产，让我们国家五十六个民族的文化展现在世界舞台上，让文化精神展现在世界舞台上。

Persistence in Achievements

Narrator: Li Guangzhao

Compiled by: Dong Lu

Supervised by: Wang Xueqin

When knowledge is genuine and sincere, practice is included; when practice is clear and minutely adjusted, knowledge is present.

—Wang Yangming

Lucky to Encounter Illuminated Painting

Chinese society in the 1960s was an era of planned economy, when work and jobs were all distributed. People had no alternative but to do what they were allocated to, and it was considered lucky for one to have a job. At that time, I was irrevocably committed to illuminated painting. Now in retrospect, I feel that I was very blessed to get to work with illuminated painting. Illuminated painting is a lacquer craft that combines both gold paint and painted lacquer, and its history can be traced back to the Hemudu culture more than 7000 years ago. Now I am one of the few remaining successors of illuminated painting in Ningbo.

At the very beginning, Mr. Cao Houde tested me, which impressed me. He knew I had learned painting before, but arts and crafts, after all, were different from painting. The purpose of the test was to know my abilities and potential. He took out a piece of thin glass, about two centimeters thick, coated with cream, and asked me to carve the different shapes of a knife, a horse and a gun, which together form a "general". When I finished it, he looked with great surprise and asked me whether I had done it before. I told him that it was my first time, but I had learned painting before. He praised me and thought I was talented.

After that, I began working in the illuminated painting workshop and I found myself really fond of illuminated painting. Some craftsmen regard their job as a way of living, so whenever they work, they feel bored and when they come to retirement, they get rid of it immediately. Different from them, I am full of passion and dedication in my work and put my mind into every single craft. After my efforts pay off, I feel proud and happy, with a great sense of accomplishment. The more I feel proud, the more I like it; the more I like it, the more I want to learn. I am determined to be a master of illuminated painting.

In *Doctrine to Students in Longchang*, Wang Yangming warns us that people should make resolutions. People will never be successful unless they possess a strong will and a firm resolution. It is far from enough to just be determined. If you are determined to be a gentleman, naturally you should strive to learn; those who don't study hard don't have strong determination. That's why I have been studying and exploring illuminated painting all this time and, finally, my efforts have paid off. In the autumn session of the Canton Fair in 1964, because of the exquisite quality and national characteristics, our products were highly thought of by foreign companies, bringing about a large number of orders, which made me feel the joy of success.

Learning and Doing Lies in the Heart

Learning and doing lies in the heart. Mr. Yangming said, "Action can truly reflect knowledge, while observations in action reflect knowledge. " There are now a lot of people who separate knowledge and action. They are convinced that knowledge comes first and only when they have possessed this knowledge, then can they start their action; consequently, they will never act nor possess the knowledge. In the illuminated painting workshop with assembly lines, each person's division of labor is different. I am a man who works with my heart and soul; in my free time, I would always ask people: "Why do you do it this way?" Gradually, I understood the whole process. Work and life are very similar; those who do their work painstakingly tend to reap greater rewards.

Craftsmanship is the sincerity of the spirit of artisans; craftsmanship is "the unity of knowledge and action". For example, everyone will have a pursuit of beauty, but everyone's pursuit of beauty is not the same. At this moment, we need to try our best to do our work, put our own ideas into the work, and make every piece of work perfect. For so many years, I have been holding the attitude of making every effort to perfect every piece of my product, expecting my products to be more and more outstanding. Sometimes, I feel irritable and fractious, unable to unite knowledge and action. Over a long time of pursuing illuminated painting, I realized that illuminated painting has become a part of my life. Slowly, I can understand Mr. Yangming's saying "Conscience lies in people's heart and mind, and conscience is people's guideline."

Now there is a saying concerning present society, and it is believed that most young people are impatient, not efficient in achievement. For me, there truly are a large number of flighty and impetuous young people, but many young people can make achievements. For them, they spend too much time in vain, idling away by looking at the stars in the night sky, so that they cannot really work in an earnest and down-to-earth way. For today's young people, I want to say: "Work needs craftsmanship. You find your direction and goal, and then, step by step, you plot your course and get out there. Those who stick to the end are likely to succeed. Now the world is in an era of diversity, and people need to seize the opportunity at this crossroad."

Learning and doing lies in the heart. Everyone must persevere to learn. At work, we learn more ingenious working skills; in life, we learn to improve our modes of behavior and ways of talking. Learning is not "going fishing for three days and drying the nets for two"; instead, learning is a long-term thing, a lifetime thing. As Mr. Yangming said, to be a person who emphasizes "the unity of knowledge and action", we shouldn't be the kind of person who is ignorant and frivolous, without thoughts or action. Meanwhile, we shouldn't be the other kind of person who is extremely lofty-minded, who only has thoughts but refuses to really practice. Therefore, knowledge and action are one, inseparable, and knowledge and action go hand in hand.

Eager to Make Contribution to Illuminated Painting

In fact, there are only a few more years that I can hold on in this field. Now my eyes are far worse than when I was young, and I can only write big words. When producing illuminated painting crafts, I do it all by feeling, because my eyes have grown so bad. But for me, there is no pity. What satisfies me is doing the beloved illuminated painting for more than fifty years. As Mr. Wang Yangming said before his death, "Being conscientious the whole life, what else can I say?" It is true.

Now my concern is the inheritance of illuminated painting. If I achieve nothing and let illuminated painting disappear in our generation, we will be judged harshly by history. Every piece of illuminated painting takes more than 20 procedures, including cooperage, plastering, prime lacquering, tracing, mud-pouring, sculpturing, gilding and so on. They are all done by hand, step by step. In general, it takes a few days to finish a small piece of product, but it takes several months or half a year to complete a grand product. Learning this craft, you are expected to tolerate great loneliness. I once saw some painted works by some students in a school for deaf-mutes in Ningbo, which highly interested me. So I invited the students to my own studio, and it occurred to me that I could find the inheritors and those who could pass on illuminated painting in these deaf students. Later, I took on several apprentices from this school during my teaching there.

Illuminated painting was highly respected in ancient times, because it has exquisite craftsmanship. For decades, I have always kept the traditional pure handmade craftsmanship. Lacquering is generally wooden-bodied, and only a few products are bamboo-bodied. Many people use chemical lacquering to save cost, but I have always insisted on using natural lacquering, which is of high cost and difficult to paint. Because natural Chinese paint has strong stability, it will not peel off easily even after a long time of use. In the past, illuminated painting handicrafts were mostly exported to overseas countries; though they are produced in Ningbo, there are few locals who really know and appreciate them. I hope that illuminated painting can be more well-known. Over the years, many investors have come here and have invited me to cooperate with them. The commercialization of illuminated painting can make it more widespread and famous, but most businessmen seek maximum profits instead of devotion and adherence to the exquisite craftsmanship, thus leaving the cooperation unsettled.

On weekends, I teach foreign friends to do illuminated painting and lead them to appreciate profound Chinese culture. People in other countries even show a stronger sense of interest, believing that this is something with our Chinese characteristics. I have always thought that illuminated painting belonged to our nation, our country, and our state. We have the responsibility to protect our intangible cultural heritage, including illuminated painting. We have fifty-six nationalities, all possessing distinctive and profound cultures. Let us promote our Chinese culture to the world stage.

做到"知行合一"

董 路
指导教师：王雪芹

如今，习近平总书记多次提到"知行合一"，提倡将思想转化为行动。而我在采访李光昭先生之后，感受到了"知行合一"的工匠精神，不仅有十年磨一剑的坚韧，还有诚心诚意做好手头事的态度。

从二十岁开始接触泥金彩漆，到现在五十余载，他没有放弃，并一直保持着对泥金彩漆的热爱。在他看来，遇到泥金彩漆是他一生的幸运，甚至把它视为自己的家人一般。试问，能热爱一件事五十余载并一直用心对待的人还有多少？二十多岁的我，深深地敬佩他那种坚持"知行合一，行胜于言"的品质以及"此心光明，亦复何言"的心境。

李光昭用一生诠释了何为工匠精神，如何做到"知行合一"。在我看来，他不仅是一个优秀的工匠大师，更是一个"知行合一"的阳明文化传播者，一生绘制的许多作品里融入了他对美的追求，体现了诚心诚意的工匠精神。关于对美的追求，他会在作品中融合自己对生活的看法，把自己对美的认识通过作品表达出来，并诚心诚意地去做好每一件作品。随着年龄的增长，他懂得了很多为人处世的道理，也拥有了很多难能可贵的品质，而他的作品就如同他的心境一样获得不断的提升。

五百年前，阳明先生提出"知行合一"，开创了"致良知"学说，影响了中国乃至国外无数的人。蒋介石在悟道阳明格言之后，遂改名为"中正"，而"中正"出自王阳明心学之"大中至正"；更有日本东乡平八郎，随身佩戴的腰牌上写着：一生俯首拜阳明。一个国家综合实力最核心的还是文化软实力，文化软实力是一个国家综合国力的集中体现，已成为国家核心竞争力的重要组成部分。这事关精气神的凝聚，我们要做到"知行合一"，把思想转化为行动，在落细、落小、落实上下功夫。

大学生是民族的未来与希望，更应该做到"知行合一"。在采访李光昭先生时，他说道："现在的大学生仰望星空的时间太长了，都不能好好地脚踏实地去做事，对他们来说，做事应该有一种工匠精神，一步一脚印，要认准方向走下去，坚持到最后的人往往都是成功的。现在是多元化的时代，在十字路口要把握住机会。"是啊，就我自己而言，也是言大于行，往往说得比做得多。在理解了"知行合一"的工匠精神之后，我不会盲目地去仰望星空，而是把踏踏实实做好眼前事放到第一位。大学生身上需要承担更多的责任，我们不需要像周恩来一样为民族之崛起而读书，但要有我们自己的理想与抱负，不断进步。

做到"知行合一"，是一件看似简单、却需要漫长过程的事。知之真切笃实处即是行，行之明觉精察处即是知。茫茫荡荡，悬空去思索，而没有行，不能知其真；懵懵懂懂，任意去做，而没有思，只是冥行妄作。做一个"知行合一"的人吧！

团队成员：叶珈妤　董　路　李　铭　项金龙

Adherence to "the Unity of Knowledge and Action"

Dong Lu

Supervised by: Wang Xueqin

Nowadays, General Secretary Xi Jinping has repeatedly mentioned "the unity of knowledge and action", and advocated the transformation of thought into practice. After my interview of Mr. Li Guangzhao, I was deeply touched by the craftsmanship as well as "the unity of knowledge and action". The essence of craftsmanship not only lies in patience and perseverance over many years, but also earnestness and conscience in doing each current project.

Mr. Li Guangzhao entered the field of illuminated painting in his twenties, and now more than fifty years have passed, but he does not give up; instead, he still loves it with an ardent enthusiasm and passion. In his view, it is his great luck to understand the field of illuminated painting; he regards it as part of his life, even part of his family. How many people are there who can love their work more than fifty years with such profound enthusiasm and passion? For me, as a young man over twenty, I deeply admire his adherence to "the unity of knowledge and action", his wisdom of "actions speaking louder than words", and his magnanimous and peaceful state of mind.

Mr. Li Guangzhao lives to interpret what craftsmanship is, and, with his life, shows us how to unite knowledge and action. From my perspective, he is not only an outstanding master of craftsmanship, but also a communicator and practitioner of Yangming's spirit of "the unity of knowledge and action"; many of his paintings reflect his pursuit of beauty and craftsmanship, including earnestness and conscience. In the pursuit of beauty, he integrates his views of life into his works, expresses his understanding of aesthetics through his works, and sincerely completes every piece of work. With age, he not only has learned a lot of truth about life, but also possesses numerous valuable qualities, meanwhile his work as well as his state of mind makes continuous improvement.

Five hundred years ago, Mr. Yangming put forward the idea of unity of knowledge and action, and created the philosophy of innate knowing (or consciense), greatly influencing countless people in China and abroad. Mr. Chiang Kai-shek, enlightened by Mr. Yangming's motto, renamed himself Zhongzheng, which was taken from Yangming's innate knowing; the Japanese general Hachiro, on his waist, carried a flat plate which read "bowing to Yangming with a whole life". The core of a country's overall strength is the national cultural soft power. The cultural soft power is the concentrated expression of a country's comprehensive national strength, which has become an important factor of the country's core competitiveness. It is related to the cohesion of essence, energy and spirit; we must adhere to "the unity of knowledge and action" and put the idea into action, fostering and practicing core socialist values.

College students, as the future and hope of the nation, are expected to adhere to "the unity of knowledge and action". During the interview with Mr. Li Guangzhao, he said: "Many college students spend too much time in vain, idling away by looking at the stars in the night sky, so that they cannot really work in an earnest and down-to-earth way. Work needs craftsmanship. They need to find their direction and goal, and then, step by step, plot the course and get out there. Those who stick to the end are likely to succeed. Now the world is a time of diversity, and people need to seize the opportunity at the crossroads." This is definitely true. Taking myself as an example, I often speak a lot but act little, forgetting "action speaks louder than words". In understanding the spirit of craftsmanship, I will not idle away by looking at the stars in the night sky, but really work in an earnest and down-to-earth way. As college students, we need to shoulder more responsibility; we needn't go to school for the rise of the Chinese nation as Mr. Zhou Enlai, but we need to have our own ideals and aspirations for continuous progress.

Adherence to "the unity of knowledge and action" is not easy, but it is a lengthy and drawn-out process. Only through simultaneous action can one gain knowledge. There is no way to use knowledge after gaining it because knowledge and action are unified as one. Let us be a person who adheres to "the unity of knowledge and action".

Team members: Ye Jiayu, Dong Lu, Li Ming, Xiang Jinlong

第三章

Chapter Three

Entrepreneurship

企业家精神

<table>
</table>

导言　　　　　　　　　　　　　　　　Introduction

中国改革开放四十年为世界贡献了一大批优秀的现代企业家,他们为创造社会财富,建立市场经济体制,确立市场经济秩序,推进平等、法治和契约精神深入人心,提升综合国力做出了巨大的贡献。当前,世界经济形势风起云涌,中国虽然处于世界经济的大风口,瞬息万变的市场以及国家整体发展战略都对企业家发挥更大的作用提出了新的要求。2017年9月下发的《中共中央 国务院关于营造企业家健康成长环境弘扬优秀企业家精神更好发挥企业家作用的意见》把企业家精神概述为:爱国敬业遵纪守法艰苦奋斗的精神、创新发展专注品质追求卓越的精神、履行责任敢于担当服务社会的精神。

《王阳明全集》主编吴光先生谈及阳明思想对现代企业家的启示时以六个意识来概括,即内圣外王的追求意识、利他向善的道德意识、立志创新的品牌意识、以人为本的人才意识、诚信立业的信用意识、和谐双赢的经营意识。这与上面提及的企业家精神有异曲同工之妙。中华文化中义利统一的经营哲学,阳明先生"四民异业同道"的商业伦理,"舍短以用长"等管理思想对于形成有中国特色的企业家精神意义非凡。稻盛和夫从阳明思想中汲取养分,提出"敬天爱人"的经营哲学,这与"自立则生,利他则久"的传统经营哲学一脉相承,自利是企业的本性,没有自利,企业就失去了生存的基本驱动力。同时,利他也是企业天性的一部分,没有利他,事业就会失去平衡,并最终导致失败。

中国经济发展步入新常态,阳明思想在商业领域的实践依然闪烁着智慧的光芒。义利统一是千年中华商帮的文化自觉,也是对商业文明中契约精神的特色诠释。义利冲突是检验企业是否奉行企业家精神的最佳时刻,曾几何时,当冲突来临时,宋汉章倾家荡产赔付了荣氏家族,宁波帮的信托精神立了起来。二十多年前,当冲突来临时,张瑞敏砸烂了已经出厂的七十六台冰箱,中国企业家精神立了起来。当前,"一带一路"背景下中国企业走出去已经是大势所趋,弘扬中国企业家精神、塑造中国企业家形象关系到实现民族复兴大业的重大梦想。

（蔡 亮 撰写）

邱智铭：事业，就是事上磨炼

Qiu Zhiming: Career Is a Matter of Dedication

邱智铭，宁波贝发集团总裁，中国制笔协会副理事长。2006年荣膺首届"十大风云甬商"与"和谐中国：年度十大影响力人物"，2012年入选"浙江年度经济人物"。他是当代中国笔业最具创新性和前瞻性的企业家之一。他倡导在现代企业管理中融入阳明文化，积极践行阳明先生"知行合一"的思想，立志将贝发集团打造成中国规模最大、实力最强、出口创汇最多的制笔和文具集团。

Qiu Zhiming is the president of the Ningbo Beifa Group and the vice president of the China Writing Instrument Association. In 2006, he was given the award for one of the first "Top Ten Ningbo Merchants" and "Harmonious China: Top Ten Influential People of the Year". In 2012, he was elected as one of "Zhejiang's Annual Economic Figures". He is one of the most innovative and forward-thinking entrepreneurs in China, advocating the integration of Yangming culture with modern enterprise management, and he is an active practitioner of the Yangming philosophy of "the unity of knowledge and action". He is determined to make the Beifa Group China's largest, most powerful and most influential export trade group which is engaged in pen making and stationery.

事业，就是事上磨炼

口述：邱智铭

整理：谢雨诗

指导教师：蔡　亮　徐志敏　曹雅娟

引 子

人须在事上磨，方能立得住，方能静亦定、动亦定。

——**王阳明**

小港青年"磨出"人生第一单

我记得那是 1993 年的春节，在当时的北仑小港。那时候我们家有一个家庭作坊，但它已经难以为继。在一次气氛凝重的家庭会议后，我从父亲手中接过这个只有三十名员工、摇摇欲坠的家庭作坊，那年我三十六岁。

几乎是一夜之间，我感受到一种无以言表的压力，家人的重托和员工的质疑让我有些不知所措，我迷惘该从哪里开始，该如何闯出一番大事业。我走访了余姚临山、温州龙湾和桐庐分水镇这三个圆珠笔厂家集中的地方，搜集样品，并把自己作坊生产的两支多色圆珠笔和三角形塑料圆珠笔搭配进去，上百种样品笔就装在两盒木箱子里。接着，我拎着这两盒木箱子装的圆珠笔，到 1993 年春季广交会上去推销。没有展位，也不是正式代表，我只能花五十元钱从"黄牛"那里买了张临时参观证，我就站在广交会场馆外和楼梯口守候，偷偷给国外客商塞名片。一天过去了，两天过去了，十天过去了，几乎没有一个客商正眼看过我拎在手上的木箱子里的"土笔"。但我仍不厌其烦地向客商递上名片，还向客商索要名片。我不知道自己从哪里来的那股不服输、不抱怨的劲头，我知道对于一个有梦想的人而言这些都是必须要经历的苦头。

熬到了第十一天，在我即将心灰意懒的时候，奇迹终于发生了！我记得第七天时曾向一名中东地区"大胡子"客商塞过名片。到第十一天时，这位来自也门、名叫穆罕默德·沙易特的客商，让我晚上 10 点去他下榻的广州白云宾馆 10 楼一个房间洽谈。我仿佛抓到了一根"救命稻草"，兴奋无比。晚上 9 点就赶到那里，但房间门口早已排起了长队，还有十多家笔类生产商同行在等候洽谈。轮到我进房间洽谈时，时针已指向次日 0 点 40 分。穆罕默德·沙易特从我的木盒子里挑出两支笔，在我本已薄利的报价上又砍价 30%多。几乎无利可图，做还是不做？最终，我咬咬牙接了单。尽管价格被砍得"血淋淋"，但这是我在广交会上"磨出"人生的第一桶金，1万打圆珠笔订单，总价1.4万美元。从此我走上了外贸之路。

事业就是事上磨炼

我到现在还在思考我是如何度过了那难熬的十天，每一天的过去对我的精神都是一种挑战，我不得不说"守仁格竹"故事带给我的力量。阳明读朱子书，欲做圣人，先修格物。就这样，阳明盯着自家的竹子，不吃不喝，想以此参透人生。到第七天，实在坚持不住，最后卧病在床。很多人觉得这是个笑话，我觉得不然，故事恰恰体现出王阳明先生"欲做圣人"的决心与毅力。探索世界首先要磨炼自我，他敢于摆脱当时社会思潮的束缚，独立地思考，提出自己的学说，以"事上磨炼"的功夫，"知行合一"地实践和传播自己的思想。应该说，没有"事上磨炼"，就没有王阳明的学说。每一个梦想家，都需要有"事上磨炼"精神，王阳明先生正是创业者和梦想家的楷模。倘若我们不去学习他这一点，而去因袭照搬他的思想，岂不是弃之精华，而取之表皮吗？

闽南人最爱说的一句话是"爱拼才会赢"。阳明先生说："人须在事上磨，方能立得住。"正是王阳明的"事上磨炼"的启示带给我人生第一个奇迹。然而，我的"事上磨炼"并非一帆风顺，我还没有好好回味成功的甜蜜，一封来自也门的加急电报惊醒了我。两个集装箱圆珠笔全部漏油，更糟糕的是客户要求赔偿4万美元，像王阳明先生最终病倒那样，我知道我碰到了麻烦事，磨炼似乎才刚刚开始。

所谓"格物致知"，质量不过关，我就创新！这一惨痛的教训让我下决心成立一个研发中心，改造生产线，提升产品质量。之后，贝发开发的中性墨水笔、直液式针管笔还填补了国内空白。并且，其镍白铜笔头技术指标达到了国际先进水平，替代进口笔头。贝发成功了，我成功了，由于产品质量过硬、款式新颖、种类繁多、交货及时、价格低廉，贝发迅速被海外众多采购商列为核心供应厂家，客户群如"滚雪球"般扩大。

只有创新，贝发才能永葆辉煌。创新就是贝发的"事上磨炼"。2015年我参加央视财经《对话》栏目，在对话现场，我谈及精密制笔机械设备在国内是片空白，只能依赖于从瑞士进口。听罢，格力电器董事长董明珠立下"赌约"：格力一年之内做出造好笔的设备。我欣然"对赌"：如果有了一流国产设备，就一定能在一年内造出中国自产的世界好笔。我知道贝发与格力合作研发成功，受益的不仅是贝发，还有整个中国制笔业。

良知是企业家的灵魂

王阳明参透世事人心，创立阳明心学，终成一代圣哲。阳明文化是五百年来中国人最精妙的神奇智慧，王阳明所说的"知行合一"中的知是良知，那么什么是良知呢？良知是一种大爱，是一种纯粹、纯净的仁爱之心，良知就是中国人的信仰。"致良知"就是"知行合一"，通过"事上磨炼"达到道德意识与道德行为的统一，不断靠近我们的信仰，无论这个过程多么漫长和艰辛。

邱智铭先生谈"事上磨炼"

良知是老祖宗传给我们最纯朴的精神财产，我的两个孩子虽是在美国出生，但我仍坚持让他们在国内长大，从小接受国内教育。我认为作为一个中国人，不能忘本，中华文化博大精深，就拿阳明文化来说，能学的东西就很多。然而现在的中国人容易忘本、崇洋，相反外国人却重视中国文化！王阳明对日本的影响甚于中国，是他在中国的贡献少了吗？不是的，是我们没有好好珍惜，没有认真挖掘这种文化的内涵。我希望国人能更重视我们的本国文化，否则还会出现"韩国人为端午申遗"这类让人扼腕的事。

我认为一个企业家的"致良知"就是弘扬有良知的企业家精神，这种精神是企业家或企业团队的价值观和品质。我认为这种精神体现在"知交尽四海，万里有亲朋"的团结精神、"永不停步，求实创新"的进取精神、"多尽实心，多干实事"的务实精神、"争创一流，敢为人先"的求精精神的整合，这应该是中国企业生存和发展的"灵魂"。网络上评价我用十年时间带领贝发登上中国制笔业之巅，完成了国外同行起码二十年才能取得的成就。我觉得自己没有那么伟大，但是我也希望能像阳明先生那样，活着被人需要，死后还能被人传颂。

邱智铭先生与团队师生合影

Career Is a Matter of Dedication

Narrator: Qiu Zhiming

Compiled by: Xie Yushi

Supervised by: Cai Liang, Xu Zhiming, Cao Yajuan

One must be trained and polished in the actual affairs of life. Only then can one stand firm and remain calm whether in activity or in tranquility.

—Wang Yangming

The First Order for a Green Hand

My father had a family workshop, but it was quite hard for many of these small workshops to survive during the 1990s. I remember it was in Beilun, a small harbor in Ningbo then, in a depressing family meeting during China's Spring Festival in 1993 that I took this workshop over from my father, which was on the verge of bankruptcy with only 30 workers. I was 36 that year.

Almost overnight, I felt inexplicable pressure. I felt at a loss with the expectations from my family members and the doubts from my staff. I was confused about where to start, and how to make it a success. I visited Linshan Town in Yuyao County, Longwan Town in Wenzhou, and Fenshui Town in Tonglu—the three concentrated places of ball-point pen manufacturers—and collected samples. I put hundreds of samples together with the products from my own workshop—two multi-color ball-point pens and a triangle-shaped plastic ball-point pen—into two wooden cases and took them to sell at the Spring Canton Fair. Without a booth and not being a formal exhibitor, I had to spend 50 yuan to get a temporary ticket from a scalper. The only thing I could do next was to wait outside the exhibition hall or at a stair landing, handing out my cards to foreign businessmen. One day passed, two days passed, ten days passed—no one stopped to have a look at the unpopular pens in the cases. But I still took pains to hand out cards and ask cards from foreign businessmen. I don't know how much courage it took to persist, but I know persistence with no complaint is important for a man with dreams.

On the 11th day, when I was about to lose heart, something unexpected happened. I remembered I had presented a card to a bearded merchant from the Middle East on the 7th day. Then on the 11th day, this man from Yemen, named Muhammad Sha Yite, asked me to go to a room on the 10th floor at ten o'clock that night at the Guangzhou Baiyun Hotel where he lived. I seemed to have caught a "lifeline", so I felt excited. I got there one hour earlier, only to find a long queue outside his room. There were a dozen pen manufacturers waiting for orders. It was already early the following morning when it was finally my turn to get into the room. Muhammad Sha Yite picked up two pens from my wooden cases, and cut the price by 30% of my low offer, which meant that transactions would be uneconomical. I asked myself whether I should accept it or not. In the end, I made up my mind to accept it despite the low price offered. That was my first pot of gold—an order of 10,000 dozen ball-point pens, which totaled $14,000. From that day on, I embarked on an export-oriented path.

Career Is a Matter of Dedication

Even nowadays, I'm thinking about how I spent those ten tough days. The passing of each day was a challenge for me. I have to admit that I got some inspiration from "Yangming's Bamboo Investigation" story. Having reading Zhu Zi(Xi)'s books, Yangming was determined to be a sage, so he needed to "investigate the world" first. Therefore, Yangming stared at the bamboo plants in his courtyard without eating or drinking, hoping to understand the meaning of life. On the 7th day, he could hardly hold on and finally he fell ill in bed. A lot of people think of it as a joke, but I don't think so. The story manifests Wang Yangming's determination of being a sage. You need self-cultivation before you are going to explore the world. Yangming dared to get rid of the bondage of contemporary traditional thoughts and put forward his own theory with independent thinking. He delivered and practiced his thoughts by the way of dedication and "the unity of knowledge and action". It can safely be said that Wang Yangming's philosophy could not have come into being without his dedication. Every dreamer needs to have the spirit of dedication. It is Wang Yangming who sets a good example for being both an entrepreneur and dreamer. If we follow his thought without understanding his dedication, we fail to get the essence of his philosophy.

People in the Minnan area believe that "struggle will lead to success" (the title of a Chinese song). Master Yangming also said, "People will reach success only after dedication." It was Wang Yangming's story of dedication that brought me my first miracle. My way to success, however, was not that smooth. An urgent telegram from Yemen which said two containers of ball-point pens leak oil woke me up before I could rest and taste the joy of success. Even worse, they claimed they needed a compensation of $40,000. I was aware that I had run into trouble, which was just the beginning of my dedication.

According to Master Yangming's saying, "achieving sagehood by investigating the world", it occurred to me that we need innovation due to the inferior quality of our products. This costly lesson made me determined to set up a research and development center, to transform the production line and improve the quality of the products. Later, the development of gel ink pens and straight liquid needle pens filled the domestic gap. Furthermore, the technique of making the nickel cupronickel nibs has reached an advanced level in the world, which can well replace the imported nibs. Beifa became a success and so did I. Beifa has been listed as one of the main suppliers by many overseas purchasers due to the high quality, novel style, good variety, prompt delivery and competitive price of the products. A growing number of customers came to us, just like a "rolling snowball".

Innovation is the key to the development of the Beifa Group, which can also be called Beifa's dedication. I attended the "Dialogue" program in the economy channel of CCTV and mentioned that we had to import sophisticated pen-making machinery from Switzerland because it was not available at home. Hearing this, Dong Mingzhu, the CEO of Green Electric Appliances Incorporation promised to develop a quality machine for us. And I made my promise too that we would produce the quality pens completely made in China with a first-class domestic machine. The combination of the two corporations will benefit not only Beifa, but the whole pen-making industry in China as well.

Conscience Is the Soul for an Entrepreneur

As Wang Yangming gained insights into the world and its people, he created the Yangming's Philosophy of Mind and eventually became a sage. Yangming culture is brilliant wisdom from the last 500 years. In Wang Yangming's "unity of knowledge and action", the knowledge here is conscience, but what is conscience? Conscience is a kind of love, a pure loving heart. Conscience is Chinese people's religion. "Realizing conscientious wisdom" is the result of "the unity of knowledge and action". By "realizing conscientious wisdom", we can achieve the unity of moral consciousness and moral behavior in a manner of dedication, no matter how long and hard the process is.

Conscience is the purest spiritual property our ancestors left us. Both of my children were born in the United States, but I insisted that they grow up in China, receiving education in their motherland. I think, as a Chinese, we should not forget our roots. Chinese culture is profound. Take Yangming culture for example, we can learn a lot from it. Many Chinese, however, forget their roots easily and admire the foreign things. Instead, foreigners nowadays attach great importance to Chinese culture. Yangming culture has had a much deeper influence on Japan than that in China. Does that mean he made less contribution in China? Definitely not! It is because we haven't cherished it, failing to explore the connotations of his culture. I hope we as Chinese people will attach more importance to our own culture so as to avoid such ironies as R. O. Korea's application of the Dragon Boat Festival for the list of world heritage.

I think an entrepreneur's "realizing conscientious wisdom" is the spread of the entrepreneurial spirit of conscience. Such kind of spirit is the value and quality of entrepreneurs or business groups. I think this spirit is embodied in the combination of the solidarity of "making friends all over the world", in the aggressiveness of "keeping going by being innovative", in the pragmatism of "dedicating yourself to the things you are doing and being realistic", and in the perfectionism of "making the first-class brand". These should be the "soul" for the survival and development of Chinese enterprises. The remarks on the Internet say that I have turned Beifa around and have made it one of the top domestic pen makers within the last ten years, which is half the time that foreign counterparts will spend. I don't think I'm that great, but I also hope to be a man like Master Yangming—needed when alive and praised after death.

做有良知的人

谢雨诗

指导教师：蔡 亮 徐志敏 曹雅娟

为何要提良知呢？明代王守仁，能文能武，官拜兵部尚书，戎马一生，却仍不忘讲学，讲的就是良知。有一次一个乡绅请他讲学，问他："除却良知，还有什么说的？"他用原话回答说："除却良知，还有什么说的！"之前我所知道的王阳明，仅仅只是高一时历史书上一笔带过的"心学大师"四字而已。直到大学的暑期社会实践，我参加了"用声音叙事"这个活动，我才开始慢慢地深入地去了解王阳明，知道为人之本，是坚守良知。

良知是个人行为的道德准绳。邱智铭先生是阳明文化的真正的践行者。无论是当他谈到事业上的事上磨炼，还是对企业人才选拔的要求，我都听他反复强调两个字：良知。良知，是人的一种天赋的道德观念。正所谓"人之初，性本善"，人之所以为人，就是因为人有独立的思想，有良知，它既是道德意识，也是人的最高本体，是人的本心。

做人难，做一个坚守良知的人更难。花花世界，很多人在钱与权的诱惑中迷失了自己。然而，邱智铭先生却在这样的诱惑下坚守了自己的良知。如他所说，他也曾追逐金钱与名利，但现在，他知道人该追求的是"合一"，知与行的合一，道德与行为的合一，个人与社会的合一。他认为人行于世，该坚守自己的良知，虽然在此过程中会受到种种诱惑，但我们要时刻谨记做事良知先行，便不会迷失自我。

良知是大爱，是一个纯粹纯净的仁爱之心。中国价值体系中最核心的因素便是"五常"，即"仁、义、礼、智、信"。邱智铭先生认为，良知是中国人的信仰。他的两个孩子虽是在美国出生，但他仍坚持让他们在国内长大，从小接受国内教育。他认为作为一个中国人，不能忘本，要有良知。中华文化博大精深，是老祖宗留给炎黄子孙的宝贵财富。

与个人相比，良知对于社会更是弥足珍贵。近些年来，孔雀绿、苏丹红、落日黄等化工原料频频"走进"我们日常食用的食品，而三鹿的"毒奶粉"更是让国人心寒。作为一名消费者，我不禁要问：企业的良知和社会责任哪儿去了？在这次采访中，令我惊讶的是邱智铭先生对我们的态度。他虽是个家财万贯的大老板，但却没有一点有钱人的架子，他一口答应接受我们这群无名的大学生的采访；他跟我们说话的时候就像一个和蔼的长辈在与我们说笑；他开设训练营帮助许多人创业；他新创办了神域健康项目……他的首要企业核心价值观就是诚信，做一个有诚信有良知的企业家，就是他的企业家精神。他认为一个企业家的"致良知"就是弘扬有良知的企业家精神，他认为人有多大本事，就有义务对社会做出多大的贡献，这种精神是企业家或企业团队的价值观和品质。

良知乃个人行走于世间的道德基础，没有良知，人同物就没有什么差异了；良知乃社会发展的要义，没有良知的社会只有一条出路，即消失，良知乃民族的黏合剂，没有良知的民族必会走向灭亡。物质，不是人类的所有，但一颗良心，才是所有人类应具有的。这次的活动让我走近了王阳明，让我更深刻地知道，每一个人都应该怀着一颗良心，用良心做事，坚守自己的良知，做个有良知的人。像阳明先生一样做到"我心光明，惟致良知"。

团队成员：贺　芸　谢雨诗　钱　昊

Being a Man with Conscience

Xie Yushi

Supervised by: Cai Liang, Xu Zhiming, Cao Yajuan

Why should we mention conscience? In the Ming Dynasty, Wang Yangming was both adept at letter and sword. He led a military life and served as the minister of the Board of War, but he never forgot to deliver lectures to spread his theory of conscience. Once, a squire asked him, "What do you have to say besides conscience?" He responded to him with the same words, "What do you have to say besides conscience?" My knowledge about Wang Yangming had been nothing more than a comment of "the master of the Philosophy of Mind" mentioned in a high school history book. I had little understanding of Master Yangming until I attended the summer practice "Beyond the Voices" at college. I began to gradually get to know Yangming and his philosophy, and be aware that to be a man, you must have your conscience.

Conscience is the moral standard for individual behavior. Mr. Qiu Zhiming is a true practitioner of Yangming culture. During the interview, he repeatedly placed emphasis on the word "conscience" when he mentioned dedication in business and his criteria for selecting business talents. As the Chinese saying goes, "all people are born kind"; conscience is a gift of morality. Because we can think independently and have conscience, we are called human beings. Conscience is a moral consciousness and a basic requirement for a human being.

Life is hard, but what is even harder is to stick to our conscience. In this earthly world, many people lose themselves in the temptations of money and power. Yet, Mr. Qiu has persisted in his conscience despite all temptations. He told us that he had never chased money and reputation, but now he knows what a man should pursue is "unity", the unity of knowledge and action, the unity of morality and behavior, and the unity of the individual and society. He believes that a man needs to stick to his conscience despite different kinds of temptation. With conscience, a man will not get lost.

Conscience is great love, a pure loving heart. The core factors in the Chinese value system are the five virtues, namely "benevolence, righteousness, courtesy, wisdom and honesty". According to Mr. Qiu, conscience is Chinese people's belief. His two children were born in the United States, but he insisted that they grow up in

China and receive their education in his homeland. He believes that as a Chinese, we should stick to our conscience instead of forgetting our roots. We have a great profound culture, a treasure our ancestors left us.

Conscience is important to individuals, but it is more valuable to the society as a whole. In recent years, malachite green, Sudan red, sunset yellow and other poisonous chemicals have frequently entered our daily food, not to mention the chilling Sanlu milk powder scandal. As a consumer, I can't help asking "Do you corporations have any conscience and social responsibility?" What surprised me in the interview was the way Mr. Qiu treated us. Rich as he is, he was never as arrogant as some rich men. When we asked for an interview with him, he did not hesitate. He was just like an elder, saying something kind and constructive to us in the interview. He opened a training camp to help many people start their businesses and founded some health programs. The core value of his enterprise is conscience. He is determined to be a conscientious and honest entrepreneur. He believes that people are obliged to make contributions to society depending on the abilities they have, which is also a value for quality entrepreneurs and enterprises.

Conscience is the moral foundation for us to live in the world. Without conscience, there would be no difference between man and animals. Conscience is quite essential for social development. A society without conscience has no way out, but vanish. Conscience is the bond that helps unite different nations. A nation without conscience will finally perish. What we human beings need to pursue is not material goods but conscience. This summer practice brought me closer to Wang Yangming, whose philosophy tells me that everyone should have conscience, and stick to it. I will do as Mr. Yangming tells us: "My heart is righteous, and the only thing I need to do is to realize conscientious wisdom."

Team members: He Yun, Xie Yushi, Qian Hao

黄君立：文化塑造精神，诚信凝聚力量

Huang Junli: Culture Makes Spirit while Credibility Makes Cohesion

　　黄君立，浙江双羊集团有限公司总经理。双羊集团有限公司是创建于 1986 年的民营企业，主要生产并出口钢管、定时器、漏电保护器、PVC 电线、橡胶电缆电线、插头电源线等。在罗国明董事长的带领下，企业不断创新、重才爱才、关爱员工、回报社会。他们的成功贵在逆势坚守，赢在理性发展。他们始终坚信企以信立，财以德聚，业以才兴。

　　Huang Junli is the general manager of the Zhejiang Shuangyang Group Co., Ltd., a private enterprise founded in 1986. Their major products include steel pipes, timers, creepage protectors, PVC cords, rubber cables, power cords and extension cords, which are sold both at home and abroad. Led by Luo Guoming, the CEO of the Group, the enterprise creates constant innovation, treasures talents, cares for employees and repays society. Their success can be attributed to their perseverance during difficult situations and their rational development. They always hold the belief that the survival of an enterprise depends on credibility, the gathering of wealth depends on virtue, and the prosperity of a business depends on talents.

文化塑造精神，诚信凝聚力量

口述：黄君立
整理：沈旭桐
指导教师：曹雅娟　徐志敏

引　子
尽心知性知天，是生知安行事。

——王阳明

栉风沥雨牧双羊，一路风雨一路歌

我们双羊的发展之路走得非常不容易，如果今天的双羊还算得上是成功的话，那么应该说，这个成功首先来自党的开放政策带来的发展机遇及党和政府、各有关部门对双羊的支持；其次，我们双羊能有今天，正是我们十八年如一日，始终坚持诚信为本、操守为重的经营原则带来的结果。罗国明董事长在企业管理中一直对职工所倡导的就是：企业的发展在于管理，企业管理的核心在于企业文化，而企业文化的精髓则在于诚信。

1986 年夏天，罗国明董事长受刚上任的乡党委书记重托，担任了乡办塑料配件厂第六任厂长。当时乡办厂只有几间破旧的厂房，几台破烂的手扳压机，不到 7 万元的总资产，现金也只有 150 元。但就是在如此艰难的条件下，双羊正式成立了。而后的创业之路，也是一波三折。

记得 1993 年上半年，双羊正在紧锣密鼓搞钢管厂基建，天津的合作方却由于种种原因，无法履行原来商定的钢管销售协议。这对我们公司而言，无疑是个晴天霹雳。我们决定自己打开销售之路。

就在我们的钢管销售刚有一点起色的时候，令人措手不及的事情再次发生，这对艰难行进中的我们而言，无疑是雪上加霜。1998 年，我们更是面临着破产的危机。但在罗董事长的坚持下，秉承对员工、合作单位负责的心，我们齐心协力，让双羊度过了最艰难的时段，迎来了丰收年。

能够留住员工的文化，才是有生命力的企业文化

我们始终秉承着一颗对员工负责到底的心，即便是在公司最困难的时候，我们也没拖欠员工一分钱。当初企业快破产的时候，罗国明董事长说过："申请破产是不可能的！那样做我是一身轻松了，可是让员工们怎么办？一下子全都没了工

125

作，他们的家庭怎么办？"因为我们对员工的负责，员工也热爱着我们企业。

关于企业文化，我们认为："文化即习惯，每个职工的言行习惯，都是企业风气的反映。"本着这种理念，员工的教育培训在双羊的企业文化建设中显得尤为重要。为提高员工生活质量，我们保证员工合理的上班时间，让他们自由地工作，使得他们的价值得到最大的体现。我们特别注重对外来员工的人文关怀，如：每周集中给该周过生日的员工送生日蛋糕和生日贺卡，假期为他们订购回家的车票，解决子女读书问题等。我们也十分注重员工的凝聚力，不排斥新员工，让每个员工在我们企业能快乐工作。

我们对员工就像朋友，不会因为我是总经理就摆架子，"万物一体""人人平等"，这八个字使得我和员工之间能更舒服地相处。我们会在保障员工利益的前提下，妥善处理员工的意见和建议，并对合理化建议进行奖励，鼓励员工积极参与企业的民主管理。尤其是一线员工，他们经常会有很好的想法与我们分享，有时候他们更是起着决定性作用。

以诚信经营企业，以慈爱回报社会

对合作伙伴的诚信体现在我们企业对产品质量的重视，我们认为"没有质量就没有双羊的明天"。在质量方面，我们从原料开始就严格把控，不偷工减料，不会因为所谓的利润就丢去我们一直坚持的"诚信"之心。由于我们双羊一贯以来在合作中重质量，讲诚信，一直坚持"致良知"，做好自己的本分，因此在客户中树立了良好的口碑，欧洲的一些大超市、大客户都与我们建立了长期的良好合作关系，双羊电缆线在全球的知名度大幅提升。由此也引来一些不法厂家假冒双羊商标生产电线进行销售。为了进一步保护知识产权和消费者权益，2010 年，我们和德国 VDE 认证机构合作，成为全球首家（目前也是惟一的一家）与 VDE 合作防伪标贴项目的电线电缆生产厂家。这个方法很成功，既保障了我们企业的名声，又保证了我们企业产品的质量。正是因为我们对产品质量的严格把控，才会有那么多外国企业找我们合作，信任我们。

企业的社会责任已成为企业发展的重要方面，所以我们也热心参与社会公益与慈善事业，对家乡各项社会事业的发展充满着一种使命感和责任感，尤其是罗国明董事长，经历过困境，更是懂得以慈爱回报社会的重要性。经济的规律也好，现实的困境也罢，都不能意味着一个商人可以远离良知！"得民心者得天下"，企业经营的成功之道必须是得人心。

不忘初心，顺应潮流

我们不能被"逐利"的心态绑架，总是想着一夜致富，看到有利可图，就不计后果，想一口吃成个大胖子。制造业是靠踏踏实实做出来的。如果没有这种心态，制造业是没有坚实基础的。

后来，我们发现一味地守旧不能满足客户的需求，所以我们成立自己的创作团队，并在我们的产品中融入自己的想法。我们开始进行产品创新，跟上时代的步伐。

黄君立总经理与团队师生合影

从资金的束缚到技术的突破，从人才的引进到产业的调整，一场场比拼，一次次考验，都帮助着我们成长。因为有真诚的关爱，所以才有凝聚的力量；因为有坚定的信仰，所以才有追随的步伐！我们做好自己的本职工作，满足客户的需求，以创新跟上时代的步伐，一步一个脚印，不骄不躁，以诚信经营企业品牌，坚守主业，转型升级，一路稳健发展！

Culture Makes Spirit while Credibility Makes Cohesion

Narrator: Huang Junli
Compiled by: Shen Xutong
Supervised by: Cao Yajuan, Xu Zhimin

As to exerting one's mind to the utmost, knowing one's nature, and knowing Heaven, these are the acts of those who are born with such knowledge and practice it naturally and easily.

—Wang Yangming

A Hard Way for Shuangyang's Establishment

Shuangyang has suffered a lot of hardship in the process of its development. If today's Shuangyang can be counted as a success, credit first goes to the governmental supports and the opportunities brought by the reform and opening-up policy, which has helped develop our foreign trade. In addition, the success of Shuangyang today can be attributed to our belief in credibility and integrity and that we do what we should do. Mr. Luo Guoming, our CEO, always emphasizes that we cannot run an enterprise without effective management; we cannot manage an enterprise without business culture, and we cannot develop a business culture without credibility.

In the summer of 1986, Mr. Luo was entrusted by the new leader of the town to be the sixth director of a plastic parts factory that was originally founded by the local government. At that time, there were only a few shabby workshops and broken arbor presses in the factory, with altogether 150 yuan of cash and total assets of no more than 70,000 yuan. It was under such difficult circumstances that Shuangyang was established. Of course, the following days would be full of ups and downs.

I remember when we were focused on the infrastructure of the steel tube factory in the first half of the year of 1993, our partner in Tianjin couldn't fulfill the sales agreement about steel tubes for various reasons. It was really a shock for the factory at that moment. Therefore, we decided to sell the products on our own.

Just when we gained some achievements in sales, something terrible abruptly happened again, which worsened the already grave situation. In 1998, we were even on the verge of bankruptcy. However, it was Mr. Luo's perseverance and sense of responsibility for employees and partners that we survived the hardship with our joint effort. Then came the spring for Shuangyang.

Vigorous Culture: The Key to Employees' Devotion

We constantly take responsibility for our employees and there were no wage arrears even in the toughest time. When we were on the verge of bankruptcy, Mr. Luo said, "We won't file for bankruptcy! If I did that, I would be relieved. Then what could my employees do? They all would lose their jobs. What would their families do?" Because we are responsible for our employees, our employees also love the Group.

In regard to the business culture, we believe, "Culture is the habit, and every employee's words and deeds are the reflection of the enterprise." Based on this belief, it is especially important to expose the employees to the training of a business culture. In order to improve the quality of life for employees, we work out a reasonable timetable and let them work freely, so that their value can be fully expressed. In addition, we give our humanistic concern to migrant workers. For example, once a week we provide a birthday cake and birthday card to those whose birthday is during that week. We will help them book tickets home. We also help them solve their children's education problem and so on. We also value the cohesion of the employees and never discriminate against new employees, so as to let them work in a pleasant atmosphere.

We treat the employees like friends, and never regard ourselves as superiors simply because we are leaders. Master Yangming's two beliefs—"unity of all things" and "everyone is equal"—enable me to get along well with employees. Bearing their interest in mind, we duly handle their complaints and suggestions, among which those reasonable ones are rewarded. We encourage employees to get actively involved in the management of the group, especially those at the production line, who often share good ideas with us and sometimes even play a decisive role.

Credibility in Management, Kindness to Society

We focus on the quality of products to show our integrity to our partners, because we believe in the motto "no quality, no tomorrow for Shuangyang". We strictly control the quality of raw materials, and never use inferior ones or turn out substandard products. We won't lose our credibility and integrity when faced with so-called profits. Due to our adherence to the principle of quality, integrity, and conscience, we have gained growing popularity among our customers. We have established a long-term cooperation with some major supermarkets and companies in Europe. Shuangyang cable has increasingly gained worldwide reputation. Some unscrupulous manufacturers, therefore, have gained profits by producing counterfeit Shuangyang wires. In order to protect our intellectual property and consumers' interests, we became the first and the only wire and cable manufacturer around the world at present that cooperated with VDE (Verband der Elektrotechnik) testing and certification institute in Germany to develop a security label in 2010. This measure has been very successful, not only protecting our reputation, but also guaranteeing the quality of the products. It is because of our strict control on products that many foreign companies are willing to trust us and cooperate with us.

Social responsibility has become an important quality for the development of a company, so we take active part in charity and social work. We are full of the sense of mission and responsibility for the development of our hometown. Mr. Luo, in particular, has a deeper understanding of the importance of repaying society since he went through so many difficulties. A businessman cannot lose conscience however tough the dilemma is. As the saying goes, "If you win all people's heart, then you win the whole world," winning the hearts of your employees ensures the success of your company.

Following the Trend with an Original Mind

We cannot become the slave of profits and neither can we dream of an overnight success. The manufacturing industry is rather hard because it requires a down-to-earth attitude, without which, there is no solid foundation in this industry.

When we gradually found that we failed to meet all the demands of customers due to our conservatism, we set up our own innovation-seeking team, and put our ideas into the products. We try to keep up with trends by focusing on the innovation of original products.

We have survived a series of challenges and tests, from shortage of capital to a breakthrough in technology, from talent introduction to product adjustment, all which have contributed to our maturity. Because of our sincere concern for our employees, we have strong cohesion amongst ourselves. Because of our strong belief, we can keep pace with the trends. We do what we should do to meet customers' demands and never stop our innovation. On the basis of credibility and integrity, we persist in doing what we should do, making constant transformation and upgrading, and now our efforts have paid off.

不骄不躁，坚守本心

沈旭桐
指导教师：曹雅娟　徐志敏

　　时代不断更替变化，我们的心也越发地浮躁，不再肯脚踏实地，只想着如何一步登天，这体现在物质上，但却侵害着我们的精神。

　　作为一个大学生，我已经开始踏入社会这个复杂的环境。不知从哪天起，我开始变得物质，变得易怒，变得不再像我自己。想要追求更多更好的东西，这没有错，错的是我什么都不想努力却想要最好的那个想法。时刻交错在自责与自负间，我变得迷惘，变得浮躁。短暂快乐后袭来的空虚，让我更加无助，我甚至开始怀疑我的大学生活。但说到底还是我不够坚持自己，不够清楚自己当初选择上大学真正的目的是什么。就像这次我的采访对象黄总给我举的一个例子一样，前几年房地产市场很吃香，不少企业家开始按捺不住自己想要一步登天的心，开始打着企业的名号，暗地里投资房地产，久而久之，他们不但没投资好房地产，也没能经营好自己的企业。黄总说："虽然赚钱很重要，但我们不能被'逐利'的心态绑架，不能看到有利可图，就不计后果，想一口吃成个大胖子。任何东西都是靠踏踏实实地做出来的，如果没有这种心态，是不会有结果的。"就像王阳明先生说过要坚守本心，我的本心、本职是学生，我要做的就是好好学习。

　　其实在这次采访前，我对王阳明先生"致良知"的认识是说什么就做什么，将知识和实践联合在一起。采访后，我才知道我所认知的王阳明精神，是如此的表面化。

　　王阳明先生说过，他不要求每个人都学习他的理论，但希望每个人心中都有良知。这一点，我从黄总那里得到了很深的感触。黄总深知他整个公司的员工对阳明精神都不怎么了解，可是他做的一切都符合阳明精神。他对企业员工负责，对合作伙伴诚信，一步一个脚印，做着自己最本职、最该做的事，这不就是阳明精神，不就是"致良知"嘛。

　　除了"致良知"，我们更需要拥有一颗"诚信"的心，只有诚信待人，才会赢得别人的信任。不但是工作，也是交朋友，更是生活，诚信做好每一件事，诚信待人、诚信做人。

　　诚信做人，不骄不躁，坚守本心，我相信这12个字会一直影响着我，教我做人，教我真正的阳明精神。

团队成员：郑秀媛　车晚静　沈旭桐

No Arrogance, No Diversion

Shen Xutong

Supervised by: Cao Yajuan, Xu Zhimin

As time goes by, we are increasingly irritable and no longer willing to work hard. We just want to find a shortcut to gain success. It is reflected in the aspect of material life, but it also does damage to our spirit.

As a college student, I begin to enter this complex society. I don't know from which day on I have become materialistic and irritable, not being like I used to be. Admittedly, it is perfectly fine to pursue more and better things, but the problem is that I hope to get all these things without hard work. I have been confused and irritable, blaming myself and justifying my conduct. Transient happiness is always followed by void, which aggravates my sense of helplessness and even makes me uncertain about my college life. In fact, what contributes to this situation, I think, is my lack of perseverance and my confusion about the purpose for attending college. My situation is, in a sense, similar to the example given by Mr. Huang, my interviewee in this summer practice. He told of the story of some entrepreneurs being tempted to make investment in the real estate business by using the company brand, aiming to make a big fortune from it. Of course, it is not unexpected that quite a lot of them finally failed in both the new business and the existing line. Mr. Huang said, "It's important to earn money, but we cannot be the slave of profits or dream of an overnight success regardless of the possible negative consequences. Bear in mind that everything should be done step by step, otherwise you will finally get nothing at all." Just as Wang Yangming always mentioned, "keep your original mind", since I am a college student now, my "original mind" is to focus on academic study.

In fact, before this interview, to me, Wang Yangming's "realizing conscientious wisdom" or simply "conscience" only meant to do as what I say, and to combine knowledge and practice. I didn't know how shallow my understanding was until I finished the interview.

Wang Yangming said he didn't want everyone to acquire his philosophy, but he hoped everyone could have conscience in their daily life. I got a thorough understanding about this point from Mr. Huang. He knows clearly that most of his employees don't know what "conscience" is, but what he does conforms to the philosophy of "conscience". He is responsible for his employees; he is honest to his partners; he does everything step by step; he does what he should do. Aren't these the practice of Yangming philosophy of "conscience"?

In addition to conscience, we also need to have the quality of credibility and integrity. Only in this way will we gain others' trust. Do everything with integrity whether it is for our job, friends or everyday life.

Keep credibility and integrity; never be arrogant and impetuous; be yourself. I think these words will have a far-reaching influence on my life, teaching me to truly practice Yangming philosophy.

Team members: Zheng Xiuyuan, Che Wanjing, Shen Xutong

蔡文迪：良知二字是参同

Monday: Conscientious Wisdom—the Secret of Being a Sage

蔡文迪，英文名 Monday，是芥末（JEMO）公司的 CEO。她是北京大学毕业生，学的是历史和外语。专业与服装并没有什么关系，但她从小对经商很有兴趣。她毕业后的目标就是创业，然后再继续读书。对她来说做什么都很有趣，关键是要新、要快。她认为透明化是历史化进程的一个趋势，而她要在这方面站到行业的前端。

Cai Wendi is the CEO of JEMO Dress-making Company in Beijing. Monday is her English name, and she is a graduate of Peking University, having majored in history and foreign language. Though her major was not related to dress making, she has been very interested in doing business since childhood. Owning her own startup firm and then furthering her study are her dreams after graduation. It is fun for her to do things that are new and fast. She believes that transparency is a historical trend in social development, so in terms of transparency, she needs to stay on the top of the business she is doing.

良知二字是参同

口述：Monday
整理：贾雅婷
指导教师：曹雅娟　徐志敏

引　子

你看到满大街都是圣人，满大街的人看你也是圣人。

——王阳明

仲尼于心

我所理解的"致良知"就是从一而终地使用优质的面料去做衣服，同时也真诚地对待我的顾客和伙伴。我不在价格和成本上对我的客人故弄玄虚，不在做衣服的过程中偷懒耍滑，用市场价四分之一的价格，供给客人同样优质的面料和一等的做工。我希望能够发展出属于我们国家的真丝衬衫品牌。惊讶吗？我国是全球最大的丝绸生产国。丝绸产量和出口量连续二十多年占全球七成，可我们居然没有自己的真丝衬衫品牌。

而关于对生产成本及定价透明的最初看法，我在 Everlane（一家著名的美国线上服装零售商，主打基本款，致力于带给人们低成本、高质量的服饰）上第一次见到这个做法的时候就觉得它非常符合我所想要的认知。我很认同 Everlane 上定价表格的做法并且由衷地对此产生敬意。正巧那时我和我的伙伴就已经有想要创办芥末（JEMO）的念头，然后我就想，我也要做一个像这样的东西。事实上它也确实给企业带来过一些好处。我一直都很强调一点，简单的事情往往能带来益处。

这项措施在一开始的时候就收到了三种不同的对待。很大一部分人并没有接触过这种做法。而这很大一部分人中的很大一部分对这项措施漠不关心，无视它。小部分人不知道我们这种做法借鉴于 Everlane，认为这项举措是创新的、与其他企业不一样，并且非常认同。另外很小一部分的人了解 Everlane，也肯定了我们的做法。造成这种结果也许是我们把国外的做法搬到国内没有很好地本土化，也许是有其他缺陷而我们还没发现。我的本意是希望大家能有意识地去思考。我希望大家能去思考行业背后的事。我们相信透明化是历史化进程的一个趋势，而我们坚持这样的事，会让大家慢慢地有这样的意识。透明化是一个渐进的过程。我们都知道许多媒体都做过这样的事。比如大家都知道网易在《成本控》的 2013

年第 12 期公开过一瓶迪奥香水的价格组成。这样的事恰恰证明了人们已经开始重视和关心行业背后的事。

随物而格

每一个创业者都不容易。像玛丽苏小说中受到上帝眷顾随随便便就能创立一个商业帝国的人在现实中是不存在的。每一个成功的企业家背后都一定有他们的艰辛努力。

就好像我们做生产成本及定价透明，我们不是想想而已。一个看上去很简单的价格目录做起来并不简单。在每一件商品上新之前，我们需要顶着压力做大量的数据分析，每一个环节、每一个步骤都要计算在内。但一个价格目录的完成并不代表着万事大吉。我们一开始的时候就遭到过美工的质疑。他认为目录太占版面又没人关注。只有去做了，我们才知道事情是怎样的。不过令我们相当难过的还是惨淡的市场反馈。接受了结果，我们还是决定坚持下去，因为我们是从自己的认知，或者说"良知"出发的。我们是对生产成本及定价透明有信心才去做的。我们想过创业路上会遇到的困难。遇到困难是很正常的事，最重要的是接下来想办法去解决它。

在开始创业的时候，我们有很多行业上的东西都不懂，又害怕受骗，于是就假装强势。事实上，我们很少被欺负。而我们装得过于强势，倒显得自己对前辈不尊重。这也是我们感到后悔的地方。我不知道我们的例子是否具有普遍性，但现在许多的 90 后与 70 后、80 后前辈一起工作时，往往过于强调自己。90 后认为自己代表了最新的眼界和观点，就觉得别人都应该听他的，把前辈的经验和稳重当作不可取的东西，这是不对的。我一开始的时候经常犯这样的错误，和前辈发生过许多不愉快的事。我浑身是刺，刺痛别人也扎伤自己。这恰恰证明了我不够强大。在我们不断地拓展见识、填充自己之后，我们就会为之前的不懂事而感到后悔。当我们足够强大后，与他人交谈时，无论他年长与否，我们都不会再像个刺猬一样了。我们会静下心来，平等地和对方交谈，然后事情就会向好的方向发展。

创业对我最大的影响就是让我变得更实在。举个例子，在有一个好想法的时候，我不会一味地沉迷于空想，而是更倾向于去行动，去把想法落实到每一个环节。在需要工具的时候，我更倾向于先使用手头上能用的，而不是想要没有的。大学生刚毕业的时候都面临着许多的选择，很多人会迷惘，不知道该怎样选。这个时候倒不如先去做，先去实践，加深理解后再做决定。同时，学生们也不能眼高手低，要正确认识自己的能力。

如保赤子

我们三个主创人在创业的时候也有过分歧。解决的办法就是四个字"求同存异"。合伙人制度一定会有分歧的。但是我们都认同我们要去做的事,所以在大方向上是没有太大矛盾的。而当初成立芥末,我们之间除了性格相投之外,最重要的还是技能的互补。我们各自有各自的管理领域,所以从自己领域出发我们会有不同的考虑。但这其实是非常正常的。我们要做的就是充分的沟通和理解,快速解决矛盾。

对于企业家应该怎样体现社会责任感这一个问题,我认为我们首先要做到的是一个普通人要做到的。我的搭档和我说,她看到一个阿姨,每次在垃圾桶里见到矿泉水瓶都会捡起来。她觉得阿姨特别辛苦,就做了一个小的垃圾桶,让大家专门来扔矿泉水瓶,方便阿姨来拿。其次作为企业家当然要对顾客负责,认真地做产品。

Monday 和她的合伙人

最后是怎样看待阳明文化对于当代社会的意义。我想每个人对于阳明心学都有自己的理解,这其中也难免出现一些分歧。但在大学,你会发现老师对阳明心学的理解很不一样,评价也不一样。出现这种情况的原因是人们对阳明文化的了解程度不同。对于大部分的普通人来说,这种古代学说看上去过于高深,难以理解。但事实上,阳明文化中有许多如"致良知""知行合一"等是非常具有实践意义的。我想,这就是阳明文化对于当代社会的意义。

Conscientious Wisdom—the Secret of Being a Sage

Narrator: Monday

Compiled by: Jia Yating

Supervised by: Cao Yajuan, Xu Zhimin

In your view the people filling the street are all sages, but in their view, you are a sage, too.

—Wang Yangming

Original Good Will

My "original good will" or "conscience", I believe, is faithfully making clothes with high quality fabrics and treating my partners and customers sincerely as well. I won't lie on the price and cost of the clothes we make. I offer clothes with equally good quality both in fabrics and workmanship, but at only one quarter of the market price. I hope to develop a brand for silk shirts which belongs to our country alone. China is the world's largest producer of silk. Silk production and export has accounted for 70% of the world's market for more than 20 consecutive years, but we haven't yet established our own brand of silk shirts. Surprised?

As for the question of what was my initial impression of production cost and pricing transparency, I thought it consistent with what I wanted when I first saw it in Everlane (a well-known American online clothing retailer with a basic style as its featured product, which is committed to bringing people low-cost, but high-quality clothing). I agree with their practice of price catalogues emphasizing price transparency and pay respect to it. It happened that my partner and I planned to start our own business at that time. Therefore, I made up my mind that I needed to practice the policy of price transparency, which in fact does bring some benefits to the enterprise. I have constantly stressed the point that simple things can always bring benefits.

This measure received three different responses in the very beginning. The large majority of people had not ever heard of this approach, among many of whom were indifferent to it and ignored it. A small portion of people did not know we had imitated Everlane, showing their approval and thinking it innovative and different from other companies. In addition, there were still a few people who knew Everlane well, and they affirmed our imitation. The reason for this situation might be partly the imperfect localization of foreign practice, or perhaps other defects we haven't found yet. My intention is to urge people to reflect—reflect on the things behind the industry. We believe that transparency is a social trend in historical development, and our persistence will help develop social awareness. Transparency is a gradual process. We all know that many have done such things before, using media. NetEase, for example, is reported to have made known to the public the price component of a bottle of Dior in the 12th issue of *Cost Control* in 2013. This practice is a powerful evidence that people have begun to value things behind the industry.

Inspecting Things Based on Its Nature

Life is not easy for every entrepreneur. The person who is always kissed by God and can easily create a business empire, just like a character in Mary Sue's novel, does not exist in reality. There must be a lot of hard work behind every successful entrepreneur.

Just like production cost and pricing transparency, more than a wish cannot be put into practice. A seemingly simple price catalogue is not easy to make. Before each item is rolled out, we need to do a lot of data analysis under tremendous pressure, taking into consideration every step and possibility. However, a complete price catalogue does not mean the end of the story. We were questioned by the art designer in the beginning. He thought the catalogues occupied too much space and no one would care. Only when we begin to do something will we know the way the things are. But what made us sad were the poor market reactions. Having accepted the results, we decided to stick to it, because it was our thought, or original good will that kept us going on. We did it because we have confidence in production cost and pricing transparency. We know we would meet difficulties during the venture, which are quite normal. What is more important is how we solve them.

At the beginning of our business, we did not know much about the industry, and we were afraid of being cheated, so we pretended to be tough. As a matter of fact, we were rarely bullied. Sometimes we didn't seem to show enough respect to seniors because of our pretence. That is what we regret now. I am not sure whether our example is universal, but many people born in the 1990s nowadays often seem to be too pushy when working with the older generation. Believing that they represent the latest trend, these people of the 1990s think others should listen to them and ignore seniors' experience and prudence. Of course, it's wrong. I used to make the same mistake, and had a lot of unpleasant contact with seniors. I was just like a hedgehog, tormenting others and myself as well with spikes. It just proved that I was not strong enough. As we continue to broaden our horizons, we will feel regret about our ignorance. If we are strong enough, we will not behave like a hedgehog anymore when talking with someone regardless of his age. Most problems can be smoothly solved after we calm ourselves down.

The greatest impact of entrepreneurship on me is making me more practical. For example, if a new idea occurs to me, I will not indulge in fantasy. Instead, I will try to put it into practice. When I need tools, I will use something at hand instead of something not available at that moment. Students are faced with many choices when they first graduate from college. Many of them will be confused, and do not know what to choose. At that time, they may as well choose something at hand and then make their decisions after practice. At the same time, students shouldn't have unrealistic expectations; they need to have a clear knowledge about themselves.

Protecting People as Their Parents

Of course there has been divergence of opinions between us—three entrepreneurs. The solution is six words: "seeking common ground and reserving differences". There must be some disagreements in a partnership system. However, we all know what we are going to do, so we do not have much difference in general. The reason why JEMO Dress-making Company could be established was not only because of something we have in common concerning our personality, but also the complementary skills that we share with each other. We each have our own management fields, so we will have different considerations from our own perspective. What we should do is fully communicate and understand one another, so as to seek an effective way to solve the differences.

In regard to the question of how entrepreneurs show their social responsibility, I think the first thing they should do is what an ordinary person should do. After my partner saw a woman pick water bottles in a trash bin, she made a small trash can to help everyone throw water bottles in so that the woman could take the bottles away easily. The second thing entrepreneurs should do is taking responsibilities for their customers and products.

The last thing is concerned with the contemporary social significance of Yangming culture. I believe everyone has his own understanding of Yangming philosophy, so differences in understanding are unavoidable. In college, you will find the teachers' concepts and evaluation are different from others. The reason for the difference lies in the different level of people's understandings of Yangming philosophy. For most common people, the ancient theory seems too profound and difficult to understand. In fact, however, there are many points of Yangming culture, such as "the extension of innate knowledge or conscience" and "the unity of knowledge and action", which are of great practical significance. I think this is the influence of Yangming culture on contemporary society.

个个人心有仲尼

贾雅婷

指导教师：曹雅娟　徐志敏

人胸中各有个圣人，只自信不及，都自埋倒了。

——王阳明

王阳明先生在逝世前留下的最后一句话是"吾心光明，亦复何言"。吾心，良知也。光明，已致良知也。"致良知"，无疑是阳明心学的核心。本次活动是以"我是阳明青年"为主题的"用声音叙事"，要求我们寻找阳明文化的践行者，我很荣幸地找到了 Monday——芥末公司的 CEO——作为我的采访对象。

Monday 在采访中说，第一次看到 Everlane 生产成本及定价透明的做法时，就觉得它十分符合自己所希望的认知，并由衷地对 Everlane 产生敬意。恰巧那时 Monday 和她的伙伴有了创办芥末的念头，她就想，她也要做一个这样的东西。于是现在我们可以在芥末的每一个产品网页上找到相应的成本展示与市场价。虽然工作量很大，也遭受过许多的不理解，但她们最终还是坚持了下来。在采访中，Monday 表示，在创业中，保持自我是很重要的一点。不论在什么情况下，都应该坚持住自己的初心。

王阳明先生认为，人性本善如赤子，而因欲念阻隔行了不善的事，使自己无知。所以，"只在此心去人欲、存天理上用功便是"。人人都有良知。冯友兰先生在《中国哲学简史》的第 26 章中写道："一切人，无论善恶，在根本上都有此心，此心相同，私欲并不能完全蒙蔽此心。在我们对事物做出直接的本能的反应时，此心就总是自己把自己显示出来。""今人乍见孺子将入于井，皆有怵惕恻隐之心"，就是证明这一点的例子。我们对事物本能的反应就是我们本性的体现，王阳明先生称之为"良知"。

这时也许就有人疑惑，每个人心中多少都会有对财富权利，乃至名誉美色的欲望。那么这也是我们的良知吗？

在我们说到欲望的时候，常常下意识地认为欲望是坏的、邪恶的。欲望的好坏对错有许多不同的表达。儒家主张欲望不可遏制，应予以满足。但儒家也不赞同纵欲，强调适当的满足。在儒家看来，"欲"本身并没有什么不好的，关键在于实现"欲"、满足"欲"的手段如何。一个人可以追求名利美色，但要有一个度，有一条底线。冯友兰先生在《中国哲学简史》中写过一个故事。有一个王阳明先生的门人，夜间在房内捉得一贼。他对贼讲了一番良知的道理。贼大笑，问他："请告诉我，我的良知在哪里？"当时是夏天，他叫贼脱光了上身的衣服，又说："还是太热了。为什么不把裤子也脱了？"贼犹豫了，说："这，好像不太好吧。"门人向贼大喝："这就是你的良知。"人人都有良知，有良知而知是非。王阳明先生的门徒说"满街都是圣人"的原因就是依本性而言，人人都是圣人。

我们要去做的，就是遵从这种"知"的指示，而不是去找借口不立刻执行，让私欲蒙蔽了自己的良知。许多人误以为"知行合一"就是把所学到的知识和实践结合起来。实则不然，王阳明先生的"知"主要是格物之知，而不是近代所指的科学知识。"知行合一"指的是认识事物的道理和在现实中运用此道理是密不可分的一回事。它主要是关于道德修养、道德实践方面的。打个比方，我们做题目的时候，知道了一种题型的解决方法并不代表着我们就能把这种类型的题目都解出来。我们要做的不仅仅是知道，还要不停地去做这种类型的题目，排除错误的地方，才能更好地掌握这种方法。如果我们没有去做题目，再碰到复杂的题目时就可能会无法解决。一旦把这类问题的方方面面都捋顺了，这方法也就真正属于我们了。这里的"解决方法"就是"知"。"不断地做题"就是"实践"。"排除错误"就是"去私欲"。当我们把方方面面都捋顺的时候，就是我们"已致良知"的时候了。正如 Monday，在创业的过程中不断地解决困难从而变得更实在了。原因是她在不断地实践中践行着这一点，实在地做事已经成了她内在信念的一部分了。

正如王阳明先生在诗中提到的"个个人心有仲尼"，每个人都有自己的良知。如果人人都能坚持住自己内心的良知，努力做到"知行合一"，不管他身份样貌，地位学识如何，他就已经是个了不起的阳明文化践行者了。

团队成员：谢雨诗　贾雅婷　高志海　沈旭桐

Original Goodwill in Everyone's Heart

Jia Yating

Supervised by: Cao Yajuan, Xu Zhimin

There is a sage in everyone. Only one has not enough self-confidence buries his own chance.

—Wang Yangming

The last words that Wang Yangming left before his death are: "My heart is righteous, so I don't have to say anything anymore." "My heart" means the inceptive insights of moral mind, or what we simply call "conscience". "Righteousness" means that he has already realized his conscientious wisdom. Realizing conscientious wisdom is undoubtedly the core of Wang Yangming's Philosophy of Mind. As a series summer practice, an activity of "Beyond the Voices" with the theme of "I'm a Young Practitioner of Yangming Philosophy" required us to search the practitioners of Yangming philosophy. I was lucky to find the CEO of JEMO Dress-making Company as my interviewee.

During the interview, Monday said she felt Everlane's production cost and pricing transparency policy was consistent with her conception and sincerely paid tribute to Everlane when she first saw it. Coincidently, Monday and her partners had the idea of founding JEMO Dress-making Company and she thought that transparency was what she wanted. As a result, now we can find the corresponding cost and market price of every item shown on the web pages of JEMO Dress-making Company. In spite of the heavy workload and misunderstandings, they have eventually survived. In the interview, Monday said that being oneself is a very important point in the business. We need to follow our own heart no matter what situation we are in.

Wang Yangming believes that humans by nature are all kind, but they will do something wrong because of their selfish desires. As a consequence, the only thing we need to do is to remove selfish desires from our heart and keep justice. Everyone has his conscientious wisdom. Feng Youlan also mentioned the similar point in the 26th chapter of *A Short History of Chinese Philosophy*: "Nearly all people, whether they are good or evil, have this kind heart. And selfish desires cannot block this kindness completely. When we make instinctive reactions, a good heart will always present itself." "All people will show their sympathy when they suddenly see a child falling into a well" is an example to prove the "original good will" theory. Our instinctive reaction to things is the embodiment of our true mind. Wang Yangming called it "original good will".

Then someone might be confused. More or less, each person has the desire of pursing wealth, power, reputation or beauty. Are these pursuits our inceptive insight of moral mind as well?

When it comes to desire, we often subconsciously think of it as bad or evil. There are many different expressions for whether it is good or not. Confucianist philosophy advocates that desire cannot be controlled but should instead be satisfied. However, Confucianist philosophy is in favor of moderate satisfaction instead of overindulgence. In the perspective of Confucianist philosophy, "desire" itself is not a bad thing, but what really counts is the way to satisfy the desire. It's not a fault for people to chase fame and beauty, but the problem is that there must be a limit or a bottom line in the pursuit of these. Feng Youlan told a story in *A Short History of Chinese Philosophy*. A disciple of Wang Yangming caught a thief in a room at night. He told the thief of the inceptive insights of moral mind. The thief laughed and said, "Tell me where's my inceptive insights of moral mind." It was a summer's day. He asked the thief to strip the clothes of the upper half of the body, and said, "It's still too hot, so why don't you take you paints off?" The thief hesitated and said, "I don't think it's appropriate." He shouted to the thief, "This is your inceptive insights of moral mind." Everyone has its inceptive insights of moral mind, and he can tell right from wrong with this moral mind. The reason why Wang Yangming's disciple said "all people in the streets are saints" is that everyone is a saint in terms of nature.

What we need to do is to follow our hearts instead of looking for an excuse to avoid doing something good, which makes selfish desire control our inceptive insights of moral mind. Many people mistakenly think that "the unity of knowledge and action" is to combine knowledge and practice. Actually, it is not true. Wang Yangming's "knowledge" is "achieving sagehood by investigating the world", rather than by modern scientific knowledge. "The unity of knowledge and action" means "knowing the truth of things" and "using it in reality" is inseparable. It is mainly concerned with morality cultivation and moral practice. For example, when we try to solve a kind of question, knowing a method does not mean we can solve all types of these questions. What we need to do is more than just knowing, so we have to keep doing exercises to eliminate the mistakes as well, so that we can grasp the method better. If we do not solve any related questions, we are likely to fail in those more complicated questions. Once we understand all the aspects of this kind of question, the method will really belong to us. Here is the "method" knowledge, "keep doing exercise" is practice, and "eliminating the mistakes" is the removal of selfish desire. Therefore, it's time that we realize conscientious wisdom when we have thorough understanding of all aspects of the question. Just like Monday, she became more practical in solving problems when starting her business. The reason is that she makes a good unity of knowledge and action, and being practical becomes a part of her faith.

As Wang Yangming mentioned in his poem "all people have original good will", everyone has his own inceptive insights of moral mind. If everyone is able to hold their own conscientious wisdom, to achieve "the unity of knowledge and action", he will become a great practitioner of Yangming culture regardless of his identity, appearance, status or knowledge.

Team members: Xie Yushi, Jia Yating, Gao Zhihai, Shen Xutong

李蕾：尽天下之学，无有不行而可以言学者

Li Lei: Learn with Practice

李蕾，浙江余姚人，浙江雅叙文化传播公司总经理。她年轻有为，通过自己的努力，一步一步地把自己的公司带向正轨。她为人热情，勤奋上进，求真务实，对自己要求很高。同时，她又有很强的组织能力和团队协作精神，注重学习，不断提升自己的业务技能，不断弥补自己的不足，并将理论和实践有机结合。

Li Lei was born in Yuyao, Zhejiang Province. She is the general manager of Ningbo Yaxu Cultural Transmission Company, young and promising. She has brought her company on track through her perseverance. Passionate, hardworking, practical and demanding of herself, she possesses a strong ability in organization and teamwork cooperation. She also attaches much importance to self-study, the combination of both theory and practice and the improvement of professional skills to make up for her weaknesses.

尽天下之学，无有不行而可以言学者

口述：李 蕾

整理：高志海

指导教师：曹雅娟 徐志敏

引 子

致吾心良知之天理于事事物物，则事事物物皆得其理矣。

——王阳明

眼中的心学

我大学学习的是中文。因为文学与哲学是不可分割的，都属于文科类，所以我接触到了阳明思想，知道了"知行合一""致良知"等等。在工作中，心学和儒家学派的思想我也有所涉及。我对于"知行合一"有一些自己的理解。

首先，在公司发展的过程中，我是一个以身作则的人，对自己的要求很高，因此给自己的压力就很大，然后感觉工作量很大，什么事都要我自己做，这样让自己感到很困惑。后来，在与一位长辈交谈中，听到了这样一句话："知而不行，乃不知。"这句话给我一种醍醐灌顶的感觉，使我感触颇深。你知道这个道理，自己在脑子里想想，却什么也不做，这都是没有用的。"知行合一"，我理解的是，我怎么做，也希望自己团队的人怎么做。我认真地做每一件事，我的团队的人也应该这么做。我是公司的掌舵人，下面的人是我的职员，很少有人能跟我做到一样。比如一些刚大学毕业的小姑娘，社会经历很少，很难跟我一样做到"知行合一"，这时候，就应该体谅她们，成功地领导她们。王阳明强调"知行合一"，"知"是指科学知识，"行"是指人的实践，知与行要合一。我坚持把自己所想的付诸实践，在工作中，"知行合一"，严格要求自己，就是这样的态度，才让我拥有了现在的生活。即使有时候我会很累，但是照着自己内心行动，还是有很多的收获。

其次，诚信在公司发展中有着重要的地位。阳明先生曾经说过："惟天下之至诚，然后能立天下之大本。"这句话强调了知行的本体实质上是一个"诚"字。我觉得，诚信应该摆在公司很重要的位置，即使是一些大企业，诚信也是十分重要的，这关系到公司的声誉。公司发展的前期，诚信也非常重要，如果没有了名誉，那拿什么去跟别人谈业务。即使在我们身边，也是非常需要诚信的，人与人相处，最基础的就是要诚信对人，彼此才会有更好的关系。如果社会上每个人都很诚信，那我们的社会就会更加和谐。

阳明心学，在我看来，是阳明先生追求回归人的本性。所谓的良知，就是不忘初心。我们现在的社会非常浮躁，包括我自己。之前新闻也报道过一个 95 后女孩王凯歆的故事。1998 年出生的她从身无分文创业到身价过亿，然后再到人去楼空，期间还参加了北京卫视的创业真人秀"我是独角兽"，使得现场五个资本大佬争抢着投资。一个月后，这家成立不到一年的公司便获得了来自三家风投公司的2000 万元投资。短短半年的时间，就经历了如此大的起伏。后来我上网查资料了解到，这位小姑娘非常霸道，甚至有些人格缺陷和心智不健全。比如公司运营数据造假，招人全看面相，以各种奇葩理由开除员工，以各种方式欺骗员工，如不给工资、不给离职补偿，甚至还包括言而无信、挥霍无度、没有家教、缺乏基本常识等等。这些导致了她最后走向了失败。这违背了王阳明心学所提到的"致良知""不忘初心"——公司发展的基本要求。

　　说到身边的阳明精神，我跟你们分享一个发生在我身边的事。我前几天认识了一位投资人。这位投资人创立基金会，从不同的人手中筹集资金。在这个过程中，投资人可以分分钟做到自己发财，因为钱都在她的手中，但是她觉得要保持自己的准则，要对得起自己的良心，所以没有乱动公司的一分钱。这与阳明先生提倡的"致良知"有相类似的地方。这位投资人自己内心有衡量标准，没有为了自己的利益而违背自己的良知，此心不为私欲私意所阻碍。但是在生活中，还是会有一些人为了自己的利益突破自己的底线。虽然这样从中获利了，但是违背了自己的初心，良知被利益吞噬。那存在于这个世界还有什么意义呢？

心学的创新

　　阳明心学中也讲到了要创新，我认为现在社会创新得非常少。对于公司创新，我更倾向于与时俱进，在原有的基础上提高。

　　心学强调"事上磨炼"。人生或多或少会遇到一些挫折，对此心学提到的坚持是非常重要的。我在书上看到过，曾经有位作家格拉德维尔在《异类》一书中指出，人们眼中的天才之所以卓越非凡，并非天才超人一等，而是因为付出了持续不断的努力。一万个小时的锻炼是任何人从平凡变成超凡的必要条件。作为创业者来说，对于每一件事，你都坚持做到最好，这结果必定会是美好的。花一万个小时学习一门语言，你也一定会做得很好。所以说坚持对于每个人都非常重要。

　　阳明精神激励了很多人，对于大学生，我也给你们一些建议，我所经历的故事或许会帮助到你们。要听从我们的内心。举个例子，一位非常喜欢摄影的年轻人，他的摄影水平并没有非常专业，无法找到一个待遇好的工作，这时候可能会有一份待遇不错、但是他并不是很喜欢的工作出现在面前。因为生活所迫，他可能会选择那份待遇好的工作，放弃了他一直喜欢的摄影。在客观条件允许下，应该坚持一下自己内心追求的一些东西，也许哪一天，你的坚持就会有意外的收获。

李蕾女士与团队成员合影

现今，国家大力提倡弘扬中国优秀传统文化，鼓励传播中国优秀传统文化到世界的其他地方。关于传播阳明精神，在我看来，或者有点不一样的地方。我身边的一些国外朋友，可能都不认识阳明先生，但是我们并不一定要把思想传输给他们，而是我们应该先自己内化思想，自己咀嚼到其中的内涵，把它变为自己的东西，然后再慢慢地讲述给国外友人，这样会有更好的效果。

Learn with Practice

Narrator: Li Lei

Compiled by: Gao Zhihai

Supervised by: Cao Yajuan, Xu Zhimin

When the Principle of Nature in the innate knowledge of my mind is extended to all things, all things will attain their principle.

—Wang Yangming

My Understanding of the Philosophy of Mind

I majored in Chinese in college. Since literature and philosophy are closely related to each other, both belonging to the liberal arts, I was provided with the opportunity to learn Yangming philosophy, for example "the unity of knowledge and action" and "realizing conscientious wisdom". The Philosophy of Mind and Confucianism are always involved in my work. I have my own understanding of "the unity of knowledge and action".

Firstly, I used to be very strict with myself at work, hoping to set an example for the staff. That, however, gave me a heavy load and a lot of pressure, for I had to handle everything on my own. I felt rather confused. Then, one day, an elderly man told me, "If you don't apply knowledge to the practice, you will never get the truth of that knowledge." These enlightening words gave me a lot of feelings. It just doesn't work if some ideas occur to you, but you don't put them into practice. "The unity of knowledge and action", in my opinion, means my employees do the things as I do. If I am serious with everything, so should they be. Unfortunately, few among them can follow my lead. When some girls fresh from college, for example, hardly have experience to follow the philosophy of "the unity of knowledge and action", I will show my understandings to them and give my advice. I persisted in my principle despite a couple of employees' failure to follow me. In Wang Yangming's "unity of knowledge and action", I think "knowledge" here means scientific knowledge, and "action" means practice, so knowledge and practice must be united. I own what I have now because I put my ideas into practice, and I'm strict with myself. I have benefited a lot from "following my heart" in spite of occasional fatigue.

Secondly, integrity plays an important role in the development of a company. Wang Yangming once said, "If you treat everything with integrity, you can gain success." Actually, these words tell us the essence of "the unity of knowledge and action" is "integrity". Integrity is related to the reputation of a company, so it should be valued by both big and small ones. In the early period of its development, integrity is also very important. Without reputation, how can you establish business relationships with others? Integrity is equally important in our daily communication. A good interpersonal relationship is based on integrity. We can't promote a business without integrity. Integrity is also required in our life. If everyone in the society has integrity, our society will be more harmonious.

Wang Yangming's Philosophy of Mind, in my opinion, is the pursuit of the return to human nature. Conscience means sticking to your original good will. We are a restless generation. There was a report in the first half of this year about a girl born in 1998 named Wang Kaixin. She struggled from a penniless girl to be a billionaire, and finally vanished, leaving an empty company. She had participated in Beijing TV business reality show of "I am a unicorn" and caused an invest competition among the five venture capitalists present. One month later, her company gained a total of 20 million yuan from three top venture capitalists. So many ups and downs in half a year! Then I consulted her information on the Internet and was told that this is a rather bossy girl, perhaps with some defects in personality. She fabricated the company data, only employed people with good looks, fired employees for odd reasons, and cheated her employees on wages and severance. She was even revealed to have little common sense and to be unreliable, extravagant, and ill-bred. These negative things resulted in her failure at last, which violates Wang Yangming's principles of "realizing conscientious wisdom" and "original good will", which are quite essential to the development of a company.

To emphasize Yangming philosophy, I would like to share with you one more story. A few days ago, I met an investor who set up a foundation by raising money from different people. Actually, such kind of investors can easily make the money theirs. She, however, persisted in her principle and conscience, just leaving the money safe. I can find the similarity between her behavior and Yangming's "realizing conscientious wisdom". This investor was not tempted by illegal profits because she had her own measuring stick and conscience in mind. There, however, will always be someone neglecting the bottom line and making profits for their own interests.

Therefore, what's the point in living in this world if your conscience is swallowed by profits?

The Innovation of Philosophy of Mind

Innovation is also mentioned in Yangming's Philosophy of Mind. I think our society is in need of innovation at present. I prefer to keep pace with the times, making progress step by step.

The Philosophy of Mind places emphasis on perseverance. There will always be setbacks in our life, so perseverance is fairly important. Gladwell once pointed out in his book *Outliers* that the reason why those geniuses are extraordinary in people's eyes is not because of any supernatural factors but because of the constant efforts that they have invested in the things they are doing. Ten thousand hours of exercise is essential for anyone to be extraordinary from ordinary. As an entrepreneur, if you do everything to its best, you can expect a result. You can also acquire a language if you spend ten thousand hours learning a language. Therefore, no shortcut, only perseverance!

Yangming's spirit has inspired many people. Having experienced a lot, I have some suggestions for college students. Follow your heart. An avid young photographer, for example, can hardly find a well-paid job because he doesn't possess the professional skills needed. Then, maybe one day he is offered a job with a good salary in which he has little interest. Compelled by the pressure, he will most probably give up what he likes and accept that job. I, however, suggest that you need to stick to your inner pursuit if your situation permits. Maybe one day, your perseverance will give you some unexpected reward.

Nowadays, our nation strongly advocates the promotion of Chinese traditional culture, and encourages the spread of traditional culture to different parts of the world. In my opinion, however, the spread of Yangming culture has something different. We may not necessarily deliver Yangming culture to foreigners, because some of my foreign friends don't even know him. What is more effective is to internalize ideas first and understand its connotation before we spread these things abroad.

感知生活，从心开始

高志海

指导教师：曹雅娟　徐志敏

　　说起阳明心学，就不得不提心学的开创者和集大成者：明代著名的思想家、文学家、哲学家和军事家——王阳明。他是陆王心学的集大成者，精通儒家、道家、佛家。在其一生中，不断发展心学，研究心学。阳明先生提出"致良知""知行合一"，在明代影响很大。即便到现在，还是或多或少地影响着我们。

　　暑假期间，非常幸运地采访到了宁波雅叙文化传播公司的李蕾李老师，与李老师进行了一番关于阳明精神的交流。李老师非常热情地跟我们讲述了她对阳明精神的理解，还有发生在她身边的故事和她的经历。在简短的交流中，李老师讲到了她个人所理解的良知，也提到了前段时间的95后女孩王凯歆如何从创业到身价上亿元再到最后的一无所有、人去楼空的故事。强调了"致良知"在创业中的重要性，不要为了自己的利益，违背自己的初心，不能让自己的良心被利益所吞噬，做事不能太浮躁。在这个社会上，人不能忘了自己的本心，要遵照自己的内心所想去做，勿忘初心。顺应了自己的本心，你会收获意外的惊喜。此外李老师还说到了坚持，强调"事上磨炼"，在成功道路上，困难会不断地出现，你要做的，就是不断地克服困难。李老师说了一句话，我至今还清楚地记得：做一件事，你付出得越多，收获的必定比没有付出的多。同时，她也以作家格拉德维尔书中的一句话为例，说人们眼中的天才之所以卓越非凡，并非天才超人一等，而是因为付出了持续不断的努力。一万个小时的锻炼是任何人从平凡变成超凡的必要条件。她说自己也不是一下子就达到现在这个地位，也是一步一步坚持下来的。当中遇到过许多困难，也有过想放弃，但是要强的她，告诉自己一定要坚持。多一点坚持，就多一点成功的希望。凡事都要尽量做到最好，坚持到最后。你最后成功的时候，回头看自己之前所付出的，必定会感到非常的欣慰。因为是你的坚持，让你最终尝到了成功的滋味。这一刻，你是最棒的！

　　采访结束后，整理着李老师跟我们讲述的故事和人生哲理，感触颇多。仔细想想自己这二十年的经历，是否做到了坚持，不到最后一秒不放弃呢？是否为人处事，坚持自己的初心，跟随自己的良知呢？是否做到"知行合一"，心中所想，真的付诸实践呢？

　　回想这几年，坚持练排球，带给了我许多触动，我也从中收获许多。跟许多小男孩一样，小时候的我非常好动，几乎很难安静地坐几分钟。在学校里，我也非常喜欢参加各种体育活动，其中，学习打排球对我来说是最开心的事。刚开始接触排球，并没有那么的简单，要从垫球、接球、发球一点点学习。刚开始的几天，手会打得很红，会害怕球。慢慢接触多了，你发现你有了自信去把打过来的球接起来，你不再害怕它。迈出了第一步，后来我就慢慢地喜欢上了这项运动，每天坚持训练，早上提前去学校训练，晚上留校再继续训练，从零基础开始，然后一点点地进步。刚开始手打得很红很痛的时候，我也想过要放弃。每一次想放弃的时候，我就会问自己，是否还可以坚持，是否想继续打球。一次一次，我都坚持了下来，就这样坚持了好多年。现在回想起来，当初的坚持还是非常有意义的。"知是行之始，行是知之成。若会得时，只说一个知，已自有行在；只说一个行，已自有知在。"自己选择坚持的，并不是嘴上说说，是需要付诸实践的。我选择继续坚持打排球，我心里想的是坚持，所以我付诸实践，继续坚持训练。这似乎印证了阳明先生所说的，"知是行的开端，行是知的成果"。这就是我对于"知行合一"的理解。

阳明心学的"知行合一"和"致良知"在现今社会还是有非常值得我们学习的地方。天理在实践中，良知亦在实践中。

团队成员：施　懿　高志海　朱嘉平

Perceive Life from the Heart

Gao Zhihai

Supervised by: Cao Yajuan, Xu Zhimin

Speaking of Yangming culture, I have to introduce the pioneer of the Philosophy of Mind: the famous thinker, writer, philosopher and strategist from the Ming Dynasty—Wang Yangming. He was a master of the Philosophy of Mind, proficient in Confucianism, Taoism and Buddhism. He put forward "realizing conscientious wisdom" and "the unity of knowledge and action". His whole life was dedicated to establishing and developing the Philosophy of Mind, which has great impact not only in the Ming Dynasty, but also in modern times.

It was very lucky for me this summer to have an interview with Ms. Li Lei, the general manager of Ningbo Yaxu Culture Transmission Company. We communicated with each other about Yangming's spirit. She told me with enthusiasm her understanding of this spirit and her experiences and some stories as well. During the interview, she told us what conscience means to her, and the start-up story of a girl born after 1995, who struggled from a penniless one to a billionaire, and finally vanished, leaving an empty company. She placed emphasis on the importance of "realizing conscientious wisdom" in business management, and asked us to follow our heart regardless of the profit or our restlessness. In this modern world, we will have some unexpected reward if we follow our heart. Furthermore, Ms. Li said perseverance and conscience are the keys to overcoming those constant difficulties on the way to success. One point mentioned by Ms. Li is still impressive to me: the more pain, the more gain. She also quoted a sentence from the writer Gladwell in his book *Outliers* that it is not something supernatural that makes a genius, but perseverance. Ten thousand hours of exercise is essential for anyone to go from ordinary to extraordinary. She said she did not gain success overnight. She has encountered a lot of difficulties, and even thought of giving up. But this strong lady told herself to hold on. More perseverance means more opportunities. Do everything to your best. In retrospect, you will feel relieved about the hardship you have suffered. You can finally taste the joy of success because of your perseverance. You are the best at that moment.

After the interview, looking back on the stories and philosophy shared by Ms. Li,

I felt a rush of complicated feelings. I was wondering during my life whether I had the courage to persist in the things I was pursing, whether I could follow my heart and stick to my conscience and whether I could keep the "the unity of knowledge and action", putting what I thought into practice?

My perseverance in volleyball in recent years really touched me and benefited me a lot. Like many boys, I was rather naughty or sometimes overactive when I was a kid. It was hard for me to sit still for a while. I liked to join all kinds of sports, among which volleyball is the most enjoyable for me. It's not simple to play volleyball at the very beginning. You should learn many basic skills. In the early days, my hands turned red after practice. I was afraid to catch the ball. Gradually, I had confidence to catch the ball through a lot of practice. My scars faded. After taking the first step, I indulged myself in this sport. I stuck to my daily training and spent extra time in the morning and evening practice, all of which led to my step-by-step progress. I also thought of giving up every time my hands hurt. At that moment, I would ask myself, "Do you like volleyball? Can you hold on?" Again and again, I held on for many years. Looking back on the past, my perseverance is really meaningful, which confirms Wang Yangming's philosophy that "Knowledge is the beginning of action" and "Action is the result of knowledge". Knowledge and action are closely related to each other. That is my understanding of "the unity of knowledge and action".

Yangming's Philosophy of Mind, "the unity of knowledge and action" and "realizing conscientious wisdom", are still of value to the present society. Morality and conscience all exist in these practices.

Team members: Shi Yi, Gao Zhihai, Zhu Jiaping

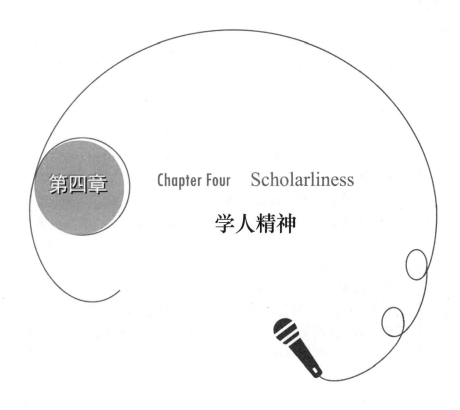

第四章　Chapter Four　Scholarliness

学人精神

Introduction

　　纯粹着、澄净着的是学人。先生曰："一心皆在天理上用功，所以居敬亦即是穷理。"学人有单纯的念头和沉着的心态，以惟精惟一的气质追求真理。《道德经》说："为学日增，为道日减。"纯粹的学人相信生而有涯，学而无涯；也相信纯粹可以化繁为简，智慧可以解决纷争，这种智慧寂然不动，廓然大公。

　　怀疑着、批判着的是学人。阳明先生曰："盖学之不能以无疑。"好奇和怀疑打开了探求真理的大门。惟求其是的批判就是对知识的敬畏和事实的尊重。所以才会有王门后学李贽曰之言："不以孔子之是非为是非。"这种书生意气、挥斥方遒的品质为创新和包容奠定了基石，有学人如竺可桢，"只问是非，不计利害"。

　　思考着、行动着的是学人。阳明先生曰："夫学、问、思、辨、行，皆所以为学，未有学而不行者也。"为学之道始于行，终于行，所以有了"知行合一"思想的横空出世，也成就了华夏文明可与世界分享的文化价值。阳明先生曰："尽天下之学无有不行而可以言学者，则学之始固已即是行矣。"习公云："时代是思想之母，实践是理论之源。"一个行动着的儒者背后，是万千步履坚定的青年。

　　忧患着、捍卫着的是学人。先生曰："善念发而知之，而充之；恶念发而知之，而遏之。惟恐吾人不闻斯道，流于功利机智，以日堕于夷狄禽兽而不觉。"这就是学人的精髓——良知，为善去恶。学人的"致良知"是"位卑未敢忘忧国"的忧患意识，是"岂因祸福避趋之"的担当，是以恻隐、羞恶、辞让、是非之心捍卫良知、捍卫底线、捍卫千古圣圣的真骨血。

（蔡　亮　撰写）

郝新林：我看到光的彼岸

Hao Xinlin: I Saw the Other End of the Light

郝新林，著名律师、心理咨询师，现任辽宁世勋律师事务所主任、大连市律师协会理事等。他积极倡导和践行阳明文化，将阳明思想带入工作和生活中。他曾带领世勋律师团队代理大连市环保志愿者协会提起的环境公益诉讼，即"7·16"中石油污染案，该案被称为"辽宁公益诉讼第一案"。之后，他与团队多次参与维护公共利益的诉讼案件，社会影响广泛，社会效果良好。

Hao Xinlin is a famous lawyer and psychological counselor. Now he is the director of a law firm called Shixun and Daliang Lawyer's Association, both in Liaoning. He actively advocates and practices the philosophy of Wang Yangming, putting Yangming's philosophical theory into work and life. He led the law team of Shixun and acted on the behalf of the Dalian Environmental Protection Volunteers Association to put forward the oil pollution case of "716"—an environmental public interest litigation committed by the China National Petroleum Corporation which was called the "No. 1 case of public interest litigation in Liaoning". After that, he and his team participated in many cases related to public interest. All of these cases have achieved a widespread influence and have had an excellent social effect.

我看到光的彼岸

口述：郝新林
整理：车晚静
指导教师：张静燕　蔡　亮

引　子

此心无私欲之蔽，即是天理。

——王阳明

我听到海的哭泣

我供职的世勋律师事务所成立于 2008 年。2010 年"7·16"的时候正是我们团队艰难的爬坡期，那时的痛苦与煎熬是来自多方面的，一言难尽。因此每每困惑或加班到午夜的时候我都开车到黑石礁海边坐坐。那时自然博物馆的转盘还没有封闭，门卫室橘黄色的灯光是那样的温暖，远方间或划过的探照灯在海面上泛起一层层银光。我总是关上车子的大灯，习惯性地躺在车上，静静地听海浪拍打礁石的声音，什么都想，抑或是什么都不想，许久许久。

然而"7·16"之后，海洋全变了，特别是 7 月 20 号的那个早上，我心痛地看到油污已侵入了黑石礁，一层层油花在海水中滚动。如果海洋也有生命的话，我相信，她一定在控诉，一定在哀号。

回到律师事务所，我立刻让助理查询了一下大连有没有环保组织，我一定要参加油污清理。当我们苦闷寂寞的时候大海给了我们无数的慰藉，当海洋受伤的时候，我们怎么能不管不顾？就这样，我参加了大连市环保志愿者协会，参与了大部分的油污治理工作。慢慢地，我成长为三星志愿者，我们世勋律师事务所成为协会免费的法律顾问、交费的会员单位，我还担任了协会策划部部长，协会的博客、微博、微信、期刊都在协会策划部的努力下推出。

或许会有人问，这么大片海域的油污，清理工作要进行到猴年马月呢？确实，油污清理的工作任重而道远，但难道因为这样就什么都不做，眼睁睁地看着被污染的海洋而无动于衷吗？既然减少油污，让海洋重现美好是每个人的初心和愿望，那为什么不顺应自己的初心放手去做呢？虽然一个人能做出的努力是有限的，但在看不到的地方，有许许多多同样贡献着自己一份力量的人们。

油污清理工作一点一点地进行着，这样的日子让我感到充实和安心。时间一天天过去，我以为自己已经忘却了"7·16"。

我感到心的呼唤

然而在 2015 年的 5 月，时隔五年之后，大连市环保志愿者协会正式向我们世勋律师团队提出要打"7·16"中石油污染案的官司。坦率地说这让我有点意外，我想过协会有可能会提出相关环境公益诉讼，但没想到杨白新会长和唐在林副会长会对"7·16"中石油污染案提起民事诉讼。接着协会就开始了有条不紊的推动工作，在得到上万份调查问卷中 96% 的大连市民的支持和经过协会和自己的一系列准备之后，我们愈发坚定了信念。

《半岛晨报》对"7·16"中石油污染案的报道

同我们预料的一样，"7·16"中石油污染案的诉讼道路注定不平坦。首先就是被告的主体问题。在普通公众眼里，"7·16"事件就是中石油导致的污染，但从法律定义上来说却远没有那么简单。这起事故牵涉了七家不同的主体，这些主体均在不同程度上与此次事故存在着法律上的联系。然而这些主体天南海北，需要一个个工商局跑，工作量很大。我们委托了当地的律师，又专程赴北京工商总局反复确认了解到主要责任人，即购买原油的中石油燃料油股份有限公司，其注册地在珠海。我们随后电话通知了大连的团队成员，马不停蹄地赶回去。

珠海方面律师传来的消息不是很好，居然没有找到中石油燃料油股份有限公司的工商档案，而工商总局又言之凿凿。我们一下子陷入了困境，团队如同困兽一般煎熬着。我们只能不断地查询搜索，几番波折之后，我们发现原因竟然是中石油燃料油股份有限公司从股份有限公司变成了有限责任公司，而变更的时间恰恰是在"7·16"之后。

之后我们面临的最大难关就是损失情况的鉴定，几次研讨会都在这里陷入了僵局。坦率地说，我们律师团队对此是无力的，而协会在这方面的资源也明显不足。

怎么办？这时候杨会长设立的信息收集组真正起到了作用。我们的协会志愿者徐巍巍在网上找到了由上海海洋大学经济管理学院温艳萍、吴传雯撰文的《大连海洋溢油事故的生态环境损害评估》，提出了九类直接损失不低于4.96亿元的海洋生态环境损失。我们非常感谢《海洋经济》杂志社的支持，同时更要感谢温艳萍、吴传雯两位老师，没有她们的文章，我们不知要在困惑中摸索多久。

在设置申请的时候，团队内部发生了一定的争议。一个是要求赔偿的这4.96亿元的诉讼时效问题，毕竟"7·16"已经过去五年了，对方的抗辩一定会集中在这个问题上。另一个是关于向社会公众赔礼道歉的诉求。"7·16"这次事件受损最大的就是600万大连人民，这不是狭隘的地方主义，这是我们真实的呼声。

王阳明先生曾说："良知之说，从百死千难中得来。"那个时候阳明先生已经成为"心学集大成者"，这是在他回忆自己寻求圣人之道的历程之时发出的由衷感叹。正是在困境中不断磨炼自我，才能够彻底地接受身心洗礼，从而脱胎换骨。我们一次次地陷入困境，一次次地感受到无路可走的煎熬和痛苦，这不仅没能让我们放弃，而是让我们更加清楚地感受到自己身上的责任，更加坚定了我们坚持下去的信心。每向前迈一步，我都能听见心底有个声音在默默地支持自己。

我看到光的彼岸

前期诉讼准备了很长时间，总算在6月5日世界环境日之前拿出最终材料递交了当事人，并于6月5日向大连海事法院提起诉讼。然而收到相关材料后，大连海事法院十余日后出具了不予受理裁定，称环保志愿者组织没有诉讼权，只有拥有海洋环境监督管理权的部门才有诉讼权。当时协会在组织我们研讨的时候，我出去到洗手间静思了许久，简直无以言表，为了能够清醒地判断和抉择，我一直自以为是地保持所谓的冷静和距离感，然而在这份裁定书面前，所有的冷静都几乎崩塌无余。

当天，我们世勋律师的团队成员海洋哥连夜写了诉状，在凌晨4点多发到我们的工作QQ群中，我在5点多改完，海洋哥又几易其稿，最终在8点之前，递交给了协会，并在协会的网站上刊登。我在群里开玩笑说，如果每个案件我们都是这么个做法，我们的业务可不得了。

第二天，协会就开始忙碌起来。经过各方协调，协会告知，中石油已确定拿出2亿元资金，专项用于大连海域的污染治理，由大连市财政局管理，各方监督使用。之后，协会放弃了上诉。至此，"7·16"已经告一段落，回头再看看我们走过的路，不禁心生感叹。

五百多年前，阳明先生为了实践怎么"格物穷理"，一连七天静坐在书院里"格竹子"，废寝忘食，直到病倒，可见先生心性之坚韧。这样的一股坚韧劲儿，让立志成圣的阳明先生不断向着自己的人生目标前进，不管遭受多少陷害贬谪，不管环境多么艰难困苦，阳明先生反而从中磨砺了身心，感悟出了与当时的主流学派不同的道理，独成一派，成为真正的圣人。

五百多年后的今天，我们团队也凭借着一股坚韧劲儿冲破重重阻碍，最后也算是获得了一个不小的成功。在日新月异的现代生活中有太多私欲左右了人的内心，因此忽略了太多本该追求的东西。而我们做这些，不为钱财，也不为什么名利，不过是顺着我们的初心，顺着良知罢了。正是因为没有物欲私欲的蒙蔽，我们才能这样坦然地走到这一步。

大连市环保志愿者协会召开"7·16"中石油污染案环境公益诉讼结果发布会

"7·16"诉讼案就这样画上了句号，用辽宁电视台的说法是一个不完美的结局和一个完美的开始。我很欣赏这句话，一大批有识之士为了公共利益参与到这次声势浩大的环境公益诉讼中，一个现实的结局却是一个理想的开始，在这里我看到了具有担当意识的学人精神，我也看到了光的彼岸。

I Saw the Other End of the Light

Narrator: Hao Xinlin

Compiled by: Che Wanjing

Supervised by: Zhang Jingyan, Cai Liang

Now as selfish human desires are gradually removed, the mind will be increasingly harmonious with moral principles.

—Wang Yangming

I Heard Weep of the Sea

Shixun Law Firm at which I worked was set up in 2008. When the "716" incident happened in 2010, our team happened to get into trouble. There was much pain and suffering in many aspects. It's a long story. Whenever I felt confused or had worked overtime until midnight, I would drive to the Heishijiao seaside. At that time, the door of the natural museum wasn't closed yet and the orange light of the guardhouse seemed so warm. Sometimes, the faraway searchlight streaked and beamed a layer of silver light on the sea. I habitually would turn off my headlights, lie on my car, and listen to the sound of the waves quietly beating the reefs. I would think everything or nothing, usually for a very long time.

However, it was totally changed after the "716" incident. Especially on the morning of July 20th, it was heartbreaking for me to see that oil contamination had invaded the reefs, with layers of oil rolling in the water. If the sea also had life, she would certainly denounce this atrocity and wail.

As soon as I returned to the law firm, I asked my assistant to check if there was an environmental protection organization in Dalian. I must participate in cleaning the oil contamination myself. When we were upset and lonely, the sea gave us countless comfort. And when it was polluted, how could we leave it alone? In this way, I joined the Dalian Environmental Protection Volunteers Association, and took part in most of the work of cleaning up the oil contamination. Gradually, I rose up as a three-star volunteer. At the same time, Shixun Law Firm had become a free legal counsel and a fee member firm. I also held the position of head of the planning department, where our blog, Weibo, WeChat, and magazine articles were published through the efforts of my department.

Perhaps someone might say that there was such a big area of oil, so how much time did we need to clean it? Assuredly, there was a long way to go to clean the oil contamination. However, should we do nothing just because of this, and look indifferently at the polluted sea? Reducing the amount of oil and making the sea beautiful again was everyone's wish and intention, so why not just do it? Although the effort of only one person was limited, there were many people who were striving to contribute their power in unknown places.

The job of cleaning the oil contamination went underway little by little. I felt rich and reassured during these days. As time went by, I thought I had forgotten the "716" incident.

I Felt the Call of the Heart

However, in May 2015, five years after the incident, the Dalian Environmental Protection Volunteers Association proposed to our team that they wanted to officially litigate the "716" oil pollution case. To be frank, I felt a little surprised. I thought maybe the association would put forward relevant environmental litigation for public interest, but I hadn't expected that Mr. Yang Baixin and Mr. Tang Zailin would want to litigate the "716" oil pollution case. Then the whole thing was carried out in regular sequence. We got 96% of Dalian citizens' support in over ten thousand of questionnaires and after some preparation, we became more steadfast.

As we expected, the road for litigation was not even. The first problem was the main body of the defendant. In the eyes of the general public, the pollution was caused by the China National Petroleum Corporation. But it was very intricate in the legal sense. This incident involved seven different companies in different legal degrees. Meanwhile, these companies were spread all over the country. Therefore, we needed to go to different Trade and Industry Bureaus. This was a very heavy workload. We entrusted the local lawyers and went all the way to the Beijing Trade and Industry Bureau to make confirmations over and over again. Then we found out that the main responsible party, China Fuel Oil Corporation, had bought the crude oil and was registered in Zhuhai. Immediately, we called our team members in Dalian and quickly went back.

Lawyers in Zhuhai brought bad news. Out of our expectations, they couldn't find the business archive of the China Fuel Oil Corporation, while the State Administration for Industry and Commerce was sure about it. We were in trouble in one blow and our team was suffering like trapped animals. The only thing we could do was to inquire and look for new clues. After several twists and turns, we finally found out that the China Fuel Oil Corporation had changed from an incorporated corporation to a limited liability company. And the change was made exactly after the date "716".

The next difficulty we faced was to appraise the loss. Several seminars were held, but we came to a deadlock. To tell the truth, our team was weak in this aspect, and the association was in lack of resources.

What could we do? The information collection group set up by Mr. Yang played an important part at that time. One of the volunteers of our association, Xu Weiwei, found an article entitled "The Evaluation of Ecological Environmental Damage of the Oil Spill Accident in Dalian" which was co-authored by Wen Yanping and Wu Chuanwen from College of Economy and Management at Shanghai Ocean University. They put forward marine ecological environmental damage of direct loss of nine kinds, which was estimated to cost no less than 496 million yuan. We felt very grateful for the support of the *Marine Economy* magazine. At the same time, we expressed our gratitude, particularly to the two teachers. Without their article, we wouldn't know how much more time we would be kept in confusion.

Some disputes emerged among the team members when we wrote the applications. One problem was the prescribed period for the litigation of 496 million which was claimed as a compensation. After all, it had been five years since the "716" incident took place. So the defense of the other party would be focused on this problem. Another problem was the request for an apology to the public. The six million Dalian people were the biggest victims in the "716" incident. It wasn't narrow provincialism; it was the true voice of the people.

Wang Yangming once said, "The theory of conscience comes from countless difficulties and sufferings." At that time, he had become "the synthesizer of the Philosophy of Mind". It was the genuine emotional thoughts he recalled on the way to seek the Tao of sages. Only because Wang Yangming hardened himself during setbacks could he completely receive the baptism of body and mind. Similarly, we got into trouble over and over again, feeling painful and tortured all the time. However, that did not make us give up; instead, we understood more clearly the responsibility that we shouldered, which encouraged us to hold on. Every step we got, I could hear a voice supporting me in silence.

I Saw the Other End of the Light

The preparation of the litigation took a long time. Finally, before June 5th, we submitted the final materials to the parties involved, and put forward the litigation to the Maritime Court on June 5th, World Environment Day. However, about ten days after the Dalian Maritime Court received the relevant materials, it decided the case would not be accepted. It claimed that the Environmental Protection Volunteers Organization had no litigation rights, while only the departments which supervise and manage marine environment had rights. When the association had a discussion with us, I went to the washroom and sank into wordless contemplation. In order to make clear judgments and wise choices, I always tried to keep calm and sober. However, in front of this written verdict, all that collapsed.

On that exact day, a member of our team named Haiyang wrote an indictment overnight, and sent it to our working QQ group at four o'clock before dawn. I amended it a little past five o'clock in the morning, and then Haiyang amended several times again. Finally, we submitted the indictment to the association before eight o'clock, and posted it on the website. As I joked with the group, if we could do every case like this, our business would have been more prosperous!

On the second day, the association became very busy. Through negotiation, the association told us that the China National Petroleum Corporation was willing to set aside two hundred million to bring the polluted sea of Dalian into control. It would be managed by Dalian Municipal Bureau of Finance and used under the supervision of several relevant parties. Shortly afterwards, the association gave up the appeal. Therefore, the "716" incident had come to a halt. Looking back to what we had encountered, I couldn't help shouting for joy.

Five hundred years ago, in order to expand knowledge via investigation of the world, Wang Yangming, sitting in the yard to investigate bamboo, forgot to eat until he became ill, which showed his persistence. Owing to this, Wang Yangming gradually moved forward toward his own goals in life. No matter how much suffering and relegation he got, no matter how hard the environment was, Yangming tempered himself, inspired by rules which were different from the main schools of thought, and became a real saint.

Five hundred years later, depending on our tenacious power, our team also broke through many obstacles, and finally gained a big success. In this protean modern life, there are numerous desires which control people's inner mind, so they ignore too many things that they should have chased. However, we did not do it only for fame or money, but followed our conscience and initial determination. As there was no material desire and selfish desire to distract us, we could enjoy our achievements.

The "716" case had come to an end. As commented by the Liaoning TV Station, it was not a perfect ending, but a perfect start. I appreciated it very much. A large number of people participated in this influential environmental litigation for the sake of public interest. A realistic ending was an ideal start. I witnessed the spirit of scholars who had the sense of consciousness, and I also saw the light of the other side.

初心不负笃学行

车晚静

指导教师：张静燕　蔡　亮

　　暑期实践采访结束后，我踏上了回家的渡轮，再一次看到了熟悉的岛屿，看到了熟悉的大海。但是眼前的海水混着浑浊的黄色，甚至有些水域还漂浮着一层诡异的暗红色，让我每看到一次便痛惜一次。想起很久以前，家乡的海洋也曾如天空一般湛蓝，海天相接，但是，不知从什么时候开始，这种美丽的海景却渐行渐远。

　　正是缘于那份对海的关切让我无意之中了解到大连市 2010 年"7·16"中石油污染案。虽然我对大连这个城市并不了解，但是"滨海之城"的美誉却家喻户晓，因此我对它一直有着好感和向往。所以当我知晓"7·16"大连新港火灾事故引发原油管爆炸，又导致原油泄漏污染大面积海域的时候，我再一次感到深深的痛惜，对大连人民沉痛的心情也能感同身受。

　　无论是谁看到"7·16"事故造成的海洋污染，心中都是沉痛和愤怒的，这便是良知，便是人的本心。良知人人皆有，而大连市环保志愿者协会和世勋律师事务所的同仁们坚定不移地诉讼"7·16"，便是"致良知"了。他们为了城市利益和公共利益，在行动中捍卫着我们赖以生存的家园。"知之真切笃实处即是行。"将对环境污染的痛切之情转换为保护环境的有为之举，这就是阳明先生所言的"知行合一"。有着"知行合一"精神的学人从来不是旁观者和抱怨者，他们一定是用知识和智慧、勇气和毅力去解决问题的，这就是我们要寻找的学人精神。

　　凡是了解大连市环保志愿者协会要打"7·16"官司的人，都觉得"7·16"案阻力太大，不可能胜诉。而事实也的确如此，"7·16"诉讼的道路上困难重重。只要牵扯到诉讼，哪怕在普通民众眼里一个简单的事实，在律师那里也是一个无比繁杂的过程，更何况一个关乎民众利益的重大案件，这就是郝律师和他的团队所面对的局面。从对涉及事故的七家不同主体单位去一个个所在地工商局详询，到对损失情况的鉴定，再到团队内部一些争议的解决，最后到诉状的完成，其中有太多的困难和焦灼。虽然郝律师只是轻描淡写地向我们讲述了诉讼"7·16"的过程，但是从他的话语里我们不难发现那段时间里他们遇到的困难之多，煎熬至极。但即便如此，他们都从未有过一丝放弃的念头。我也在采访中问过郝律师，到底是什么精神和动力使他们在遇到如此多的困难时始终坚定自己的信念，专注于"7·16"的诉讼,只考虑如何克服而不是放弃?当时郝律师的回答让我想到了《传习录》里的一个故事。阳明先生的弟子陆澄曾向他请教"主一"的功夫应该怎样做到,而先生回答他:"主一是专主一个天理。"一心只在天理上,对于郝律师他们来说,诉讼"7·16"就是一个天理。我想郝律师他们正是用这种"主一"的精神和态度对待"7·16"的。因为他们知道,要给大连人民一个交代!

环境污染和破坏的事件常常见诸报端,我们一方面扼腕长叹,另外一方面却似乎无能为力。久而久之,我们的感慨变成了漠然和麻木。是因为我们都没有良知吗?不是的。我们或许是不够重视,或许是潜意识里认为自己只是普通人,不是专家,我们无能为力。但真的是这样吗?我们真的什么都不能做吗?大连市环保志愿者协会诉讼"7·16"就是最好的榜样!"知行合一"的学人精神求诸自我,求诸行动去唤醒。

又或许很多人认为不能给自己带来利益的做法是不值得的。现代生活的步伐太快,在纷繁复杂的互联网信息时代,我们有时会一味地追求外物而忘记了本心。我们经常会迷惘,因为我们不知道自己真正想要的是什么。殊不知正是因为我们太过追求外物,这种私欲蒙蔽了我们的良知,让我们无法做出顺应内心选择的行动。阳明先生曾说:"人人都有良知,人人都是圣人。"但是"致良知"这个"致"的关键过程正是现在我们所欠缺的。

其实我们应该如何"致"良知,我们早就知道了。从小我们就被教育要"从我做起,从小事做起",但是很多人早已把这句话抛到了脑后。无数的事实证明,正是每一个人一点一滴的积累,才会有日后的巨大改变。或许在你眼里只是阻止了一个游客向大海丢垃圾这样一个小小的举动,岂不知这个举动能让大海免受多少灾难和痛苦!我们能做的,就是珍惜那些未被污染的海洋,同时也不要让已经蒙受灾难的海洋痛上加痛!

我敬佩那些为了我们共同生活的家园默默付出的人们,他们不图名利,只是想让大海重现曾经的风采。我相信会有越来越多的人参与到这一行列中来,做到"致良知",实现良知和实践的高度统一。大连市环保志愿者协会的朋友们、郝律师和他的团队可以听到大海的哭泣、听到内心的召唤然后从简单的清洁活动转变到提起诉讼,这个过程他们也用了很久。为了那片曾经蔚蓝的海洋,他们用行动成就了辽宁省首例环保公益诉讼。现在我依然会乘坐轮渡回到我岛上的家,不同的是,我开始思考自己未来可以为这片海做点什么。

团队成员:车晚静 郑秀媛 沈旭桐

Learn and Practice Steadfastly to
Comply with My Initial Determination

Che Wanjing

Supervised by: Zhang Jingyan, Cai Liang

I went home by ship after the interview that summer practice. I saw once again the island and the sea that were so familiar to me. However, the sea I saw in front of me was mixed with turbid yellow water. In some areas, an uncanny layer of dark red floated on top. I regret every time when I see it. A long time ago, the sea in my hometown was also as blue as the sky, stretching to meet the horizon. I don't know when this beautiful seascape started to fade away.

Because of my special concern for the sea, I unwittingly learned something about the "716" oil pollution incident in Dalian in 2010. Although I knew little about Dalian, a coastal city, it was widely known in China. Therefore, it left a favorable impression on me and I was always yearning to go there. So when I learned that the "716" fire accident had caused an oil pipe explosion in Dalian, and of the resulting marine pollution, I felt deeply regretful. Meanwhile, I could also feel the painful mood of the Dalian people.

Everyone was grieved and angry when they saw the marine pollution caused by the "716" incident. This is conscience; it's the true mind. Conscience is possessed by everyone. However, volunteers in the Dalian Environmental Protection Volunteers Association and lawyers in Shixun Law Firm unswervingly litigated "716", which is a good exhibition of the extension of conscience. They took firm action to protect our home in the interest of the city and the public. "Practice helps judge truth." They converted the painful emotions about the environmental pollution to the action of environmental activism. This is "the unity of knowledge and action" advocated by Wang Yangming. These kinds of people who abide by "the unity of knowledge and action" never complain or just look on. They take advantage of their knowledge, wisdom, courage and perseverance to solve the problem. This is the scholarly spirit that we are seeking.

Anyone who knew that Dalian Environmental Protection Volunteers Association was going to litigate the "716" incident thought it was too difficult to win. It was true. There were so many obstacles on the road of the lawsuit. As long as the litigation was concerned, one bare fact in the eyes of common people would be a very complex process to lawyers. What's more, it was a case closely related to public interest. This was the situation that Mr. Hao and his team were facing. From the inquiry of the seven companies which were connected with the "716" incident in different Trade and Industry Bureaus, to the authentication of the loss, to reaching the agreement about the controversial issues, to the accomplishment of the indictment, they encountered many difficulties and anxieties. Though Mr. Hao understated his accomplishments, through his words, we could trace what they had suffered. Even so, they never thought of giving up. In the interview, I also asked Mr. Hao what had motivated them to stick to doing what they did and why they only thought about overcoming instead of quitting. His answer reminded me of a story in *Instructions for Practical Living*. Wang Yangming's student, Lu Cheng, once asked him how to concentrate. And the answer was, "Just concentrate on one heavenly principle." For Mr. Hao and his team, it meant to concentrate on the litigation. They knew they had to give Dalian people a reasonable explanation!

Actually, environmental pollution and destructive incidents in news reports are quite popular these days. On the one hand, we feel great regret; on the other hand, we can hardly do anything. As time passes by, we become indifferent and insensitive. Is that due to our lack of conscience? No. Maybe we pay too little attention to it. Or perhaps subconsciously we think we are ordinary people, not experts, so there is nothing we can do. Really? Can't we do anything? The litigation of the "716" incident brought by the Dalian Environmental Protection Volunteers Association was the best example! This scholarly spirit originates from ourselves, and waits to be awakened by action.

Maybe a lot of people think that anything that doesn't bring any benefits to themselves isn't worthy of doing. Nowadays, the pace of modern life is too quick. Especially in this complicated Internet age, we will sometimes chase money so blindly that we forget the true mind. We are usually at a loss, because we don't know what we really want. Actually, we ask for too much, and this desire distracts our conscience. As a result, we can't really follow our heart. Wang Yangming once said, "Everyone has conscience; everyone can be a saint." However, what we lack is the action we take to attain conscience.

As a matter of fact, we already know how to attain conscience. From childhood, we were educated to "begin from myself and begin from small things". But many people have already put these words aside. Countless facts prove that every little bit of accumulation will lead to big changes. Perhaps in your view, you have only done a very trifle thing by stopping a visitor from throwing rubbish into the sea, but maybe you can't see that what you have done has protected the sea from many disasters and sufferings! Try to take good care of the unpolluted sea and never make the polluted sea suffer any more!

I admire those people who have made great contributions to our common home. They have no aspiration for money or fame, but just want to help the sea return to its past grace. I'm convinced that more and more people will join us out of conscience, to realize a high degree of unity of conscience and practice. It was not only people from the Dalian Environmental Protection Volunteers Association, but also Mr. Hao and his team, who could hear the weeping of the sea, sense the call from their hearts and turn from simple clean-up to litigation. This process has lasted for a long time. For the sake of the blue sea, they took action and accomplished the first environmental public interest litigation of Liaoning. As for me, each time I still return home by ship; the difference is that I have started thinking about what I can do for the sea in the future.

Team members: Che Wanjing, Zheng Xiuyuan, Shen Xutong

王渊源："双语游侠"的文化交流之旅

John Gordon: The Cultural Exchange Trip of a "Bilingual Ranger"

　　王渊源，英文名 John Gordon，来自美国北卡罗来纳州，毕业于维斯里安大学东亚研究系，人称"双语游侠"，汉语与英语说得一样棒。他曾担任新航道国际教育集团副总裁一职，主持过中央电视台国际频道《快乐中国——学汉语》等节目；业余时间喜欢球类运动，非常热爱中国文化，致力于文化交流工作。

　　John Gordon, former vice president of New Channel International Education Group Limited, comes from North Carolina, the United States. He graduated from the Department of East Asian Studies at Wesleyan University. A "Bilingual Ranger" as he is called, his Chinese is as good as his native language, English. He has hosted such programs as "Happy China—Learning Chinese" in the CCTV International Channel and some others. He loves ball games in his spare time, and loves Chinese culture. He has devoted himself to cross-cultural communication work.

"双语游侠"的文化交流之旅

口述：王渊源
整理：胡 双
指导教师：张静燕 蔡 亮

引 子

知者行之始，行者知之成：圣学只一个功夫，知行不可分作两事。

——王阳明

行动中爱上中国

古人时常提到"知行"二字。曾有阳明先生的弟子问道，我不解"知行"怎么就合一了，我也可以学问思辨而不去实践啊？王阳明先生是这样回答的，"行"就是认真地去做事，学问思辨也是"知"，你这个探求的过程就是"行"，所以"学问思辨"的过程就是"知行合一"。

关于"知行合一"，王渊源先生跟我们分享了他的一些经历：总有很多人问我为什么要来中国。其实，最早的时候完全是出于好奇，但是后来我慢慢爱上了中国和中国文化，决定致力于文化交流工作。我认为很多误会和冲突都是因为缺乏沟通和了解而起的，所以我想帮助中国人更了解外国人，帮助外国人更了解中国人和中国。在 2006 年的时候，我真的很高兴 CCTV 和《快乐中国——学汉语》能给我这样一个交流的平台，让我的想法落实到了行动之中。

我在维斯里安大学的时候接触了哲学方向的书籍，阅读了英文版的《老子》《大学》《中庸》等，也看过一些中文版，当时担心可能会理解得不大透彻。我最初接触东方哲学时，遇到的第一个问题是：中国的哲学到底是不是一种哲学？像《老子》，主要讲的是一些道理，西方的哲学则注重逻辑性。而阳明先生批判朱熹的理念，拿他的说法去考证，检验它够不够扎实，然后在这个过程中得到新的想法、新的方向或者是强调的东西，这一方面与西方哲学有些相似。我喜欢中国哲学的一个原因是，它能即刻让我得到启发。

初识阳明之良知

说起阳明文化，可能大多数的外国人都不知道，从推广的角度来看，这是好事也是坏事。如果将"知行合一""致良知"等思想解释给他们听，他们也不会觉得特别陌生，这些思想都可以跟西方主流思想结合起来。但是两种思想的相同点和不同点也要讲清楚，有些也许是从更好的、更有价值的角度；同时也要搞清楚推广的目的，是想将这个思想变成大众流行文化还是想要影响西方的哲学界。

简单地讲，"知行合一"若是强调实践便是主流思想了，同时"致良知"也是西方哲学自古以来经常讨论的人的本性是善还是恶的问题。当然也有不同的学派，但主流思想还是强调善的。

心外无物，心外无理

提及如何看待主观意识在我们生活或者学习过程中的作用，我觉得从某种程度上来说，自己的主观意识是自己惟一拥有的东西，要依靠它，同时也要关注外在看法、客观因素以及一些别人的主观想法和观点。很多时候别人的主观意见也是我们主观意识的一个镜子，更加开放地考虑别人的观点以及学会倾听别人的意见，会让我们更加接近真相。

随人分限所及，量力施教

我在教学的过程中当然也会强调因材施教。比如有的学生不能适应大班的教学，就需要根据他个人特点调整教学方式，包括我现在做的微信公众号：清晨朗读会。虽然现在这个微信号只是每天提供不同的练习材料，并没有针对不同学生的水平，但是我会在后台或者留言中获取一些建议。其中重要的一点是要和学生有交流和沟通，才能决定怎样做对学生是合适的。同时这也是一个很好的循环，在交流的过程中也能根据学生的需求时刻调整。在这里也给自学者一个小小的建议，自学的关键是要反思，要接受语言学习的痛苦和压力。语言学习不可能一蹴而就，接受因为听不懂而感到难受的过程，这样才能获得进步。

具有公益精神的园丁

新航道的"成功之道"大型公益巡讲以及我现在做的清晨朗读会，最初是从一个希望帮助别人的小小愿望开始的。我选择教育行业，一方面是受到了家庭的影响——我的父母都是老师。另一方面，在上大学期间有一个契机，当时有机会去教雅思，我觉得这很有意思，能帮助更多的学生出国留学。我个人觉得，教育是一种比较直接的帮助别人的方式，能帮助他们学到想学的东西；教育也是个很好的事业。我希望我做的事情对别人有所帮助。我也喜欢和学生交流，和他们一起成长。

一个美国青年的"中国梦"

我在2015年做巡讲的时候提到过，我小时候经常听到周围的人讲"美国梦"。

现在在中国，又经常听到一个词"中国梦"。我在想，当时的"美国梦"指的是什么？现在的"美国梦"又有什么含义？"中国梦"应该怎么去理解呢？它与"美国梦"又有什么区别呢？还有我这个美国人怎么会到中国来寻梦呢？

美国青年的"中国梦"巡讲

小时候没有人告诉过我"美国梦"是什么，它是一种文化产物，如果不明说可能也会有一些了解。我当时对"美国梦"的一个大概了解是：只要你努力，就能够为自己和自己的家庭创造出一个更加美好的未来，一代比一代过得好。这个"美国梦"的结果往往是有一所房子，有自己的小花园和一个 white picket fence（白栅栏）。

"中国梦"这个说法我在近几年听说得比较多，它的产生应该跟这些年中国经济的发展和大家对未来的向往有一定的关系，那么"中国梦"是什么？没有white picket fence，但也是希望能够通过自己的努力养家糊口，创造更好的未来，一代比一代强。我记得我回妻子老家的时候，每次祭祖，她父亲总是反复地说，一代比一代强。他从山区出来，看到自己的孩子都建立了各自的家庭，找到了自己发展的方向，因此感到非常欣慰。

当然，"中国梦"作为文化和理想的产物，是不是也有自相矛盾的地方？是否也有它的盲区？我想是有的，也希望大家能够对这些矛盾和盲区保持警惕，但同时我知道，"中国梦"这个概念的存在既代表着社会的一种愿望，也代表着一部分现实。

如此看来，"美国梦"与"中国梦"有很多相似的地方，也许就是传说中的 One World, One Dream（同一个世界，同一个梦想）。不管是哪个国家的人，都希望能够通过自己的努力创造更好的未来。我希望我们所生活的环境能够提供一个越来越公平的平台让人们寻梦，相信不管是美国人还是中国人都在往这个方向努力。任重而道远。

当然，我这个美国人来到中国，也是想给自己创造更美好的未来。在养家糊口的同时，寻找其他方面的满足和人生的意义。

我在中国已经生活了十多年，回想我做过的事情，从留学生转型为帮助美国留学生习惯中国生活的老师，再转为帮助中国学生学好英语的老师，最后成为希望帮助更多的中国学生成功地学好英语、成功地出国留学并进一步了解世界的创业者，一条很明显的主线是重视跨文化交流。我一直坚信更多的这种交流对我们大家的未来很重要。彼此之间正面的接触越多，不管是通过学习、旅游还是商务活动，都会增加彼此之间的理解，都会减少产生冲突的可能性。我很高兴能够参与这个过程，并希望以我小小的力量促进这个过程。我说不清楚这是"中国梦"还是"美国梦"，但是我会很珍惜。

The Cultural Exchange Trip of a "Bilingual Ranger"

Narrator: John Gordon

Compiled by: Hu Shuang

Supervised by: Zhang Jingyan, Cai Liang

Knowledge is the beginning of action and action is the completion of knowledge. Learning to be a sage involves only one effort. Knowledge and action should not be separated.

—Wang Yangming

Love China through Action

People in ancient times often referred to the two words, "knowing (knowledge) and doing (action)". One day, a student of Wang Yangming asked, "I don't understand how 'knowing and doing' can be united. I can just learn, ask, and make intellectual inquiries without practicing." To this question, Wang replied in this way, "Doing means that you do things seriously, and when you're learning and thinking, you are also knowing. This process of pursuing is 'doing'. Therefore, learning and making intellectual inquiries is also 'the unity of knowing and doing'."

With regard to "the unity of knowing and doing", I can share you with some of his own experience: A lot of people have asked why I came to China. In fact, it was out of curiosity at first, but then I slowly fell in love with China and Chinese culture, and I made a decision to focus on cultural exchange. I think many misunderstandings and conflicts arise from lack of communication; this is why I want to help Chinese people understand foreigners better and help foreigners know China and Chinese better. In 2006, I was so happy to get a chance to host CCTV's "Happy China—Learning Chinese" program which really gave me a big platform to communicate, and to implement my ideas into action.

When I was in Wesleyan University, I read some books about philosophy, including the translated versions of *Laozi, The Great Learning, The Doctrine of the Mean*, and some of the Chinese versions of them, but I doubted whether I could understand them well enough at that time. The first problem that I met with when I was learning Eastern philosophy is: Is Chinese philosophy a kind of philosophy? Taking

Laozi for example, it mainly talks about some principles, but Western philosophy is more concerned about logicality. However, Wang Yangming criticized Zhu Xi's philosophy, taking his statement to research, to see if it was solid enough, and in this process, he also got some new ideas, new direction or something to emphasize. It is quite similar to Western philosophy. If there is a reason why I like Chinese philosophy, it is because it can enlighten me quickly.

The First Encounter of the Intuitive Knowledge of Wang Yangming

As far as Yangming culture is concerned, most foreigners may know little about it. From the perspective of promotion, it is a good thing, but also has its bad side. If the ideas of "the unity of knowing and doing", "realizing conscientious wisdom" and so on, are explained to foreigners, they may not feel so unfamiliar, since these thoughts are well integrated with Western cultures. But making the similarities and differences of the two cultures clearer is also important. Some of these ideas may be understood from a better point of view. At the same time, knowing the promotional purposes is necessary as well. Whether we want it to be a popular culture or an influence to Western philosophy is of vital importance.

To put it simply, if the idea of "the unity of knowing and doing" lays stress on the importance of practice, it can be classified as mainstream ideology. Meanwhile, "realizing conscientious wisdom" is also a debate of the theory as whether human nature is good or evil. Certainly, there are many different schools, but mainstream philosophy usually emphasizes the goodness of human nature.

The Mind Is Identical with Objects

When it is mentioned how our subjective consciousness works in our life, or the role of it in the learning process, I think, to some extent, our own subjective consciousness is the only thing we have, and on which we can rely. Meanwhile, we should focus on external opinions, objective factors, and thoughts and opinions of other people. More often than not, others' opinions will be a mirror of our own subjective thinking. Thinking about others' points of view and learning to listen to others' opinions will take us closer to the truth.

Teaching Students in Accordance with Their Aptitude

I always stress students' aptitude in my teaching process. For example, if a student can't adapt to traditional large-class lectures, it is important to adjust my way of teaching to satisfy his demand, including what I'm doing right now in WeChat called "Reading aloud in the morning". It only provides English learners some different exercises each day, without considering their different knowledge levels, but I also got some advice from the background message boards. It's essential to communicate with students to decide which way is appropriate for them. At the same time, a good recycle is formed in the process of communication as to adjust flexibly according to students' needs. There is a tip for self-learners: the key to learning English by oneself is to keep reflecting and withstanding high pressure and great pain in learning.

A "Gardener" with Public Spirit

The free speaking tour "The Road to Success" made by the New Channel International Education Group around the nation and "Reading aloud in the morning" WeChat ems-cnpl began from one of my tiny wishes to help other people. There are two reasons why I chose education as my career. On the one hand, I was influenced by my family—as you know, both of my parents are teachers. On the other hand, I got an opportunity to teach IELTS when I was at the university. I found it really meaningful to be able to help more and more students study abroad. Personally speaking, I feel that teaching is a more direct way to help others, to help them learn what they want to learn; teaching is also a good career. I hope what I do will benefit other people, and I love communicating with students, growing together with them.

An American's "Chinese Dream"

As I mentioned when I made the speaking tour in 2015, as a little boy, I often heard people around me talk about the "American dream". Now in China, the words "Chinese dream" are frequently mentioned. I am always asking these questions: What was the "American dream" in the past time? What is the meaning of the "American dream" today? How can the "Chinese dream" be interpreted? What is the difference between the "Chinese dream" and the "American dream"? And why do I, an American, come to China to chase down my dream?

When I was young, no one told me what the "American dream" was. It is actually a cultural product, and we may also learn something without any explanations. A brief understanding of mine at that time was that as long as you work hard, you will be able to create a better future for you and your family, and a better life for the next generation. To realize this "American dream" is to have a house, have your own small garden and a white picket fence.

The "Chinese dream", which is frequently heard in recent years, must have something to do with China's economic development and people's yearning for a brighter future. So what is a "Chinese dream"? Even though there is no white picket fence, Chinese people hope that they can support their families through their own efforts, create a better future and a better life for the next generation. I remember that every time I go back to my wife's hometown and every time we worship the ancestors, her father always says repeatedly, "Each new generation excels the previous one." He came from the mountain areas. Seeing his children establish their own families and have their own direction of development, he feels very grateful.

However, is the "Chinese dream" a product of culture and ideal? Is it self-contradictory? Does it also have its blind areas? I think there are some. But I also hope that we can be vigilant against these contradictions and blind areas. I also know, at the same time, that the existence of the "Chinese dream" represents an aspiration for society, as well as a part of reality.

In that case, there are many similarities in the expression of the "American dream" and the "Chinese dream". Perhaps they are exactly what the legendary "One World, One Dream" means. No matter from which country, people all want to create a better future through their own efforts. I hope that the place where we live can provide a fair platform for people to pursue their own dreams; I believe that both Americans and Chinese people will work for this goal, though there is still a long way to go.

Of course, I'm an American who has come to China to create a better future for myself. At the same time, I'm looking for satisfaction and the meaning of life.

I have lived in China more than ten years. During these years, I have transferred from an overseas student to a teacher who helps American students adapt to life in China and helps Chinese students learn English better. Eventually, I wish to help more Chinese students learn English successfully, succeed in studying abroad and learn more about entrepreneurs all over the world. Looking back to what I have done, I never deviate from intercultural communication. I've always believed that more of this kind of communication will be very important to our future. The more positive contacts between us, whether through learning, travel or business activities, the more understanding we can obtain, and the less conflicts will there be. I am very glad to participate in this process, and I hope that with my drops of strength, I can help promote this process. I am not sure whether this is a "Chinese dream" or an "American dream", but I will cherish it.

格物致知以求善，跨越文化以求同

胡　双

指导教师：张静燕　蔡　亮

　　我曾在闲暇时刻读过一则阳明先生的小故事。初春时节，先生为学生讲学时，一老农求见。然而他并不是来求学的，而是来与先生做一笔生意的，老农因家里拮据故而希望将田地抵换现金。先生一听，觉得君子应成人之美，怎能趁火打劫？于是他借给了老农一笔现金，并没有约定还款日期。老农十分感谢先生的好意。几日后，先生与学生游玩时发现一块风水宝地，竟是那老农前些日子想要交换的田地。先生懊悔之余，幡然醒悟，便有了四句教，即"无善无恶心之体，有善有恶意之动；知善知恶是良知，为善去恶是格物"。

　　人人都有善恶的观念，人人都有良知，但是为什么有的人被世人厌恶，有的人却被世人爱戴呢？我们需要像阳明先生所说的一样，要"知行合一"，用格物的方式去"致良知"，去践行自己的良知。

　　此次我很荣幸能够采访到王渊源先生，一名致力于英语教育的师长。他是一个美国青年，但是他拥有自己的"中国梦"，并非常珍惜这个梦想。他曾经说过："我这个美国人来到中国，当然也是想给自己创造更好的未来，但是我在养家糊口的过程中也找寻到了人生的意义。我坚信跨文化交流的重要性，同时认为多交流能够促进彼此间的理解，减少冲突。我非常高兴能够参与这个过程，也希望自己小小的力量能够促进这个过程。"这是良知的体现，是践行良知的具象化。他真真切切地投身到了这份事业中，为了减少不同文化之间的冲突、加深不同文化之间的友谊而贡献出了自己的力量。不管是一个美国青年的"中国梦"，还是一个中国人的"中国梦"，我们都渐渐地明白何为良知并且亲自践行。

　　出于好奇，他来到了中国，爱上了中国文化。他帮助外国人更加了解中国，也帮助中国人更加了解外国，让不同文化背景下的人们在交流中共同进步、理解彼此。当在一档电视节目中首次见到这位汉语讲得非常棒的美国人时，我不由自主地惊叹他的汉语水平之高。后来他来我们学校做了一次令我印象深刻的讲座，与我们分享了他学习汉语的过程并鼓励我们坚持学习英语，也为我们提供了些比较好的方法。

　　不仅如此，王渊源老师通过公益讲座无偿地分享他的求学经历，为广大因学习英语而苦恼的中国学子们提供了他的经验。同时，我也关注了他的清晨朗读会微信公众号。他每天不间断、准时地为英语学习者提供一些英语学习的材料。他非常乐意与学生交流，希望通过交流和学生们一起成长。

像王渊源先生一样成为文化交流的"桥梁"的人很多，令我印象最深的美国的赛珍珠女士，她的作品《大地》改变了当时西方人对中国的印象，当时瑞典学院对她的评价也非常高，这个例子现在也是适用的，我们只有通过实实在在地交流才能互相理解，求同存异。这是一个开放的多元化的时代，我们需要更多人以善意看待不同的文化，去理解和包容。而我作为一名英语系学生，我也很高兴以微薄之力促进这一进程。

作为阳明文化的初学者，我对阳明文化的认识非常粗浅。但是通过这次采访，我更多地了解了王阳明先生，这些了解不仅仅只是停留在高中历史课本对于阳明先生的一些简单描述，以及对心学的一些介绍。同时我也希望，这次的阳明文化之旅是一个很好的开始。这不仅仅是一场短期的旅行，更是中国历史文化的悠久魅力和它对我的长期熏染带来的启迪。阳明文化贯穿了我们的历史，是千年中华传统文化的一部分，需要我们去继承和发展。而且要更加细致地理解心学集大成者王守仁先生的观点和理念，单是知道"知行合一"和"致良知"并不能真正地理解和践行这一理念，关键要像先生所说的一样要"格物"。在实际践行过程中了解阳明文化的意义，更加深刻地思考阳明文化的现世意义。我们的未来想必是兼收并蓄，贯古通今，融合中西的。因此我很感激这次采访机会，让我能够在实际行动中了解这位心学大家王阳明先生，了解他的理念背后的故事，加深了我对这些理念的认识，真的是受益匪浅。

团队成员：朱嘉平　胡　双　车晚静　李　铭

Investigate to Realize Conscientious Wisdom and Bridge Cultural Gaps to Seek Similarities

Hu Shuang

Supervised by: Zhang Jingyan, Cai Liang

In my leisure time, I once read a little story about Wang Yangming. In early spring, when he was giving lectures to students, an old farmer asked to see him. However, this farmer did not come for his lectures. He came there to make a deal with Wang Yangming. Because of his poverty, the farmer wanted to sell his farmland for some money. Hearing this, Wang Yangming thought that a gentleman was always ready to help others attain their goals rather than profit by their ill luck. So he lent some money to the farmer with no agreement for refund date. The farmer felt very grateful. A few days later, when Wang was traveling with his students, he found a geomantic treasured site which was the farmland the old farmer had wanted to sell. He felt very regretful, but that four-sentence doctrine occurred to him: "Every life is born with no good or evil. When we're thinking, our consciousness decides them. If you can differentiate between kindness and evil, that's intuitive knowledge. And learning the true meaning of goodness and evil is based on the understanding of nature."

Everyone has his own concept of what is good and what is evil; everyone is born with his intuitive knowledge, so why are some people hated, while others are loved? We should do as what Yangming said, to realize "the unity of knowledge and action", and to practice our intuitive knowledge by studying the nature of things.

I was honored to have the opportunity to interview Mr. Gordon, a teacher who devotes himself to English education. He is an American, but he has his own cherished "Chinese dream". He used to say, "I'm an American who came to China. Certainly, I want to create a better future for myself. However, in an attempt to support my family, I have found the meaning of life as well. I'm convinced that more and more cultural communication is very important to us in the future. The more positive contacts between us, whether through learning, traveling or business activities, will increase the understanding between us, and also will reduce the possibilities of conflicts. I am very glad to participate in this process, and hope to promote this process with my effort." It is intuitive knowledge itself and an embodiment of how he put practice into reality. In order to reduce the conflicts among different cultures, deepen friendship, he has devoted himself to this career. Be it an American's "Chinese dream" or a Chinese's "Chinese dream", slowly but surely, we will know what "intuitive knowledge" is, and can practice it at the same time.

Out of curiosity, he came to China and fell in love with Chinese culture. He helped foreigners have a better understanding of China and vice versa. He enabled people with different cultural backgrounds to make mutual progress through communication and understanding each other better. I met this American, whose Chinese was very good, in a TV program for the first time and I was amazed by his good mastery of Chinese. Later, he came to our school and gave students an impressive lecture. He shared his process of learning Chinese and encouraged us to stick to our English study. He also offered us some good approaches.

Besides, Mr. Gordon also shared his learning experiences for free through public welfare lectures for many Chinese students who were feeling frustrated by English learning. At the same time, I also followed his morning reading club on WeChat ems-cnpl. On a daily basis, he unremittingly provides English learners with some materials for English learning and at just the right time. He is happy to exchange with students and hopes to grow with them through communication.

There are many "bridges" across cultures like Mr. Gordon and Ms. Pearl Buck, the latter of whom is the most impressive to me. Her masterpiece *The Good Earth* changed Westerners' impressions of the Chinese. The Swedish Academy gave high appraisal to her works. Till now, this example is still appropriate. Exchanging or communicating with each other is the only way through which we may understand each other, see our differences and keep our similarities. In this world of vast variety, it is necessary for more and more people to see different cultures with good will, and to understand and tolerate them. As an English major, I am very happy to facilitate this process through my small efforts.

As a beginner in the field of Yangming culture, my understanding of it is strikingly little. But through this interview, I learned more about Wang Yangming. These understandings go beyond the mere descriptions of him in my senior high school history textbook, which also give some introductions to the Philosophy of Mind. At the same time, I hope this interview is a good start of our Yangming trip. It is not just a short-term trip, but an enlightenment derived from the rich charm of Chinese history and my absorption in it. Yangming culture has penetrated our history and as a part of traditional Chinese culture for several thousand years, it is our duty to develop and inherit it. As a result, we need to do further investigation and analysis to have a better understanding of Wang Yangming's views and concepts. It is not enough for us to merely know the theory of "realizing conscientious wisdom" or "the unity of knowing (knowledge) and doing (action)". The most important thing is to practice it. It is necessary for us to understand the meaning of Yangming culture in the process of practice, and to think more clearly and deeply about its meaning in modern society. The coming future must be an era of the incorporation of diversity and harmony between the ancient and the present, and between the West and China. I greatly appreciate the opportunity of this interview; it helps me to know more about Wang Yangming, and to understand the stories behind his concepts and views. It deepens my knowledge of these concepts, which really has benefited me a lot.

Team members: Zhu Jiaping, Hu Shuang, Che Wanjing, Li Ming

栾成斌：修身立德，"知行合一"

Luan Chengbin: The Cultivation of a Person's Morality Is "the Unity of Knowledge and Action"

栾成斌，西南大学历史地理学博士，贵州大学历史与民族文化学院、中国文化书院、阳明学院专职教师，校聘副教授，贵州大学阳明学院"史记""阳明学概论""资治通鉴"等课程开课教师，先后为教育部第101期全国高校辅导员骨干培训班、贵州大学—香港大学双向文化交流启动仪式等活动开展优秀传统文化讲座。

Luan Chengbin, doctor of historical geography of Southwest University, is now a full-time teacher and associate professor in the College of History and Ethnic Culture, the Academy of Chinese Culture, and the Yangming College of Guizhou University. Besides that, Dr. Luan started teaching several classes such as "Records of the Grand Historian", "An Introduction to Yangming Doctrine" and "History as a Mirror" several years ago. As an outstanding researcher of Chinese traditional culture, Dr. Luan has been asked to give lectures to the 101st College Counselors Backbone Training Class held by the Ministry of Education and at activities such as the opening ceremony of Guizhou University and the Hong Kong University Bi-directional Cultural Exchange.

修身立德，"知行合一"

口述：栾成斌

整理：李 铭

指导教师：张静燕 蔡 亮

引 子

仁人者，正其谊不谋其利，明其道不计其功。

——王阳明

路漫漫其修远兮，吾将上下而求索

我认为弘扬阳明文化具有很大的必要性。在当今这个国际竞争激烈的大环境下，我们需要弘扬党和国家在伟大斗争时期所展现的先进文化，突出我国在综合国力竞争中的精神优势，从不同视角、不同高度、不同层次弘扬社会主义价值观。阳明文化在我们所要达成的这个文化目标中起到了统筹全局的作用，在文化传承与传播的过程中能够推动社会文化氛围，形成天时地利人和共生共存的和谐局面，从而推动中华传统文化的发展。

文化的传承与传播需要一个环境。以我在贵州大学阳明学院任职的经历来说，以阳明学院为代表的这类通识学院对于建立学生对多种学科的深入了解具有不可替代的作用。以阳明心学为例，很多大学生在接受通识教育之前，对它的了解往往局限于其为唯心主义思想的代表，很少有人脱离课本去深入了解其根本内容。从您所提到的受访同学对它的理解中也可见端倪——很多同学对于阳明文化的了解仅限于高中课本对于阳明心学的寥寥数语：

"王阳明早年对程朱理学的'格物致知'深信不疑。他曾面对翠竹，穷格七天七夜也没有得到其理，反而因思虑过度而致疾。从此，他开始质疑朱熹理学。后来，王阳明从禅学研究中受到启发，始知'圣人之道，吾性自足'。并用'心外无物，心外无理'来否定'格物致知'说。在镇压农民起义时，他进一步悟出'破山中贼易，破心中贼难'的道理。

"王阳明更多地吸取了佛教'心外无佛，即心是佛'的思想，宣扬'心外无物''心外无理'的命题。在认识论上，他提出'致良知'和'知行合一'学说。他认为良知是存在于人心中的天理，是人所固有的善性，但良知往往被私欲所侵蚀，所以要努力加强道德修养，去掉人欲，恢复良知的本性。他的'知行合一'，认为知和行都产生于心，因此要用良知来支配自己的行为实践。王阳明的'知行合一'并不能科学地说明人的认识和实践的关系。自明朝中期以后，陆王心学得到了广泛传播。之后的宋明理学历经几百年的发展，对中国社会政治、文化教育以及伦理道德都产生了深远影响。"

这样的介绍，于应试而言尚且不足，更不要说去理解吃透一门学科、学习一种文化、感受一位大家的精神世界了。

话虽这么讲，但是我们文化课程的教学条件已经足够进行深入的国学文化教育：在硬件方面，现在大学的传统文化课堂已经达到了相当高的标准，各类设施对于日常教学已很充足；在软件方面，众多学校的通识教育都具有不同的长处。但是，各个学校通识教育存在的缺点也显而易见。就我所任职的贵州大学阳明学院而言，在阳明文化教育和传播的过程中存在着一些问题，这些问题可能不是非常普遍，但却极具代表性，我将它概括为以下几点。

1. 教学内容需要得到丰富，我们需要打造公共领域教学计划；2. 实现通识教育中的精品化过程仍然任重而道远，就像盖楼一样，需要各方面不停地进行累积与磨合；3. 我们缺乏一种必要的激励政策以提高同学们的学习积极性，而这就需要我们提高传统文化知识学习情况在学生个人综合考核中的权重。

律人当以律己为先

之前我也有提及，在我们的同学之中有相当大一部分人对于阳明文化的了解仅限于"知行合一""致良知"，现在让我分享一下在工作中所遇到的实际例子吧。

我们知道陆王心学中有"存天理，去人欲"这样的表述，对于时值青春期的同学们来说，若只看字面意思，阳明文化便被打上了一层"压抑人性"的标签，变成了落后文化了。但是实际上阳明先生是如何解释这句话的呢？

"存天理，灭人欲"这句话语出朱熹，很多时候我们学习一些思想家的思想文化，都是在脱离原典的情况下进行的，这样便不免断章取义。有时，这种理解的错误甚至使我们得出与事实完全相反的答案，造成文化传承过程中出现缺漏乃至错误的现象。"饮食者，天理也；要求美味，人欲也。"朱熹在《朱子语类》中给出了他自己对于天理和人欲的区分，用现在的话来解释朱熹老先生的话就是：合理的便是天理。由此可见，在文化学习中，我们并非缺少去了解并理解它的途径，而是我们自身是否愿意花费时间去学习这种文化。

对于阳明文化的传承者而言，培养对阳明文化的兴趣非常重要。这对我们为人师者提出了更高的要求。如何帮助我们的学生培养对于阳明文化的兴趣呢？我觉得首先老师们需要对我们所要传授的阳明文化有准确透彻和有趣味的理解，这不仅仅是课堂对我们的要求，也是我们对文化传承这一伟大社会职责的担当。"给人一碗水，自己一桶水"，这句话是对老师工作很好的阐述。然而我对自己的要求是，我为人师，不仅仅要有这一桶水，还要保证这一桶水是一桶清澈的活水，这也是我刚刚提到的老师本身需要具有对文化深度了解的必要性。

文化苦旅

在现代社会中，不仅是阳明文化，还有很多中国古代传统文化元素都具有很大的现实意义。这是因为从本源上讲，上至奴隶社会，下至当今时代，同样的水土养育着同样的一群人。古时候曾有一本民歌集——《诗经》，其中很多章节都表现了当时人们脚踏实地地对幸福生活的追求与对欲望的克服，这也是中华民族一直以来前进的动力。

对于阳明文化的对外传播，我觉得是完全没有问题的。阳明文化产生于明朝的中后期，正值三教合一的时期，表面上看这三教差别很大，实际上它们对于人生终极价值的追求是相通的。用马斯洛学说来解释的话，都是将个人价值的自我实现作为人生的最高价值追求。由此可见，佛、儒、道文化圈中的国家其实都能够从阳明文化中找到自己的影子。作为一种方法论，阳明文化对来自不同文化氛围的人群都具有普世的指导意义，而这种意义是不会因为民族文化的不同而阻隔的，是更偏向人类的共性的。尽管如此，阳明文化作为一种文化，其民族特色是难以被不同文化人士所接受的，这就需要一个过程。我将这个过程分为三步。第一步，听得懂。也就是对阳明文化进行透彻准确的讲述，使学习者对阳明文化的本源具有初步的了解。第二步，接着讲。结合时代意义与时代特征，将阳明文化与现实联系起来，引起学习者的学习兴趣。第三步，对着讲。在这一步中，我们需要结合不同的文化背景进行跨文化的交流与沟通，通过传统文化的阐释将知识归纳转化成智慧。这个过程没有终点，它本身就是阳明文化发光发热的继续。我个人觉得，这样的过程发掘了阳明文化的生命力，使我们得到的智慧生生不息。就此看来，学人精神其实已经在上面的过程中体现出来了。但是光有学术的进步是不足以被称为学人精神的，我为它增加了一个新的要求："修身立德，知行合一。"这样合起来就是我心中的学人精神了。我心里所憧憬的社会，正是将这种学人精神推崇至社会精神高度的社会，当这样的精神成为人们思想世界的指导时，便是我心目中的大同社会了。

The Cultivation of a Person's Morality
Is "the Unity of Knowledge and Action"

Narrator: Luan Chengbin
Compiled by: Li Ming
Supervised by: Zhang Jingyan, Cai Liang

The man of the highest virtue confines himself to what is right and proper, and does not plan for his own advantage; he exhibits the truth of the doctrine, and does not devise schemes for acquiring fame and merit.

—Wang Yangming

The Way Stretches Endlessly Ahead: I Shall Search Heaven and Earth

I think it is very necessary to carry forward Yangming culture. Under fierce competition in the international world, we are required to develop our advanced culture cultivated during the period of struggle by our Party and our country, to stress our spiritual superiority in the competition of overall national strength, and to advocate our socialist values from different angles, different heights and different levels. Yangming culture has played an overall role in reaching this cultural goal. It has helped in building a harmonious atmosphere of culture in the process of cultural inheritance and transmission to promote the development of China.

Cultural inheritance and transmission takes place in a proper environment. As you know, I have been teaching in the Yangming College of Guizhou University. In my opinion, schools for general education established in several universities play an irreplaceable role in establishing a profound understanding of a variety of disciplines in students. Let's take Wang Yangming's doctrines as an example. Before students receive some general education about it, we find that many of them understand it in a quite limited range as a representative of idealism, while few students try to further their understanding of the basic contents apart from their textbooks. As we can also learn from those students interviewed, many students know about the philosophy of Wang Yangming from the several words found in their high school textbooks:

"In his early years, Wang Yangming firmly believed in 'studying the nature of things' of the Neo-Confucianism. He once observed bamboo, agonizing seven days and

195

seven nights without getting anything except for a serious illness due to anxiety. From then on, he began to question the Neo-Confucianism. Later, Wang Yangming was inspired by his Buddhist studies, beginning to understand that 'the principles of the sages lie in their self-satisfaction' and trying to negate 'studying the nature of things' by 'the truth lying in one's conscience'. During the suppression of the peasant uprising, he further realized the truth that 'it's difficult to keep your mind always clear'.

"Wang Yangming learned a lot of ideas from Buddhism, such as 'Buddha exists nowhere but in your heart', to promote his own ideology. In epistemology, he put forward the theory of 'conscience' and 'the unity of knowledge and action'. Yangming believed that 'conscience' as the inherent goodness of people, was a heavenly principle existent in their hearts. However, 'conscience' was often eroded by desires. That's why we should try to strengthen our moral cultivation to get rid of our desires and restore our goodness. In his theory of 'the unity of knowledge and action', all the knowledge and action stemmed from one's inner heart. So it is advisable to use 'conscience' to control our dominant behavior. However, Wang Yangming's theory cannot scientifically explain the relation between knowledge and action. After the mid-Ming Dynasty, Lu and Wang's thought spread widely. Later, the Neo-Confucianism, after several hundred years' development—has a profound impact on Chinese social politics, cultural education, ethics and morality."

This introduction is obviously not enough for tests, let alone for understanding a discipline, and for getting acquainted with a culture. Certainly, it would be impossible for us to perceive the spiritual world of a master.

Even so, the teaching conditions that we have for cultural curricula have enabled us to provide students with an in-depth traditional Chinese culture classes. In the aspect of hardware, now the traditional cultural teaching in universities has reached a very high standard and facilities for daily teaching are quite sufficient; in the aspect of software, the general education in many schools has its own strengths while the shortcomings are also obvious. For instance, in Yangming College of Guizhou University, where I work, there are some problems in the process of teaching and propagation of Yangming culture. These problems may not be very common, but they are representative. Here I would summarize them as follows:

1) The teaching content needs to be enriched. It is necessary for us to build a teaching plan in the public domain.

2) There is still a long way to go in the development of excellent courses in general education. Just like building a house, accumulation and participation from all

parts are quite essential.

3) There is a lack of a necessary incentive to improve the students' enthusiasm for learning, and this requires us to improve the weight of traditional culture learning in the students' individual comprehensive assessment.

If You Want to Discipline Others, Discipline Yourself First

As I have mentioned before, the understanding of a great number of my classmates about Yangming culture is refined to "the unity of knowledge and action" and "realizing conscientious wisdom". Now, let me share the examples I have encountered in my work.

We know that in Lu and Wang's thought, there are such statements as "keeping the natural law and abolishing the selfishness". For adolescent students, if it is understood in a literal way, Yangming culture can be labeled as an "oppression on human nature", which can be very backward. So, how, in fact, did Wang Yangming explain this statement?

"Keeping the natural law and abolishing the selfishness" is a statement from Zhu Xi, a famous philosopher in the Song Dynasty. Actually, when we learn some ideologies from some philosophers, we often make a deliberate misinterpretation out of context. Sometimes, this kind of understanding errors even leads us to a direction completely contrary to the real answers, which results in gaps and even mistakes in the process of cultural inheritance. "Diet, heavenly principle; delicious food, human desire." Zhu Xi gave his explanation of the differences between heavenly principle and human desire in his *Classified Utterances of Zhu Zi*. Now, we may explain Zhu's statement like "What is reasonable is heavenly principle". Thus, in the study of culture, it is not that we lack ways to learn and understand it, but whether we are willing to learn it.

To those bearers of cultural inheritance, it is very important to foster their interest in Yangming culture. This has brought forward higher requirements on teachers. So, how can we help foster students' interest in Yangming culture? First, teachers should have a thorough, accurate and fascinating understanding of Yangming culture. This is not just the requirement in school education, but also the great social responsibility for cultural inheritance. "To give a bowl of water to your student, you should already have a bucket of water." This sentence is a good reflection of a teacher's job. However, as a teacher, I need more than a bucket of water, but a bucket of clean running water. This is also what I just mentioned about the necessity of teachers' cultural understanding.

Cultural Perplexity in Agonized Travel

In modern society, not only Yangming culture, but many other ancient traditional culture elements have great practical significance. As for the origin, from the slavery society of antiquity to contemporary time, people have lived with the same environment. In the ancient time there was a collection of folk songs—*Book of Songs*, many chapters of which show us people's pursuit of a happy life and their desire to overcome difficulties. It has long been the incentive for the Chinese nation to move forward.

For the transmission of Yangming culture, I think it is absolutely no problem. It originated in the semi-late Ming Dynasty, the period when the three religions incorporated into one. On the surface, they are very different religions, but actually their pursuit of the ultimate value of life is interlinked. In Maslow's theory, they are all a personal value of self-fulfillment, which is seen as the highest value in the pursuit of life. Thus, those countries, under the influence by the cultures of Buddhism, Confucianism and Taoism, can find themselves influenced by Yangming culture. As a methodology, Yangming culture had a means of universal cultural instruction for people from different cultural flavors, and this kind of significance, which would not be blocked due to the differences in national culture and the barrier, is more common in humans. Nevertheless, the national characteristics Yangming culture contains are difficult to be accepted by people of different cultures. This requires a process. I will divide this process into three steps. The first step is to understand. It is a thorough accurate account of Yangming culture, so that learners can have a preliminary understanding of its origin. And the second step is to talk. With the incorporation of the significance and characteristics of time, Yangming culture is linked with reality, which arouses students' interest in learning. The third step is to speak. In this step, we need to combine different cultural backgrounds to conduct cross-cultural exchanges and communication and through the interpretation of traditional culture, to convert knowledge into wisdom. Yet there is no limit to this process. It is the continuation of the shining part of Yangming culture. Personally, I think such a process will help explore the vitality of Yangming culture, so that we get the wisdom of life and growth in nature. In this view, the scholarly spirit has in fact been reflected in the above process. But academic progress itself is not enough to be called a scholarly spirit, so I added a new requirement to it: the cultivation of our morality and the unity of knowledge and action. These two combined together are, in my mind, the scholarly spirit. The society I long for is one that promotes the scholarly spirit with the social spirit. When such a spirit becomes the guiding ideology of the world, in my mind the utopian society will be achieved.

文化创造未来

李　铭

指导教师：张静燕　蔡　亮

　　在此次社会实践中我采访了贵州大学历史与民族文化学院、中国文化书院、阳明学院专职教师，校聘副教授栾成斌老师。老师用易于理解的方式解答了以阳明文化为重要组成部分的中国传统文化的一些问题。他用自己的切身经验告诫我：作为文化的传承者，我们需要对阳明文化有准确透彻的理解。因为文化作为人类社会珍贵的精神财产，除了具有推动人类社会进步的巨大力量，同时也存在着将主流思想引入歧路的可能。我曾经读过刘慈欣先生所著的一部科幻小说，小说中对于文化灾难的可怕性描述在未来的背景下被无限放大，甚至关乎国家与民族的存亡。的确，科幻小说具有虚拟性，但其中所做的逻辑推理是非常合理的，值得为我们的未来敲响警钟。努力加深自己对于阳明文化的理解，不仅仅是对阳明文化这一传统文化瑰宝的尊重，更是对创建国家和民族美好明天的要求。老师告诉我，现在很多人对传统文化的传承并不看好，抱有悲观的态度，这是错误的。我们可以发现在现代社会的各行各业里，仍然不乏学习并实践阳明文化的建设者，从文化传播的角度来说也可以将他们称为不自觉的文化传承者。从以此为业的专家教授，到不经意间实践知行的能工巧匠，这些人在这个社会中将自己的经验与对文化的独特感知汇聚一体，并用这种文化赋予自己的劳动成果以源源不断的生命力。是的，人们的劳动成果不仅仅是一种物质财产，其中被赋予的文化与精神，在人类社会中是极具共鸣的。

　　所以，我觉得，很多人所担忧的传统文化衰亡问题，在文化未出现断层的情况下，是很难出现的。但是，这并不意味着不存在这种可能性。在不同文化剧烈碰撞的今天，我相信具有强大生命力的中华文化能够守住自己的根源，在世界民族文化之林开出一片绚丽的花海。

　　在此次阳明文化的探究之旅中，我收获了以前不曾接触过的与阳明文化有关的想法。其中一些是与我年岁相仿的大学生群体的想法，而另一些则来源于老师以及专业阳明文化研究者。这些不同的想法在我脑海中碰撞融合，构成了现在我脑海中阳明文化的整个框架图。尤记得第一次看到书上关于阳明先生事迹的介绍，那时我对阳明先生及其学说并无深入的理解。而现在我们的同学之中有相当大一部分人对于阳明文化的了解还是仅限于阳明格竹的故事与后人总结先生的"知行合一"与"致良知"。

直到现在，很多人仍然把"存天理，去人欲"解读为对人类天性的抑制，对于时值青春期的我们来说，若只看字面意思，阳明文化很容易被误解为抑制人性的落后文化。很不幸，在对栾老师的采访中我也犯了这样的低级错误；与此同时我又觉得自己非常幸运，栾老师非常耐心地指正了我的这个想法，栾老师说："存天理，灭人欲"这句话语出朱熹。很多时候我们学习一些思想家的思想文化，都是在脱离原典的情况下进行的，这样便不免断章取义。有时，这种理解上的错误甚至使我们得出与事实完全相反的答案，造成文化传承过程中出现缺漏乃至错误的现象。"饮食者，天理也；要求美味，人欲也。"朱熹在《朱子语类》中给出了他自己对于天理和人欲的区分，用现在的话来解释朱熹老先生的话就是："合理的便是天理。"作为朱熹先生学说辩证的继承者，阳明先生对这个问题的想法与朱熹先生并无不同。事实上，中国古代传统文化一直鼓励人们用自己的努力去改变自己的生活，使自己在符合"天理"的前提下追寻人生幸福。我们将阳明先生发现本心的人生态度与这种中国传统民族精神相结合，很容易就能发现阳明文化乃至中国传统文化所具有的对人追寻幸福的激励作用，这是我国民族精神中必不可少的一部分。

作为阳明文化传承者的我们其实很幸运，因为从根源来看，阳明文化与很多民族文化都存在共通之处：对道德的不倦学习，对人生幸福的不停追寻，对人类本心的自我发掘，对学习的不懈态度。这些为人类这个大群体所共同接受的思想，会以它们强大的生命力推动阳明文化成长前进，为人类未来的精神家园添砖加瓦。

团队成员：李　铭

Culture Creates the Future

Li Ming

Supervised by: Zhang Jingyan, Cai Liang

My interview during my social practice activity with the full-time teacher and associate professor, Dr. Luan Chengbin, of the College of History and Ethnic Culture, the Academy of Chinese Culture, and the Yangming College of Guizhou University benefited me a lot. Dr. Luan answered my questions about traditional Chinese culture with Yangming culture as major constituent parts in an easy and comprehensible way. He warned me with his own experience that as the inheritors of culture, we need to have an accurate and thorough understanding of Yangming culture, because culture, as the precious spiritual property of human society, not only has great power to promote the progress of human society, but also has the possibility of leading mainstream ideology into the wrong path. I once read a science fiction book written by Mr. Liu Cixin. The novel infinitely magnified the description of a terrible cultural disaster with the background of the future, which was connected to the survival of the country and the nation. Indeed, science fiction is fictitious, but its logical reasoning seems quite reasonable as a warning for our future life. Efforts to enhance our understanding of Yangming culture not only respects this traditional cultural treasure, but also requires us to create a better tomorrow for our country and nation. Dr. Luan told me that many people are not optimistic about the heritage of traditional culture. That is, they hold a pessimistic attitude, which is wrong. It can be found that in all walks of life in modern society, there is still no shortage of learners and practitioners of Yangming culture. From the perspective of cultural communication, they can also be called "unconscious cultural inheritors". No matter who the experts and professors are in this field, or the skillful craftsmen who practice the ideology unconsciously, these people have integrated their own experiences and unique perception of the culture, and it is this culture that endows continuous vitality to their work. It is true that the fruits of people's labor are not merely a kind of material property. The culture and spirit endowed are very resonant in human society.

Therefore, I think the decline of traditional culture about which many people are worried will not disappear in time as long as cultural dislocation does not take place.

However, this does not mean that there is not such a possibility. Nowadays, in the face of fierce collision of different cultures, I am convinced that Chinese culture with its strong vitality can hold on to its own roots, and blossom brilliantly out of the forest of the world's culture.

In this explorative tour of Yangming culture, I learned many ideas relevant to it that I had not heard of before. Some of these ideas are possessed by college students similar to my age, while others are derived from teachers and professional researchers of Yangming culture. These diversified ideas collide and mix in my mind to constitute a whole framework of Yangming culture. I still remember the first time I read the introduction to Wang Yangming's deeds in a book; at that time my understanding of this great scholar was quite shallow. However, now many of my fellow students' understanding of Yangming culture is still limited to Yangming's story of "studying bamboo" as well as "the unity of knowledge and action" and "realizing conscientious wisdom" summarized by his descendants.

Up to now, many people still interpret "Heavenly Principle and Human Desire" as an inhibition of human nature. To those of us who are in our adolescence, merely from the literal meaning, Yangming culture can be easily mistaken for such a backward culture. Unfortunately, during the interview I also made such a stupid mistake. But at the same time, I felt lucky to be patiently corrected by Dr. Luan as he said that the statement "Heavenly Principle and Human Desire" was derived from the famous philosopher Zhu Xi. More often than not, some philosophers' thoughts and cultures are learned without referring to their original sources as the proper context, and thus are misinterpreted. Sometimes, these misunderstandings may result in answers completely contrary to the fact, leading to gaps and even errors in the process of cultural inheritance. "Diet, heavenly principle; delicious food, human desire." Zhu Xi gave his explanation of the differences between heavenly principle and human desire in his *Classified Utterances of Zhu Zi*. Now, we may explain Zhu Xi's statement like "What is reasonable is heavenly principle". As a successor of Zhu Xi's dialectical theory, Wang Yangming has much in common with Zhu Xi in this issue. In fact, traditional Chinese culture has always encouraged people to make their own efforts to change their lives, pursuing their own happiness in accordance with the premise of "heavenly principle". If we combine Wang Yangming's life attitudes with traditional Chinese national spirit, it is easy to find that the inspiration offered by Yangming culture and traditional Chinese culture in their pursuit of happiness is an essential part of our national spirit.

As the inheritors of Yangming culture, we are actually very lucky, because from its origin, Yangming culture and many ethnic cultures have a lot in common: the tireless study of morality, the non-stop pursuit of happiness in life, the self-discovery of human conscience and an unremitting learning attitude. These ideologies are commonly accepted by large groups of people. They will push forward the growth of Yangming culture with their strong vitality and make great contributions to the future spiritual home of mankind.

Team member: Li Ming

谢建龙：吾心光明，世界光明

Xie Jianlong: The World Is Full of Light when My Heart Is Bright

谢建龙，浙江宁波余姚人，明代名臣谢迁后人，现任浙江余姚市历史文化名城研究会秘书长，常年致力于研究和宣传余姚当地名贤的工作。在任职期间，他著有《东山历代名人传记》《朱舜水的故事》等作品。

Xie Jianlong, descendant of the Ming Dynasty's famous Prime Minister Xie Qian, was born in Yuyao, Ningbo in Zhejiang Province. As the secretary-general of the Institute of Historical and Cultural City of Yuyao, he has been dedicated to the study and promotion of Yuyao local celebrities during his tenure. He has written *The Biographies of Celebrities in Dongshan*, *The Story about Zhu Shunshui* and other works.

吾心光明，世界光明

口述：谢建龙

整理：朱嘉平

指导教师：张静燕　蔡　亮

引　子

博学之，审问之，慎思之，明辨之，笃行之。

——王阳明

王阳明故居：独特的气质

王阳明故居坐落在浙江省余姚市龙泉山北麓，阳明西路以北，武胜门西侧。现存的王阳明故居并非完全是古迹，其中一部分是经过重新修建的复原品。那些得以保存下来的古迹，向我们展示了明朝时期士大夫阶层的生活。

"在绍兴还有个王阳明的'伯府'，但绍兴未能重视保护，远远没有我们余姚做得好。"在参观余姚王阳明故居时，谢建龙老师如此说道，语气中带有一些自信。

在联系余姚市历史文化名城研究会的时候，研究会得知我们几位学生想要参观王阳明故居并做采访后，十分热情地答应了，并且承诺对于故居或对于这次参观有什么问题或者要求他们都会全力满足。

于是我联系到了谢建龙老师。在来余姚之前，我的心里有些期待，有些好奇，也有着一些惴惴不安，但和谢老师见面并且短暂寒暄之后，谢先生的随和让我放下了心中的不安和紧张，然后，他便滔滔不绝、如数家珍一般向我们介绍起王阳明故居来。

故居是免费对外开放的，其中瑞云楼被改建成陈列馆。整座故居大致是按照古代士大夫阶层的生活情况布置的。

"王阳明故居的主体建筑是瑞云楼，也就是王阳明出生的地方，其实不是王阳明家的财产，而是王家向莫氏租借的。王阳明在此度过了他的童年时代。王阳明的父亲王华在明宪宗成化十七年（公元1481年）中了状元之后，皇帝就在绍兴为王华修建了状元府，那时王家就搬迁了过去。"谢建龙老师边走边向我们详细地介绍这座故居背后的故事。这座故居虽然经过修缮，但却看不出明显的修缮痕迹，尤其是从大门通往轿厅的那条石板路，虽然整体重修过了，却也经过了历史的变迁，充满了故居的历史厚重感和神秘感，让人与它接触的一瞬间就进入对历史风云进程的想象当中。由此可见，在游历这里的时候，我的心中是怎样的一种体验：

当我第一眼看到它时，除了斑驳好像没有词语可以贴切地形容这么一条石板路。虽然络绎不绝的人流与它非常的不相称，但这条石板路很符合这里的气质，莫名地让人肃然起敬。

余姚的王阳明故居保存的状况良好，内部的陈设将明代士大夫生活展示出来，每年也会接待来自五湖四海的参观者，接受他们的欣赏。

海峡两岸间的"阳明情谊"

瑞云楼在清乾隆年间曾毁于火灾，后来长期没有得到重建。因为阳明心学在日本有非常重要的影响，改革开放后，经常有日本友人来余姚寻访瑞云楼遗迹，当地的有识之士遂呼吁重建瑞云楼。于是在 20 世纪 80 年代，余姚市政府在原址上面重建了瑞云楼。故居修复后，来这里参观的日本友人就更多了。

"在王阳明心学产生之前，统治人们思想的是宋明理学，主张'存天理，灭人欲'。而王阳明心学强调，在行事的过程中，人的心占据着主导的地位——心就是主观能动性。阳明心学一经产生，犹如石破天惊，把人的思想彻底解放，由此也遭到当政者的仇视，被视为异端邪说，屡遭打击。但是阳明心学传到日本后，却风靡一时。正因为有阳明心学的指导，之后日本通过明治维新走上强盛的道路。"谢老师不仅说了王阳明心学与日本的渊源，还说了心学和中国台湾地区之间的联系。

"上个月，我们刚刚接待了中国国民党主席办公室一行，他们来到余姚就是为了拜谒王阳明故居，来瞻仰一下王阳明先生。"

这是一种很微妙的联系，它超越了政治经济文化的限制，成为海峡两岸之间联系的纽带：信仰和思想使得海峡两岸的人们站在了一起。真可谓是一种"阳明情谊"。

两岸间的"阳明情谊"不光如此。后来我与谢老师建立了微信联系，谢老师通过微信向我发出了邀请，希望我可以参与 2016 年冬至在余姚谢氏宗祠举行的祭祀仪式。因为谢建龙老师是明朝宰相谢迁的后人，所以他对于这次祭祀活动格外重视。谢老师表明，这是自 1949 年以来举行的最隆重的祭祀活动，到时候会有时任国民党主席洪秀柱亲自题写的匾额在谢氏宗祠悬挂起来，说罢便用图片向我展示了这块匾额。

匾额上书"森秀江东"，落款"余姚泗门谢氏宗祠惠存，中国国民党主席洪秀柱题"。

"森秀江东"四字精妙，字面盛赞余姚所拥有的王阳明在内的传统先贤文化，同时也将两岸人民中共有的那种"阳明情谊"表达得真真切切。我作为一个旁观者，此时竟也能体会谢老师对于先贤文化的珍惜。

"致良知"传承面临严峻的形势

在我之前的所有印象中，做研究的是非常神秘的一群人。这个群体似乎和普通大众有着太大的跨度。他们也许大多有着奇怪的脾气。但在与谢建龙老师的会面及参观王阳明故居的过程中，我们发现谢建龙老师是比较随和的一个人。参观过程中我们和谢建龙老师攀谈起来，在谈及老师的工作时，我问起了如何看待自己工作职责的问题，他这样回答："我做的工作其实非常简单，我们将余姚的先贤的生平以及思想编纂成书，向外界宣传，让大家都能够了解，能够欣赏这种文化。至于十分深层的现实意义，那是这一行业中真正的大学者所研究和探讨的内容。"

文化是民族的脊梁，名贤的思想是其中重要的一个部分，了解和学会欣赏，是正确认知传统文化的起步。谢老师以及其他文化传播的工作者所做的事情，无疑是对于人们的思想的启蒙和探索。

"现在的文化的传承往往流于形式，文化的形式已经和文化的内涵完全割裂开来。"

在之后的回访中，谢老师说起了那次王阳明故居一游结束之前，看到的故居外的情形。故居外聚集着非常多的游客，谢老师说，如果没有人为他们讲解，他们会走马观花一样将这座老宅看个大概，对于王阳明思想的内涵一知半解，看过了却毫无收获。无论是对于王阳明故居的全力保护还是全面开放，都很难解决现在人们文化常识缺失的问题，文化的传承面临着严峻的形势。

谢老师在回访中还提及了他曾经有一次在东北观看东北传统的祭祀仪式跳大神的经历。他说道，现在的人们对于跳大神的印象无非就是几个看似疯子的家伙张牙舞爪地跳着莫名其妙的舞蹈，他们并没有体会到的是这种看似荒诞迷信的祭祀仪式中的内涵。这些舞者为什么要这么做？这么做到底有什么历史渊源？它与过去的人们的生活会有什么紧密的联系？对于诸如此类的问题，观众们一无所知。

在回访的最后，谢建龙老师表达了一些他自己对于文化的传播的看法，大致意思是这样的：不论是这次的主题王阳明，还是我所研究的其他余姚的先贤，或是整个传统文化，对于当今社会对文化的此种态度，作为一个文化的传播者，我这一代的工作者有着不可推卸的责任。

在我看来，文化的传播面临如此严峻的形势，不光光是工作者的责任，文化的接受者也要为此负责。

在王阳明故居一游即将结束之际，我将"用声音叙事"以前的成果赠送给谢建龙老师，谢建龙老师在寄语卡上写下了这样的一句话："吾心光明，世界光明。"这句话让我想起了一句十分相似的话："你若光明，这世界就不会黑暗。"

今天来到王阳明故居与谢建龙老师的交流让我明白了很多，也让我第一次接触了像谢建龙老师一样的文化传播者。文化传播是个光明的职业，因为它让世界的现在和未来都充满光明。

"这是对你们大学生的勉励，在未来的道路上你们会遇到各种各样的麻烦和挫折，这个时候你只要记住这句话，只要你的心是光明的，世界也是光明的。"

带上谢建龙老师这句话，我们离开了王阳明故居。

The World Is Full of Light when My Heart Is Bright

Narrator: Xie Jianlong

Compiled by: Zhu Jiaping

Supervised by: Zhang Jingyan, Cai Liang

Studying extensively, inquiring accurately, thinking carefully, sifting clearly, practicing earnestly.

—Wang Yangming

Wang Yangming's Former Residence: Unique Temperament

The former residence of Wang Yangming is located in Longquan Mountain, north of Yangming West Road, and west of Wushengmen, Yuyao City, Zhejiang Province. The buildings are not entirely what they used to be, and some of them are restorations. These old things which have been preserved showed us the life of the bureaucratic class in the Ming Dynasty.

"There is also a former residence of Wang Yangming in Shaoxing, but people in Shaoxing do not pay attention to its protection. What they did in Shaoxing is far from the protection we do in Yuyao." When we visited the former residence of Wang Yangming in Yuyao, Mr. Xie Jianlong told us these words with a tone of great confidence.

I contacted the Institute of Historical and Cultural City of Yuyao about the interview. When the research institute learned that several students wanted to visit the former residence of Wang Yangming, they enthusiastically agreed and promised to meet our requirements to answer all the questions that might rise.

So I made an appointment with Mr. Xie Jianlong. Before I came to Yuyao, my heart was filled with expectations. I was curious, anxious and expected. But in actuality, Mr. Xie was easy-going, which made me feel at ease. He is so familiar with Wang Yangming that he could introduce the former residence of Wang Yangming in detail.

The residence is free and open to the public, and one of the buildings, called the Ruiyun Building, has been converted into a museum. The whole building was arranged according to the life of ancient scholarly bureaucracy.

The main building is the Ruiyun Building. This building did not belong to Wang Yangming. His family borrowed it from the Mo's family and Yangming spent his childhood here. After Wang Yangming's father Wang Hua won the award of Number One Scholar at the Ming Dynasty in 1481, the emperor built a house for him in Shaoxing, and then Wang Yangming moved there. As Xie Jianlong walked along, he gave us a detailed introduction of the story concerning the old house. Although the house was renovated, there were no obvious signs of repair, especially on the stone road from the gateway to the hall. It has gone through plenty of historical changes and is filled with a heavy sense of history and mystery, which immerse people in the imagination of this historical revolution. Then, what a special experience I got when I visited here is that at the first sight of such a stone road, no words other than "mottled" could be used to describe it. Although it does not seem appropriate with the constant stream of visitors all day, the stone road here is consistent with its temperament, giving out a sense of awe.

Obviously, the former residence of Wang Yangming in Yuyao was preserved in good condition, which shows us the life of the Ming Dynasty scholars. Every year, the residence receives appreciative and admiring visitors from all corners of the world.

The Yangming Connection between Both Sides of the Taiwan Straits

The Ruiyun Building had been destroyed because of fire and it nearly could not be repaired for a very long time. The preservation of Wang Yangming's Former Residence owes a lot to the Japanese. After the reform and opening-up, a lot of Japanese people came here to visit the former residence. At that time, some of those, who were knowledgeable, made great efforts to protect it. In the 1980s, the whole house was rebuilt by the government. After this, more Japanese came here to visit.

"The main philosophical trend before Wang Yangming's philosophy is Neo-Confucianism, whose opinion is 'to hold natural justice and exterminate desire'. Wang Yangming thought that the mind is the most important part when people are dealing with things and the mind is a subjective initiative. Wang Yangming's philosophy caused a great sensation and the theory was resisted by the governors. When the theory was spread to Japan, it became popular. Under the guidance of Wang Yangming's philosophy, Japan became stronger and stronger through Meiji Restoration." Xie Jianlong not only talked about the origin between Wang Yangming's philosophy and Japan, but also the connection between Wang Yangming's philosophy and Taiwan of China.

"A few months ago, we received some representatives from the presidential office of the chairman of the Kuomintang (KMT). They came to Yuyao to visit the former residence of Wang Yangming, and to pay tribute to Mr. Wang Yangming."

This is a very delicate relationship, which transcends the limits of policy, economy and culture, and has become the link between the two sides of the Taiwan Straits: It is the belief and idea that make people on both sides of the Taiwan Straits unite together. It is really the so-called Yangming connection.

The "Yangming connection" is more than just this. Mr. Xie and I have been in contact by WeChat. On WeChat, Mr. Xie sent an invitation to ask whether I could participate in the ceremony held on the winter solstice in the Yuyao Xie Ancestral Hall. Mr. Xie Jianlong is the descendant of Prime Minister Xie Qian in the Ming Dynasty, so he paid special attention to this festival. He suggested that this is the most solemn festival since 1949. The personal handwriting of former KMT chairman, Hong Xiuzhu, would be hung in the hall, so he showed me the tablet.

There are four Chinese characters—"Sen Xiu Jiang Dong"—on the board, and at the end of which inscribed, "Kept by Yuyao Simen Xie Zong Ancestral Hall, Chinese KMT chairman Hong Xiuzhu".

This remarkable inscription not only praises Yuyao's traditional sage culture, but also distinctly expresses the sincere Yangming relationship between people living on both sides of the Straits. As a bystander, I could already see what a cherished heart Mr. Xie has.

The Inheritance of "Conscience" Faces a Grim Situation

In all my previous impressions, researchers are a very mysterious group of people. This group seems to be greatly different from the general public, as most of them may have a strange temper. But when I met Xie Jianlong, in the process of visiting the former residence of Wang Yangming, I found that he was quite easy-going. During the visit, Xie Jianlong chatted with us and I asked him what he thought about his own responsibilities in his job, he replied, "My job is very easy. I put the life experience and thoughts of those Yuyao sages into books and show them to the outside world so that everyone can understand and appreciate this culture. The profoundly practical meaning of their thoughts is what the academicians will discuss and do research on."

Culture is the backbone of the nation, while the famous ideas of sages are one of the most important parts of it. Understanding and learning to appreciate is the starting line for the correct understanding of traditional culture. What has been accomplished by Xie Jianlong and other workers is undoubtedly the enlightenment and exploration of people's thoughts.

"Now, cultural heritage is often a mere formality and the form of culture has been completely separated from its connotation."

During my return visit, Mr. Xie talked about what we saw in front of the residence at the end of our trip. "There were so many tourists," Xie said, "if nobody explains it to them and they just look around by themselves, and they will know nothing about Wang Yangming or his thoughts. Although we open the residence to the public, it is difficult to solve the problem of people's lack of cultural knowledge. Cultural heritage is facing a grim situation."

Also during that return visit, Xie mentioned that once he had watched a ritual ceremony called Tiaodashen in the northeast of China. He said when it comes to Tiaodashen, people always think that it is just a kind of strange dance performed by some crazy people. However, they may not know the connotation of this seemingly absurd and superstitious ritual. Why do they do this? What is the historical origin? Does it have anything to do with the lives of people in the past? And so on. The audience may know nothing.

In the end, Xie Jianlong expressed his own views about the dissemination of culture. The main idea is whether it is about Wang Yangming or some other sages in Yuyao, or the traditional culture as a whole. As society has taken such an attitude about culture, culture workers of my generation have to take the responsibility.

In my opinion, facing such a severe situation, it is not only the responsibility of culture workers, but also that of the recipients of the culture.

Before we left, I presented our books as previous achievements to Xie Jianlong, who then wrote this sentence on the card: "My heart is bright; the world is full of light." This sentence reminded me of a very similar sentence: "If you are bright, the world will not be dark."

Actually, the discussion about Wang Yangming during this visit enabled me to understand a lot. It was my first time to connect with such cultural communicators like Xie Jianlong. Culture communication is a bright career because it makes the world's present and future full of light.

"This is to encourage college students like you. In the future you will face a lot of troubles and frustrations. As long as you remember this sentence and your heart is bright, the world is full of light."

So, with this sentence, we leave the former residence of Wang Yangming.

精神的实践是对文化最好的传承

朱嘉平

指导教师：张静燕　蔡　亮

2016 年暑假，我对谢老师进行了一次回访。在回访中，他提及了曾经有一次在东北观看东北传统的祭祀仪式跳大神的经历。他说道，现在的人们对于跳大神的印象无非就是几个看似疯子的家伙张牙舞爪地跳着莫名其妙的舞蹈，他们并没有体会到的是这种看似荒诞迷信的祭祀仪式中的内涵。这些舞者为什么要这么做？这么做到底有什么历史渊源？它与过去的人们的生活会有什么紧密的联系？对于诸如此类的问题，观众们一无所知。

"现在的文化的传承往往流于形式，文化的形式已经和文化的内涵完全割裂开来。"

这是在这次对谢建龙老师进行回访时，谢建龙老师说到的一句让我产生共鸣的话，这句话是我在参与这次社会实践活动的所见所闻当中体会最深刻的一点：文化的传播流于形式，精神内涵的传承正在面临着十分严峻的形势。

这让我想起了几个月前看到的一个视频。在北京卫视《传承者》的节目中，一个鼓艺表演节目结束之后，几位青年代表对这一个节目发表自己的看法。有的人说这是小众艺术，有的人说没有特点。青年们的争论最后变成激烈的争吵。此时的陈道明突然起来怒斥几位青年代表，说道："你们或许有很高的知识，但对于传统文化，你们连常识都没有！"

事实确实如此，几位青年气势汹汹地争论了一大堆，但他们讨论的问题也仅仅是停留在这个鼓艺表演的表面：它的形式。对于鼓的高超的表演技巧、鼓的丰富的表演方法、鼓和中华文化的紧密的关系等等问题，他们从来没有思考过，从来没有调查过，因为他们对这些一无所知。

在回访的最后，谢建龙老师表达了一些他自己对于文化的传播的看法，大致意思是这样的：

不论是这次的主题王阳明，还是我所研究的其他余姚的先贤，或是整个传统文化，作为一个文化的传播者，对于当今社会对文化的此种态度，我这一代的工作者有着不可推卸的责任。

世人对于一种文化的误解固然是和谢老师那样的文化传播工作者在工作上的失误有着直接的关系，但在我看来，错误往往不会是单方面导致的，其中更有着文化接受者的责任。现在的社会娱乐文化当道，快餐式的文化消费习惯导致人们渐渐不会在遇到事情的时候加以思考，加以判断，对于一种文化无论是传统的还是外来的认识越来越浅薄，人们越来越重视文化形式所展示的娱乐性和趣味性，与此同时，欣赏层次也随着认识的浅薄而降低，让现在的文化空有形式，缺乏灵魂。

1986版《西游记》家喻户晓，导演杨洁在节目中被问起它红火三十年长盛不衰的原因，她说道："说实在的我没有想到《西游记》会红火三十年，《西游记》的精神应该健康地传下去。要说为什么，因为我们在搞艺术。"在杨洁的眼中，《西游记》的完美演绎，就是对于西游精神的传承。为什么1986版《西游记》如此轰动？不光光是演员对表演技巧的严格的要求，更是一种对于传统文化中所拥有的坚忍、脚踏实地的"西游精神"的理解和坚持，让这部电视剧真正有了它的灵魂。

这次社会实践活动的主题是"我是阳明青年"。我们采访了企业家、工匠、专家学者，还有慈善家，他们都是传承者。与普通的文化受众不同的是，他们将王阳明的思想精神和中国传统文化的内涵融入自己的生活工作的每一件事情，不管是有心还是无意，他们因此所做出的贡献都是不可忽视的。当然还有参与这次社会实践活动的我们。这次与谢老师的接触让我了解到了将文化传播作为职业的这一类人的生活和思想，也让作为学生的我由此明白了：形式的传播不能永恒，惟有精神的实践才可以让文化永远葆有旺盛的生命力，从而长久地传承下去。

团队成员：朱嘉平 李 铭 车晚静 胡 双

Spiritual Practice, the Best Way for Cultural Inheritance

Zhu Jiaping

Supervised by: Zhang Jingyan, Cai Liang

In the summer vacation of 2016, I had a return visit to Xie Jianlong. At this return visit, Mr. Xie mentioned a special time when he had ever watched a ritual ceremony called Tiaodashen in the northeast of China. He said when it comes to Tiaodashen, people always think that it is just a kind of strange dance performed by some crazy people. However, they may not know the connotation of this seemingly absurd and superstitious ritual. Why do they do this? What is the historical origin? Does it have anything to do with the lives of people in the past? And so on. The audience may know nothing.

"Now the cultural heritage is often a mere formality and the form of culture has been completely separated from the cultural connotation."

At the return visit, what Mr. Xie said has stricken a chord with me. This sentence may be the most important and the most impressive to me during this social practice activity. Cultural transmission is often a mere formality and the heritage of the cultural connotation is facing a serious situation.

This reminds me of a video a few months ago. In the program of "Heritage" in Beijing Satellite TV channel, after a drum art show, several young representatives expressed their views on this program. Some said that this art is for small minority and some said the program did not have any characteristics. The debate among these young people finally turned into a heated argument. Suddenly, Chen Daoming angrily refuted these young people. He said, "You may have very rich knowledge, but you do not have any common sense about traditional culture!"

Indeed, although the young people argued a lot, what they discussed only stays at the surface of this drum performing art: just its form. They ignored the superb performance skill of drums, rich ways of performing and its close relationship with Chinese culture and so on. They never thought deeply and investigated, because they are completely ignorant about it.

At the end of the return visit, Mr. Xie Jianlong expressed some of his own views on the spread of culture. Following is the general meaning:

Whether it is about Wang Yangming or some other sages in Yuyao, or the traditional culture as a whole, as society has taken such an attitude about culture, culture workers of my generation have to take the responsibility.

However, even though people's misunderstanding on traditional culture is closely connected with the cultural workers, in my opinion, mistakes are often not unilateral. Culture receivers should also take the responsibility for it. In nowadays society, the entertaining culture is in power; habits of fast-food cultural consumption gradually make people not think and judge when they confront things. Their understandings of a culture, wherever it comes from, are getting much shallower and people always pay more and more attention to the interestingness and entertainment exhibited by culture. At the same time, people's level of appreciation is going down along with the shallow understanding, which makes culture superficial and a lack of soul.

The 1986 edition of *Journey to the West* is known to every household. The director, Yang Jie was asked why this TV series could be booming for 30 years. She said, "Indeed, I did not expect it can be popular for 30 years. The spirit of *Journey to the West* should be inherited. It is because what we are really doing is making art." In the eyes of Yang Jie, the way to show the spirit of *Journey to the West* is just to perfectly practice it. Why can the 1986 edition of the *Journey to the West* cause a sensation? It is not only because of the strict requirements on the skill, but also an understanding and persistence of the "journey spirit" which is tough and down-to-earth. This makes the TV drama have its own soul.

The theme of this social practice is "I'm a Young Practitioner of Yangming Philosophy". We went to interview the craftsmen, entrepreneurs, experts, scholars and philanthropists. They are all inheritors. What makes them to be different from the common receivers is that they have integrated Wang Yangming's thought into everything in their own normal life, whether it is intended or not. Accordingly, their contributions cannot be ignored. Of course, we as participants are also included. This communication with Mr. Xie enables me to understand the life and thought of cultural workers like Mr. Xie. As a student, from this activity, I understand that culture transmission as a formality cannot stay forever, but only spiritual practice can make traditional culture energetic and everlasting.

Team members: Zhu Jiaping, Li Ming, Che Wanjing, Hu Shuang

第五章

Chapter Five

Public Service Spirit

公益精神

导 言

Introduction

公益精神，是为公共利益和福祉的奉献精神，这种精神是个体履行社会契约精神的心理自觉，也是个体与世界构建对话系统的行动方案。阳明先生"万物一体之仁"的思想即是滋养公益精神的哲学基础。他说："以天地万物为一体，其视天下之人，无外内远近，凡有血气，皆其昆弟赤子之亲，莫不欲安全而教养之，以遂其万物一体之念。""视天下为一家，中国犹一人"情怀是阳明先生"致良知"思想的具体表现形式，公益行为为个体从生存需求向自我实现需求迈进提供了现实路径和情感通道。

阳明思想中的亲民思想对公益精神的形成同样有启迪意义。阳明先生在著名的《亲民堂记》中写道："吾以亲民为职者也，吾务亲吾之民以求明吾之明德也夫！"他视热爱人民为职责所在，更视为民服务为光明道德追求的必由之路，所以才能做到"惩己之忿，窒己之欲，舍己之利，惕己之易，明己之性"。亲民思想的敬畏百姓之意跃然纸上，同理，公益精神是人作为社会成员敬畏自然、敬畏他人、敬畏内心的表达。古语道：天有德降甘霖润万物，地有德生五谷养众生，人有德经四方济苍生。时代呼唤社会、个体和包括大学在内的组织探索弘扬公益精神的载体和方法，不同行业和领域的公益人士也正在通过他们的公益行为改变着中国。

技艺之道，惟精惟一；天得一则清，地得一则宁，工匠得一则生。所谓工匠精神，大道至简，一以贯之；即守一德、专一经、执一艺，修之于身而化之于行。工匠精神对于制造业从业者而言就是固本培元，本即发展的根本和生存追求，元是发展的元气和生命追求。工匠精神是一种沉着、精益求精的心性，是对心性长久磨砺之后形成的气质，秋山师承中"守破离"三法则，即匠人安身立命的策略，也是匠人由术入道的升华。

（蔡 亮 撰写）

余志伟：听从内心，成就梦想

Yu Zhiwei: Act upon Your Conscience and Build Your Dreams

余志伟，浙江大学宁波理工学院管理学院教授。他热爱教育事业，严谨治学、爱生敬业、教书育人、为人师表，在平凡的教学岗位上默默坚守；热爱公益，践行公益，曾带队赴川西支教，协助管理学院成立公益创业中心，创立益立方公益创业班；专注教学，获得青年教师教学技能竞赛第二、三等奖；勇于创新，组织"企业家进课堂"，提出并践行"分享式学习"；关注社会价值，通过班导师、社团指导教师等角色传递价值、影响年轻人。

Professor Yu Zhiwei from the School of Business, Ningbo Institute of Technology, Zhejiang University, is dedicated to his teaching, with a love for his students, a passion for education and a rigorous approach to academic research. He also devotes his efforts to public welfare in practice. He not only organized an assistance teaching team in Sichuan, but also assisted the school with the establishment of the Center for Social Entrepreneurship and started courses in Yi Lifang Social Entrepreneurship. Being devoted to teaching, he received second and third prizes in Young Teachers'

Teaching Skills competitions; being creative, he explored a new teaching approach with entrepreneurs, introduced it into the classroom, and proposed the Experience-Share Learning Mode in class. He spreads an individual's social value among young students as a tutor and an adviser of students' associations.

听从内心，成就梦想

口述：余志伟
整理：高梦婷
指导教师：阮　征

引　子

须先有根然后有枝叶，不是先寻了枝叶，然后去种根。

——王阳明

初识公益求真知

说到公益，其形式有多种多样，众所周知的有红十字会，民间的很多活动也都在公益的范畴之内。与公益结缘，更多的可能还是归结于我的性格。年轻的时候为一些事而愤懑不平，随着年纪的增长，我便想去做一个建设者，做一些行之有效的事情，试图去改变一些现象。同时，我的本职工作是教书育人，成为老师之后也接触到了很多事很多人，一些机缘巧合也促使我做公益。在某个瞬间某个人可能就能改变你的想法。比如在 2012 年，我去了天童寺，在那里遇到了一个日本老人——佐伯文雄。他在退休后自学中文并成为中文硕士。他热衷于中国文化，曾只身来到中国去寻找在唐代很盛行的金粉文字的传承人。听到之后我内心受到了很大的触动。令我十分佩服的是他能够在老年时期通过自学并实地考察去完成自己的心愿。当时我也请他为我写了八个字：听从内心，成就梦想。正是这几个字，在我心中埋下了坚持的种子，听从内心，从内心出发。就是王阳明先生所说的"致良知"。

作为一名教师，我认为公益的字面定义是"公共利益"。在当前的教育体制下，我们追求的即是成绩，从某种程度上也可称为功利。随着时代的变迁，应试压力一代比一代大，从小学起学生就要面对各种压力，不能输在起跑线上。到了大学，大家都是机械性地应付考试，或是为了拿奖学金而去学习，更有甚者会采取一些不合理手段去达到自己的目的。在这种教育背景下，有太多的功利者。钱理群老先生对此的形容即是：精致的利己主义者。在我看来，每个人从根本上来说是一个社会人，社会人所强调的是共同利益。我们所希望的是，大家都生活得更好，社会共同进步，这即是公益。我作为一名教师，公益与教育两者恰好可以结合。前几年，我也曾摇摆不定，参加公益需要大量时间，但作为教师我也需要大量精力去完成学校的教学工作与科研指标。但是，后来我与同伴们发现，公益与教学研究可以合二为一。在学校里，我们开设了公益创业班。我所主讲的三门课程，运营管理、创新创业实务、互联网思维商业模式创新都与公益有联系。在上个学期，我们申请了一门名为"公益创新实务"的课程作为全校的选修课。因此，公益与教学是能够很好地结合的。

余志伟先生在讲解

践行公益致良知

在参加了支教等公益活动后，感触愈发深刻。我认识到我们在参加公益活动时有一个误区，总是站在自己的角度去看待受助方。我们所认为的方式并不能为对方所接受。每年参加完公益活动后，我们的团队都会思考并分享心得。我认为我们不应对自己所做的好事沾沾自喜，而是应该着眼于真正对受助方有益的事。例如在支教时，我们希望把知识与好的资源带给受助的孩子们。但是这对他们来说也有负面影响，一些当地的孩子可能在支教队伍走后不适应当地的师资力量与学习氛围，产生抵触情绪。因此我们需要发展公益教学的可持续性。第一，教育的本身在于家庭，我们在支教时也进行了家访并且召开了两次家长会与家长交流。第二，教育的可持续性需要政府支持，我们也请当地机构许诺为学校配备更好的资源。在往后的公益活动中，我们将更好地将自己的想法与当地实践结合，让他们真正地受益。

我们在学校里开设了益立方公益创业班，选拔三十名学生加入，目的是培养公益创业类的人才与懂得运作公益项目的人才。在基金会的支持与指导下，我们制订了培养模块与框架。同时我们会以公益界的名人为主，邀请他们与学生进行交流和指导。从某种程度上来说，公益创业班不是个班级而是一个团队。在这个团队中，每个学生们都有志于从事公益并且注重团队精神。许多公益活动顺利进行，也得益于我们强大的学生团队与师资力量。如何去传递爱与如何影响下一个人也是我们这一团队所需要考虑的。

　　如今，公益事业正如火如荼地进行，发展前景十分美好。一些民间的公益组织会起到很好的引导作用。随着公益事业的发展，越来越多的人会渴望有所担当，建设更和谐的社会。在公益蓬勃发展的同时，当代市场规则并不是很完善，因而会有许多人、组织、机构等破坏规则，以公益之名获取不正当利益。例如乞讨，最初只是被生活所迫的人在乞讨，而现在则出现了许多职业的"乞讨人"。黑格尔曾说过："存在即合理。"破坏市场规则的行为的存在在某种程度上来说是好事。在市场规则并不是很完善的情况下，有人破坏规则，就必然会有人去完善规则。这有助于公益这个行业更好地发展。公益行业的发展需要公益精神的延续。公益精神的延续首先需要政府重视，加大宣传与资金投入，其次需要社会支持、草根组织壮大。最重要的是个人，每个人都应自立自强，做好自己，学会传递爱并去影响下一个人。这样公益精神才能在当代青年中不断延续下去。

余志伟先生与团队成员合影

王阳明先生在心学体系中强调了"知行合一"的行事方法，主张"致良知"，良知与实践的统一。在岁月大河的淘洗中，阳明心学能够传承下来必然有其包容性与适应性并且具有普世价值。在我的观点里，"知"为世界，"行"为自己，"知行合一"即是世界与自我的统一。每个人在成长过程中会试图认识真正的自己并将自己完全融入这个世界，这个过程也是"知行合一"的过程。不能认清自己或有过高的个人标准不能与世界融合则不能称为"知行合一"。在 2013 年至 2014 年间我曾到美国，在半年的时间里试图寻找中西文化的差异。而后来我认识到，无论何种文化之间，都是同多于异。虽然美国不贩卖活禽，都是将其处理好之后再售卖，饮食更偏向于科学化，而中国饮食则是更偏向于经验化，但是中西文化即使"形"不同，"神"，即内在，也是相同的。每种文化的出发点都是一个：使生活更美好。因此在更多的时候，我们应追求融入，感受不同文化，这便是"知行合一"。通过投身于公益事业拥有了一个好的名声并不重要。在这个过程中，寻找自我，"致良知"，才是真正至关重要的。"三人行，必有我师。"同行者与受助者都能成为我们的老师，让我们提升自己。公益不光是一项事业，更是提升自我的方式。

Act upon Your Conscience and Build Your Dreams

Narrator: Yu Zhiwei

Compiled by: Gao Mengting

Supervised by: Ruan Zheng

There must first be roots before there can be leaves and branches. One does not seek to find leaves and branches and then cultivate the root.

—Wang Yangming

Starting My Way to True Knowledge with Public Welfare Service

Public welfare ranges in forms from the Red Cross which is well known around the world to various localized folk activities. Engaging in public welfare is relevant to my personality. When I was young, I tended to be cynical with regard to things that were unfair. However, as I grew older, I learned to channel my feelings into constructive and effective actions in order to bring about change. As the same time, my teaching career has offered me a range of contacts and opportunities to experience, which also leads me to public welfare. It is true that the right person might change your mind at the right moment. For example, in 2012, I got acquainted with an old man from Japan in Tiantong Temple, who received a self-taught Master's Degree in Chinese language after he retired. Keenly interested in Chinese culture, he once came to China alone to look for inheritors of gilt scripts which were popular in the Tang Dynasty. I was greatly moved by his determination in this undertaking and his courage in pursuing his dream through self-study and doing field research in China far away from his hometown even in his senior years. It was he who wrote me the eight Chinese characters "听从内心，成就梦想", which means acting upon your conscience and building your dreams. Moreover, it was these eight Chinese characters that gave me the motivation to persist. In my view, these eight characters mean the same as what Wang Yangming referred to as "realizing conscientious wisdom".

As a teacher, I understand public welfare literally as "shared benefit". Under the current system of education, what students pursue is high grades. To some extent, it is a utilitarian view. With changing times, the present generation suffers from more exam pressure than ever because the tension begins in elementary school with the idea that none wants to lose at the starting line. It is common to see that students in college now study by memorization just for tests, or who learn well in order to win scholarships even by unreasonable means. Given this educational background, no wonder so many utilitarian-minded people exist. Qian Liqun once described these people as exquisite egoists. In my opinion, each person is fundamentally a social being who shares common interests. We all hope for a better life for each person and progress for the whole of society. This is public welfare. What exactly I can do as a teacher is to integrate public welfare with my career in education. A few years ago I used to hesitate, for fear that public welfare activities would cost me a lot of time and energy that could supposedly be used for school teaching and scientific research. Later, our team found that public interest and teaching research can be combined. Therefore, we set up the entrepreneurship class. Three courses I take charge of are Operation Management, Innovative Business Practices, and Innovation of Internet-based Business Modes, all of which are relevant to public welfare. Last semester, we set up a course named "Public Welfare Innovation Practice" as the school elective course open to different majors. In this way, my efforts in public welfare are combined with my teaching career.

Realizing Conscientious Wisdom through Practice

I have been getting more involved and having more thinking since I engaged in public welfare activities such as volunteering to teach in a remote rural area. I realize that a gap often exists between us public welfare volunteers and recipients of our help, because we mostly offer a helping hand from our own perspective without asking the recipients about their needs. The way we offer help is not always well accepted by them. From time to time, our team members will get together to reflect with pride and satisfaction on our experiences of public welfare activities each year. However, I think we should not become complacent about our efforts. Instead, it's more critical to do something truly helpful for the recipients. For instance, when we teach in a rural area, we bring knowledge and good resources to the children. But it must be admitted that our good deeds could also bring negative effects to them. Each time after we leave those rural children, some of them may become dissatisfied with the local teachers and the learning atmosphere, even resisting learning in their school. So we need to develop the sustainability of such volunteering assistance teaching. Firstly, education itself starts with family and depends on family to a large extent, so we conduct home visits and hold two parent-school meetings to communicate with the parents. And secondly, sustainability of education requires government support, so we also request promises from the local institutions to ensure better resource supplies for the school. In future public welfare activities, our practices will be better adapted to the local situation in order to benefit children there to the best degree.

In our school, we set up a class named Yi Lifang Social Entrepreneurship and selected thirty students to join us in order to train their talents for social entrepreneurship and to better understand the operation of public welfare projects. With the foundation's support and guidance, we created a training module and framework. At the same time, we invited celebrities in public welfare to our class to interact with and give guidance to the students. To some extent, this social entrepreneurship class is not a class but a team. In this team, each member is dedicated to public welfare development with a team spirit. At present, many public welfare activities are going smoothly, which is benefited from our strong teamwork with students and teachers. What we need to consider next is how to invite the next person to engage in public welfare by delivering love.

Currently, public welfare is developed in full swing and has great prospects. Some folk public welfare organizations take a very good leading role. With the development of public welfare, more and more people are becoming passionate about being personally responsible for creating a more harmonious society. While at the same time, since the present market rules are deficient, some people, organizations and institutions are attempting to make improper profits for themselves in the name of public interest regardless of market rules. Beggars are supposed to be those who beg for survival, but now turn out to be professional beggars for wealth. Hegel once said "what exists is reasonable". In a sense, it is a good phenomenon to see violation of the market rules because in such a condition with imperfect rules there must be someone who is attentive to improving them, which is the right way to better develop public welfare. What's more, the development of public welfare involves the continuation of public spiritedness. To continue public spiritedness, the government's efforts to enhance publicity and funding are fundamentally necessary, and the support from society and grassroots organizations is also needed. But most important of all is the individual. Everyone should be independent, self-reliable, self-disciplined and learn to how to influence the next person with love. Only in this way, can the public spiritedness be passed on to the younger generation.

Wang Yangming emphasizes the way to realize "the unity of knowledge and action" and advocates practice aiming at "realizing conscientious wisdom". In the years through history, Wang Yangming's Philosophy of Mind has been well inherited and universally valued because of its inclusiveness and adaptability. In my opinion, "knowledge" means the outside world and "action" means oneself. "The unity of knowledge and action" refers to the harmony between the world and oneself. A person's growth is realizing the true self and adapting well to the world, and this is also the process of "the unity of knowledge and action". Anyone who does not know himself well or who has too high expectations of the world which are far from reality, cannot achieve "the unity of knowledge and action". I was in the United States for half a year from 2013 to 2014 with the aim of looking into the differences between Western and Chinese cultures. Unexpectedly, I realized there are more commonalities than differences between any two cultures in the world. In the United States, people don't sell live poultry but clean it before sale in a methodical way while the Chinese diet tends to be more experience-based. After all, even if Chinese and Western cultures are different in form, the core values are similar. The starting point of every culture is to make life better. Therefore, we should feel open to different cultures with the pursuit of integration among them most of time. This is also "the unity of knowledge and action". It is not the fame that we've built through engagement in public welfare, but the process of knowing oneself and "realizing conscientious wisdom" that counts. As we often say that we can always find something to learn from people who keep us company, team members and recipients can also be our teachers to help us improve ourselves. Public welfare is not only a career, but is also the way to self-improvement.

身体力行，为求真知

高梦婷

指导教师：阮　征

　　转眼之间我们已经度过了两年的大学时光。回首过去的两年，感觉自己不曾存在于这所大学，每天只是上课、吃饭、睡觉，默默无闻，不曾做过什么引以为傲的事。因此我参加了"用声音叙事"社会实践，渴望去突破、提升自己，希望在大学四年的时间中不留遗憾。

　　在参加这次"用声音叙事"社会实践之前，我对于王阳明先生的了解仅限于高中历史书本上对心学体系的一个大概介绍。同时，我也是第一次作为一个采访人进行采访活动。对于性格较为内向的我来说，采访是一个很大的挑战。在前期准备中，我通过上网查找等方式寻找王阳明先生的资料以及他毕生所推崇的理念，进而对王阳明先生有了一个更深入的了解。王阳明先生不仅仅是心学体系的创始人，更是一个教育家、公益家。在心学体系中，最著名的就是"致良知""知行合一"。

　　何为"致良知"？何为"知行合一"？王阳明先生对其的解释就是在实际行动中实现良知，行动与良知得到统一。王阳明先生在《传习录》中说，只有先有虔诚的心，才会有结果。比如树木，虔诚的心是树根，那体现出来的具体事项就是树叶，必须先有根才会有枝叶，而不是先寻求枝叶，然后才去种树根。人也是如此，只有先拥有一颗善心，才会做出大大小小发自内心的善事。而我的采访对象，管理学院的余志伟老师，在不知不觉中做到了这几点。余志伟老师的本职工作是教书育人，但是他也已投身于公益事业很多年，如赴川西支教、建立"益立方公益学院"等。

　　"用双脚度量，用双耳聆听，用双眼洞察，用心感悟。"这是余志伟老师写给阳明青年的寄语。我们对于一件事的理解不应只是停留在纸上谈兵的阶段，自己切身实践才是最重要的，用双脚、双耳、双眼去感知。通过实践，开阔视野，多角度考量，才能真正将其理解透彻，从而做到"知行合一"。公益也是如此。嘴上说说不是公益，身体力行才是公益。如某位在中国乃至国外都被热议的公益人物，许多人批评他是作秀，将自己过度暴露在闪光灯下。但从本质上说，他是真正的公益人，他确确实实地用钱与物资帮助了那些需要帮助的人。和那些只是纸上谈兵的人来比好了太多。如今公益势头发展正旺，许多平民百姓都加入了公益的行列。例如在微博上，我们总能看到许多募捐请求与网友们自发组织的捐款活动。

每个人捐款的数目有多有少，但用意都是一样的，捧着一颗善心希望能够温暖他人。正如王阳明先生所认为的有叶必先有根，做善事的出发点是有一颗善心，然而却有人利用他人的善意来敛财，恰巧与王阳明先生主张的"存天理，去人欲"相反。这些人保存私欲，抛弃天理。

一两年前，天津曾发生过一起轰动全国的爆炸事件，人员伤亡严重。一方有难，八方支援。很快就有许多人通过各种渠道送去物资。在微博上，有一个网友谎称自己的父亲在爆炸中不幸遇难，在医院中见了父亲最后一面。她利用网友的同情心骗取了大量的捐款。随后这一骗局被揭穿，网友们愤怒的同时，更多的是伤心。打着公益的幌子，利用别人的善心来敛财，可能是世界上最可耻的事了吧。如今街上的假乞丐比比皆是，新的公益骗术层出不穷，国人的善心正在被消磨。但若是换一个角度来看，各种骗术的出现也证明了现在社会上的善良大于恶意，许多人看到别人有困难时不是选择事不关己高高挂起，而是会伸出援助之手。一个人的力量可能微不足道，但一个人可以影响身边的人。在这个过程中，越来越多的人加入这个队伍中，公益的队伍发展壮大，社会因此也更加美好和谐。我们不应因社会上的恶意而放弃去帮助真正有困难的人。不忘初心，方得始终。帮助他人，同样也会得到别人善意的回馈。

我们在人生的道路上会遇到各种各样的人和事，正如余志伟老师所说：用双脚度量，用双耳聆听，用双眼洞察，用心感悟。身为当代青年，对于事物片面的理解是不够的，我们应放下偏见，身体力行，探求真知。在这个过程中也许会有困难，但困难也正是一种磨炼。酸甜苦辣才是生活。

团队成员：高梦婷　单娇巧　贾雅婷

Value the Practical Process of Personally Pursuing True Knowledge

Gao Mengting
Supervised by: Ruan Zheng

Time flies, and it has been two years since I left home for college. Looking back, I felt that I had hardly proved my worth in this college because I had just led a routine life by taking classes, having meals, and resting there without any real achievements I could feel proud of. This is one reason why I joined this social activity named "Beyond the Voices", hoping for some personal development so I would not have regrets during my four-year college life.

One the one hand, before my participation in this social activity, my limited knowledge about Wang Yangming came from a brief introduction to the Philosophy of Mind in a high-school history textbook. On the other hand, it presented a big challenge to me, an introvert, for this was the first time that I had conducted interviews as an interviewer. To prepare for this interview, I searched online for information about Wang Yangming and his ideas so that I came to know that Wang Yangming was not only a founder of the Philosophy of Mind but also an educator and someone who was devoted to public welfare. In terms of the Philosophy of Mind, the two theories that are the most widely-accepted are "realizing conscientious wisdom" and "the unity of knowledge and action".

What do "realizing conscientious wisdom" and "the unity of knowledge and action" refer to exactly? Wang Yangming's explanation is realizing conscientious wisdom through actual action and thus achieving the unity of action and conscience. *Instructions for Practical Living* records what Wang Yangming once said that achievements result from a devout heart. Taking a tree as an example, the root is the devout heart with leaves as concrete and real reflections. It is the law that the root breeds branches and leaves, and the reverse is not true. This is also the case with human beings, whose devout hearts guide them to do good earnestly. In my view, the interviewee, Professor Yu Zhiwei, understands and realizes this law in his life. Besides his teaching work, he has been devoted to public welfare for many years by supporting teaching projects in the west of Sichuan and setting up the Yi Lifang Social Entrepreneurship Academy.

"Measure with the feet, listen with the ears, watch with the eyes, and experience by the heart" is the note that Professor Yu wrote to us young students. Our comprehension about something can be better gained through our personal practice with our feet, ears and eyes rather than mere paper talk. Only through practice can we understand the world completely with broad horizons and multiple perspectives, consequently achieving "the unity of knowledge and action". This rule holds true when engaging in public welfare for it is not achieved only by saying but through practicing to put the ideology into reality. For example, there is such a public welfare character who has aroused hot debate in China and even elsewhere in the world. Many people criticized him for his excessive exposure to the media. However, I think he is firstly a real public welfare character because he contributed money and supplies to help those in need. Compared to those with mere paper talk, this man did better. At present, public welfare is prospering in China with more and more ordinary people engaging in it. For example, we see someone requests a donation and thus donating activities are organized voluntarily by netizens on Weibo. No matter how much people donate, what is certain and common is their warm and generous heart towards others. A good heart is the starting point of doing good deeds like a tree's root to grow branches and leaves according to Wang Yangming. However, some people take advantage of others' goodwill to raise money, which is contrary to Wang Yangming's proposition to uphold justice, and to refrain from selfish desire.

A sensational explosion happened a year or two ago caused a lot of casualties in Tianjin. On hearing about the disaster, people from every corner offered a helping hand. Soon after, lots of supplies were sent there through various channels, while a netizen successfully defrauded others of a large amount of online donations with her lie that her father died in the explosion. Netizens felt sad more than angry when the fraud was exposed because it is among the most shameful acts to make money under the cover of public welfare. Nowadays, most beggars along the street everywhere are pretenders and new deceptions emerge from time to time. Human kindness is been sapped. However, we may view the appearance of new deceptions as evidence that people have more kindness to help others in trouble rather than distrust and indifference for others. One person's strength may be insignificant but he can influence someone around him. In this way, more and more people will join the team and the team of public welfare will be much stronger and able to make our society more beautiful and harmonious. We should not give up helping someone who really has difficulties because deceit exists in our society. Only when you bear your aspirations in mind can you achieve your goal.

Be kind to others and you will also deserve others' kindness in return.

We will surely meet various kinds of persons and fresh incidents in life when we move forward. As Professor Yu says, we need to measure with the feet, listen with the ears, watch with the eyes, and experience by the heart. As contemporary youth, we are not supposed to understand the world with prejudice. Instead, practice paves the way to true knowledge, on which we may meet difficulties of any kind. However, it is these encounters that make life colorful and meaningful to our growth.

Team members: Gao Mengting, Shan Jiaoqiao, Jia Yating

钱旭利：心向善——不为"慈善"而慈善

Qian Xuli: Benevolence—Human Nature, Not for Fame

钱旭利，宁波鄞州区人大代表，宁波盛光包装印刷有限公司总经理，曾任鄞州区慈善总会副会长。2008 年个人向汶川地震捐款 20 万元。2010 年斥资 1000 万元创立安百利慈善扶贫基金会，荣获第二届宁波慈善个人奖。

Qian Xuli, the general manager of Ningbo Shengguang Packaging and Printing Co., Ltd., was once elected as a deputy to the People's Congress in Yinzhou District, Ningbo City for her care and contributions to the whole society. For the same reason, she also served as vice chairman of the Charity Society of Yinzhou District. In 2008, she personally donated 200,000 yuan to victims of the earthquake in Wenchuan, Sichuan in China. In 2010, she established the Ann Bailey Charity Foundation with a total of 10 million yuan for the poor. Therefore, the second Ningbo Personal Charity Award was given to her for her contributions.

心向善——不为"慈善"而慈善

口述：钱旭利
整理：贺　芸
指导教师：阮　征

引 子

真知即所以为行，不行不足谓之知。

——王阳明

海外中国传统思想文化认知与传播

我初中毕业后就去澳大利亚求学，一去就是七年。当初选择去澳大利亚求学是因为澳大利亚是一个移民国家，对于各种文化都秉持开放的态度。一个国家的文化受欢迎程度是与其国家实力成正比的。同时，国家文化的推广也能体现一个国家历史、文化、文明层面的软实力。中华文化作为世界公认的四大古文明之一，对于西方人士一直具有神秘的吸引力。不过在宣传、理解上，东西方还需做进一步交流。比如，我们把儒家道家思想归结为哲学，而西方人都普遍认为，儒家是宗教，一般都称为儒教。从影响力和发展历史上看，儒学贯穿着整个中国社会历史发展进程。虽然王阳明的心学也属于儒家学说，但是心学起步较晚，影响力有限。在科举取士的环境下，渐渐研究儒学的人少了。而王阳明融汇了"儒释道"三家的思想，又提出"知行合一"的理念。"知"是件很容易的事情，具体要恪守执行却不是每一个人能做到的。

我觉得阳明学本身内容就具有深度。要学习阳明学，如果没有朱程理学、儒学、道家思想这些传统文化底蕴作为基础，在理解上也是很难的。

如果站在推广的角度上，我觉得受众目标首先要明确。阳明学适合有一定阅历、有一定知识的精英阶层。在学习阳明学后，就能把理论和过往经历结合在一起分析，得出体会"知行合一"。所以，在推广方式上可能需要更精准地抓取目标，培养第一批种子会员，然后通过种子会员形成传播。大学生其实就是非常好的种子群体。

慈善在生活的点点滴滴

青春期时，很多同龄人都热衷于追星，而我的偶像从来都只有一个，我的父亲。从小我就对自己要求很高，自己给自己施加压力，凡事力争第一。我父亲一直是我的榜样，他的言行举止就是我们家最好的家训。比如在工作中，他总是与人为善，常说："人胜我，勿生嫉妒。人弱我，勿生鄙吝。"而父亲总是支持着我，心疼着我，父亲告诉我万事要慢慢来。我在2006年学成归国，在父亲的公司做他的助手。父亲凡事都是亲力亲为，坚持着"走动管理"并且十分关心员工儿女的教育。父亲坚持从小事做起，2015年开工的金磐楼盘，刷墙体用了二十一道工序。当我问起这些努力是否能被顾客看见时，父亲告诉我为人有道，为商也应有商道。所以我和父亲在带领企业高速稳健发展的同时，还对社会公益事业倾注了巨大的热忱，"责任、爱心和奉献"是我的人生追求和盛光企业文化的重要内涵。

我一直耳濡目染，所以在我刚开始接触慈善时，并不为外界所谓的"慈善"或者任何褒扬的头衔，只是有需要帮助的人出现在我生活中，我会力所能及地提供帮助。我做事从来都是由心出发，当初以1000万元成立基金会，到现在已经投入了近6000万元了。

此外，当我在我家小区看到有些小宝宝因为湿疹而难受时，我都会邀请他们的父母把宝宝带到我们公司来接受免费治疗。当然也会有被误解的时候，有些人认为我是为了赚钱，有些人觉得我是在做推销。不管怎样，宝宝治愈后，他们的家人会露出幸福的微笑，我也感同身受。在参与"心灵海"活动时，有一个"1对1"助学活动，起初我资助了一个孩子，到后来十几个孩子我都资助了。我觉得能够帮到孩子学习，帮他们实现梦想是一件非常温暖的事情。我曾收到过一个我资助的四川男孩写的感谢信，在字里行间，我能感受到满溢的兴奋和感激之情，我会告诉自己做的一切都是值得。

采访钱旭利

知行合一，自我探索

我了解王阳明是从明朝历史开始的，后续主要通过钱穆先生的《阳明学述要》进行了一次扫盲。我个人认为每个人都应该看一些关于哲理的书，我们看哲理，学习哲理，就是为了找寻这个世界上的真理。哲学上的三大问题"我从哪里来""我要到哪里去""我是谁"，其实就是一个自我认识、自我成就的问题。当一个人明白自己要成为一个什么样的人，对于社会、对于国家，甚至对于人类、对于自然，该去做什么，怎么去做，那他的人生就不会虚度，也不会因为各种阻力各种困难而放弃。这样的人生就变得有目标、有使命，最后变得有价值，也就是我们常说的自我实现。

我觉得阳明学的本质是提倡理论与实践相结合。我党提出的"实践是检验真理的惟一标准"，我个人认为与"知行合一"的本意是一样的。

向钱旭利赠书

阳明先生提出的"致良知"，其实就是让我们每个人从自己内心深处去寻找"理"。"理"在于人的内心，不在于外部环境对于你的要求。在当下社会，这点有非常实际的意义。比如食品生产安全，我是一个企业家，我关心自己生产的产品质量是否安全可靠，是否让客户用得放心、安全。我认为，国家的标准是一个最低标准。你是选择要求自己企业以高标准生产，把消费者当自己家人一样让他们用得放心，还是追求利润，得过且过？这都取决于你内心的"理"。

王阳明先生曾经说过，心外无理，心外无物，天下一切都在你心中，受你控制。我是认同这种观点的。俗话说，赠人玫瑰手有余香。心中秉持一种"善理"，你看到的社会就都是善的。我们做一些回馈社会的事，出发点就是从内心觉得每个人都献出一份安心，那这个社会就会充满爱，就会更和谐。

我热爱读书，我把书分为几类。看历史书就好像在看社会案例，我们现在在社会上的交往过程中遇到的麻烦，都可以在历史案例中寻找到解决办法或吸取教训。看专业知识类的数据，主要是考虑工作上的应用，学习的是方法论，使用中一定要切记不能生搬硬套，要根据具体情况具体分析。还有名人传记、经典小说，主要是以陶冶个人情操为主。我希望自己成为一个对社会、对国家有用的人，并时时用这个想法来激励自己。

钱旭利女士与团队成员合影

我觉得在当下社会环境中，我们国人的物质水平已经很高了。古语说"仓廪实而知礼节，衣食足而知荣辱"，接下来对精神层面的需求会变得越来越多，像《百家讲坛》这类栏目的热播，就说明人们对于精神食粮有多饥渴。我觉得，随着大众对中国传统文化的学习的深入，他们的反思就会越来越多，学得越深就会对知识越加渴望。我认为阳明学是有一定深度的东方哲学，随着国学基础的提升，大家接触阳明学的可能性就会更大。在未来，我一定还会秉持"路漫漫其修远兮，吾将上下而求索"的精神。探索求知，就是抱着一颗对学术谦卑、对知识敬重、对真理渴求、对自我反思的心，不断前行、不断践行的过程。

一生低首拜阳明。我觉得，看一个人是不是"阳明青年"，要看其心，更要看其行。你觉得我是吗？

Benevolence—Human Nature, Not for Fame

Narrator: Qian Xuli

Compiled by: He Yun

Supervised by: Ruan Zheng

Knowledge is what constitutes action and unless it is acted on, it cannot be called knowledge.

—Wang Yangming

Awareness and Transmission of Chinese Traditional Ideology and Culture Overseas

I have been in Australia for seven years to pursue my study after my graduation from junior middle school. I chose to study in Australia because I thought Australia is a nation of immigrants, open to a diversity of cultures. The popularity of a nation's culture is proportional to its national strength. Meanwhile, promotion of a national culture also reflects a nation's soft power in history, culture and civilization. Chinese culture, as one of the four great ancient civilizations in the world, appeals to Westerners with its mystery. However, something more has to be done for further understanding and exchanges between the East and the West. For example, we take Taoism and Confucianism as a philosophical outlook, while people in the West generally regard Confucianism as a kind of religion. Regarding influence and historical development, Confucianism has been largely presented throughout the whole process of China's social development. Wang Yangming's Philosophy of Mind also belongs to Confucianism, but the Philosophy of Mind started late and exerted an impact to a limited degree. In the context of the imperial examination system in Yangming's era, the number of researchers in Confucianism was decreasing. However, integrating Taoism, Buddhism and Confucianism, Wang Yangming came up with the concept of "the unity of knowledge and action". Comparatively speaking, it is much easier to understand things, while complying with the knowledge-in-action is hard.

In my opinion, Wang Yangming's philosophy itself is profound and difficult to understand if there is no knowledge about the traditional cultures such as Neo-Confucianism, Confucianism and Taoism as the basis before learning Wang Yangming's philosophy.

242

In terms of promotion, I think the right target audience is very critical. The philosophy of Wang Yangming is better understood by those elites who have a certain experience and certain knowledge. When learning about the philosophy of Wang Yangming, they can combine the theories with their past experience in order to realize "the unity of knowledge and action". Therefore, better promotion may start with the right target audience, who might spread the thoughts as seeded members. College students are actually very good seeds.

Charity Is Anytime Anywhere

Unlike other peers who love famous stars as their idols, my hero since my teenage years has always been my father, my only hero. I was always self-disciplined and put pressure on myself by setting high goals for myself, and always striving for the first place. My father has always been my role model and his demeanor set the values for the whole family. At work, he is always kind to others and often says, "I'm neither jealous of whoever is better than me nor stingy to whoever is weaker than me." For me, my father would never hesitate to give his support and love. My father taught me to be patient for everything takes time. When I returned back after my study in Australia in 2006, I worked as my father's assistant in his company. This is when I came to know him better. My father sticks to hands-on leadership and manages the company by walking around among the staff. He is also very much concerned with the educational situation of his staff members' children. He sticks to his strict standards in every detail at work and in life. Buildings of the Gold Pan Estate started in 2015 have been painted under the strict supervision with 21 painting procedures, which was really complex and consuming. When I doubted whether those efforts could be appreciated by customers, my father told me that principles and disciplines for a social human were also applicable to commercial businesses. My father and I devote great enthusiasm to public welfare besides our efforts for the rapid and steady development of enterprises. "Responsibility, Love and Dedication" is the essence of my life and the core of Shengguang corporate culture.

Influenced by my family, when I first got involved in charity, I was not one to chase after titles or compliments. As long as I came across someone in need of help, I would do my best. I do all this from the bottom of my heart. Up to now, I have put nearly 60 million yuan into the charity foundation established with 10 million yuan at the very beginning.

Seeing some babies in my neighborhood who have suffered baby eczema, I would invite them to get free treatment in our company. Sometimes my offer of help would be misunderstood as making money or promoting sales. Regardless, I feel satisfied because the babies were finally cured and they smiled. In a charitable activity named "Sea of Good Heart", I financed one child to attend school and later more than ten other children. I feel warmth in my heart when I see I can do something to help children realize their dreams. I have even received a thank-you letter from one boy I financed in Sichuan, and I could feel his excitement and gratitude from the lines. This also tells me that everything I do is worthwhile.

To Explore with "the Unity of Knowledge and Action"

The first time I got to know about Wang Yangming was when I read the history of the Ming Dynasty. Later, I read more about him in *A Survey of the Philosophy of Wang Yangming* by Qianmu. In my view, everyone should read some books on philosophy which help us learn the truth of the world. The three typical philosophical questions—"where I come from", "where I am going" and "who I am"—are actually questions about self-awareness and self-growth. If a person is clear about whom he wants to be, then he knows what to do and how to do it for society, the country and even for human beings and for nature. Surely, he would neither waste his life time nor give up because of various difficulties. Such a kind of life with clear missions and goals is proved to be valuable experience of self-realization.

In my opinion, the essence of the philosophy of Wang Yangming is the combination of theory and practice. I believe our Party's claim that "practice is the sole criterion for truth" means the same as "the unity of knowledge and action".

Wang Yangming's "realizing conscientious wisdom" actually means looking for principles in one's inner mind out of one's own choice rather than by demand of the external environment, which is of practical significance in the present society. Taking food safety for instance, as an entrepreneur, I am most concerned with whether the quality of our own products is safe and reliable enough to satisfy my customers. In my view, the state standards are the lowest standards; while whether we are going to pursue a higher level of production for consumers or to make profit at the lowest cost, all depends on our own principle.

Wang Yangming says that everything in the universe is in one's mind and under human control. This is what I agree with. Besides, the old saying goes that presenting a rose to others, the hand has a lingering fragrance. If we uphold the principle of a good heart in mind, the world is also good to us. We promote activities to give back to

244

society from the bottom of the heart with the hope that society is more harmonious and filled with love if everyone gives his bit of love to society.

I love reading different kinds of books. I read history books to learn about social cases so that I can find solutions or learn from the historical cases when we encounter troubles in society. Theories from professional books are to be applied to work practice. The essence of methodology in these books is expected to be adapted to specific situations. I read biographies and classic literature in an attempt to cultivate my sentiments. Frequently I feel motivated by the passion to be useful to society and the state.

As the saying goes, "Well fed, well bred." I think people in our country now have improved a lot in terms of material life, so the spiritual needs to become more and more significant, which is obvious with the popularity of cultural programs such as *Lecture Room*. I believe that with the further study of our traditional Chinese culture, people reflect more on their life. The more they reflect, the more ignorance they realize and the more knowledge they feel thirsty for. The philosophy of Wang Yangming is a profound oriental philosophy. With the promotion of traditional Chinese culture, people will be more frequently exposed to the philosophy of Wang Yangming. It holds true for me even in the future that "The way ahead is long; I see no ending, yet high and low I will search with my will unbending." Exploration of knowledge is to keep practicing and reflecting on oneself with a humble and respectful heart for knowledge and the thirst for truth.

I would devote myself to learning Wang Yangming's philosophy all my life. To judge whether a person is a practitioner of the philosophy of Wang Yangming, I think, we have to see both his mind and his actions. Do you think I am one of them?

上善若水

贺 芸

指导教师：阮 征

采访钱旭利女士前，我对采访这样一位成功的优秀女性是满怀期待又十分紧张的。而作为一个女大学生，我对钱旭利女士充满尊敬。此次"用声音叙事"的主题是探访阳明青年的践行者和传播者。在我眼里，钱旭利女士正是这样一位不折不扣的阳明文化的践行者。

耳濡目染

钱旭利女士初中毕业便远赴澳大利亚深造，一去就是整整七年时间。聊及为什么是澳大利亚时，钱女士说因为澳大利亚是一个移民国家，对于各种文化都秉持开放的态度，而且一个国家的文化受欢迎程度是与其国家实力成正比的。一个女生孤身在外的艰辛，没有经历过的人是不知道的。而正是对自己的严格要求成就了今天的钱女士。

在其他女生沉迷于追星，陶醉于各种偶像的魅力时，钱女士的偶像自始至终都是她的父亲。钱女士的父亲是个为商有道的企业家，从钱董的"走动式管理"以及凡事亲力亲为的管理中钱女士了解到了要与人为善，要"人胜我，勿生嫉妒；人弱我，勿生鄙吝"。而谈及母亲，钱女士所能想到的第一个词就是"善良"。母亲路边帮载人、助学服务员等等事迹都让钱女士记忆尤深。正是这样的耳濡目染才让钱女士走上了行善之路，走上了阳明文化的践行之路。

自我探索

在当下的社会环境中，我们国人的物质水平已经很高了。古语说"仓廪实而知礼节，衣食足而知荣辱"。现在正是国人寻求精神层面的需求的重要时期，人们对于精神食粮十分饥渴。你就会有一种感觉，大众对中国传统文化学习得越深入，他们的反思就越多，学得越深就越渴望知识。阳明学是有一定深度的东方哲学，随着国学基础的提升，大家接触阳明学的可能就会更大。在未来，我一定还会秉持"路漫漫其修远兮，吾将上下而求索"的精神。探索求知，就是抱着一颗对学术的谦卑、对知识的敬重、对真理的渴求、对自我的反思的心，不断前行，不断践行的过程。

作为当代大学生，我曾向钱女士发问："您认为我们大学生有哪些可以参与的慈善活动吗？"钱女士说，慈善在于生活的点点滴滴，将你自己心中的善意从小事中发散出去，久而久之，这样的小爱就会成为你的习惯。人不应该为了虚无的头衔去做事，也不用为了让别人知道自己所做的善事而去做好事。只需由心而发，做自己力所能及的，去帮助自己遇到的需要帮助的人。人们常说赠人玫瑰，手有余香，从钱女士的言行中，我不难体会到她是位充满爱的女性。钱女士心之所向是善，所以她便这样去做了，这就是"知行合一"，这就是阳明精神。

在工作之余，钱女士热爱读书，沉浸于黄金屋中，偶尔烹茶自饮。其实人生在于不断地探索，我们过多地注重于向外探索，往往忘了自己本心最需要的是什么。人需要自我探索，不断审视自己，提升自己的精神世界，从而更好地为人处世。无论身处何地，官居何位，做事的出发点应为善，实践方法应是"知行合一"。

作为大学生，应该不停地学习充实自己，自我探索，与人为善。在学习与参悟阳明文化的过程中，能够学以致用，希望有一天自己能成为像钱旭利女士这样上善若水的人，能够做到"知行合一"，一生低首拜阳明。

团队成员：贺　芸　钱　浩　谢雨诗

The Best of Men Is Like Water

He Yun

Supervised by: Ruan Zheng

Before the interview, I was expectant and nervous about the coming meeting with such a successful young lady. On the other hand, as a young college girl, I admire her so much. The theme of this interview, as part of "Beyond the Voices", is "I'm a Young Practitioner of Yangming Philosophy". In my eyes, Qian Xuli is the very one.

The Family Influence

Ms Qian Xuli studied in Australia for seven years after graduation from junior high school. Australia was her choice because, in her opinion, it is a nation of immigrants, open to all kinds of culture. The popularity of a nation's culture is also proportional to a nation's strength. The hardship for a girl overseas alone is unknown to people who have no such experience. It is her strict self-discipline that makes her achievements today.

In her adolescence, she kept her father in mind as her idol when her peers were crazy for stars. Her father is an outstanding entrepreneur with his principles of walking-around management and hands-on leadership, from whom Ms Qian learned to be kind to everyone. Her father said, "I'm neither jealous of whoever is better than me nor stingy to whoever is weaker than me." When asked about her mother, Ms Qian said the best word to describe her mother is "a kind lady". Those incidents of her mother's offers of rides to strangers and financial assistance to servers are still fresh in Ms Qian's memory. It is such a positive family influence that leads Ms Qian to the charitable practice of being kind.

Her Self-Growth

As the saying goes, "Well fed, well bred." I think people in our country now have improved a lot in terms of material wellbeing, and thus the spiritual needs become more and more significant, which is obvious with the popularity of cultural programs such as *Lecture Room*. I believe with the further study of our traditional Chinese culture, people reflect more on their life. The more they reflect, the more ignorance they realize and the more knowledge they feel thirsty for. The philosophy of Wang Yangming is a profound oriental philosophy. With the promotion of traditional Chinese culture, people will more frequently be exposed to the philosophy of Wang Yangming. It holds true for me even in the future that "The way ahead is long; I see no ending, yet high and low I will search with my will unbending." Exploration of knowledge is keeping practicing and reflecting on oneself with a modest and respectful heart for knowledge and thirst for truth.

As a representative of contemporary college students, I asked Ms Qian, "Which charitable activities do you think our students are expected to participate in?" Ms Qian said that charity is anywhere, anytime in our daily life, like spreading the good will in everyday trifles. As time goes on, we may form a habit of doing others a favor. It is not advisable for people to make efforts merely for fame, nor for their popularity with others. Just do good from the bottom of your heart and do what you can do to help people who are in need. The old saying goes that presenting a rose to others, the hand has a lingering fragrance. From the words and deeds of Ms Qian, I can feel that she is a loving woman. She does good as she pursues in mind "the unity of knowledge and action", the spirit of Wang Yangming.

In her spare time, Ms Qian loves reading, addicted to "the golden room" and sometimes brews tea for herself. In fact, life is a process of constant exploration. We focus too much on exploring the outward and forget what is really needed for our true mind. People need to explore themselves and examine themselves constantly so as to enhance their spiritual world for a better lifestyle. Regardless of who we are in society, the starting point of our kind actions should be our good hearts, with which we practice "the unity of knowledge and action".

It also holds true for our college students that we should keep learning to fulfill ourselves and explore our good hearts by growing. In the course of studying the philosophy of Wang Yangming, we have to apply what we learn to our real life. I do hope that one day I will achieve my best like Ms Qian by realizing "the unity of knowledge and action" under the influence of the philosophy of Wang Yangming.

Team members: He Yun, Qian Hao, Xie Yushi

王文：公益——靠近灵魂，感悟幸福

Wang Wen: Doing Public Good Makes My Happy Soul

王文，1986 年 11 月生，毕业于江南大学。作为闻名公益圈的青年才俊，他在 2005 年上大学的时候就为失学的苗族少女奔波，发起春晖使者行动，推动大学生参与乡村建设。他曾说过，公益慈善不是简单的施舍救助，而是通过一种新的方式营造一种新的社会关系。王文现任灵山慈善基金会秘书长、上海灵青公益发展中心理事长。基金会以"弘扬慈善文化，净化世道人心"为理念，主要项目涵盖教育援助与改革、青年公益人才培养、社区治理与服务、公益发展支持等多个领域。

Wang Wen, born in November 1986, graduated from Jiangnan University. In 2005 when he himself was still a college student, he rushed about to raise financial support for girls of Miao nationality who were about to drop out of school. Very passionate and outstanding in public service, he launched a program named

"Messenger of Spring Light", aimed at promoting college students' participation in rural reconstruction in China. He explains that practicing charity is not just offering relief goods, but creating new social relations in a new way. He is currently the secretary-general of Lingshan Charity Foundation and the director of Shanghai Lingqing Philanthropy Development Center. The philosophy of the foundation is to spread the culture of charity and to purify souls of mankind with projects covering various fields such as education support and reform, young welfare personnel training, community management and service, and the support to the spread of public benefit.

公益——靠近灵魂，感悟幸福

口述：王　文
整理：盛晶艳
指导教师：阮　征

引　子

圣人之道，吾性自足。向之求理于事物者误也。

——王阳明

公益的初心：肩膀比脑袋更重要

我是在 2005 年进入大学的。其实一开始也没有特别强的目的性说一定要做公益，只是因为自己进入了大学，觉得需要做一些特别的事情来证明自己的存在感，这就包括所谓的公益实践。而当时在校园里也没有太多的人在做公益慈善，大部分人对公益慈善都是没有概念的，直到我们在学校里看到了一群大学生的调研报告，意外接触到了一群深山里面的孩子。这是一群来自贵州省贵定县某村的苗族女孩，她们大多数人十五六岁还在上小学，上完小学就会选择辍学。其中有一个女孩令人印象深刻，她已经找到了愿意资助她上学的人，可是她的父母在她很小的时候就给她订了娃娃亲，并且收取了聘礼礼金，所以女孩被迫放弃学业，这件事情对我的触动很大。当时我的目的很简单，就想走进大山，去帮助那群苗族女孩，去改变她们的命运。然后走着走着，我才发现其实我们把公益这件事情想得过分简单了。后来要真的走进大山的时候，我遇到了非常多的困难，首先我要找到这样一群愿意一起去的人，其次我需要设计出一系列的内容，例如我们要如何帮助她们。况且我当时还是一个刚进校园的大一学生，我的想法还被很多人嘲笑。其实我从大一提出这样的想法，到大一结束也没有成形。

但在大二的时候，我把这个想法付诸实践了。我找到了一群志同道合的人，但是我们还是得不到学校以及社会上的支持，我们变得很无奈。最后支撑我们下去的理由已经变得不是因为那群苗族女孩儿了，也不是我们的理想，而是自己吹出去的牛。因为当时把这个想法公之于世之后就有老师、学长不停地来询问，所以自己说出去的话，自己要把它完成。到后来，我们这群人就在学校各地找饮料瓶子、废弃的书本，一起收破烂儿筹资。就这样的一个过程，让我们这群原来认知有限的人成为很好的朋友。当然在我们走到大山里之后，和我们想象的不太一样，最吸引我们的也许是青山绿水以及那群苗族女孩儿。但事实上，她们和我们一样，都自然地生活在自己的生活中，不是一群苦巴巴的人在等着我们去拯救。我们能做的就是融入她们的生活去了解她们，所以说其实大学生要去做这样的公益，并不能对这些需要帮助的人造成多么多么大的影响，而更多的是我们自己一起去经历了特别多未知的挑战，一起想办法把挑战完成，一起去了解我们所经历的人、事以及整个中国的状况。所以我们当时就去了解当地的生活状况，然后晚上坐在一起聊这一天所经历的事情。而且因为我们是第一批走进她们村的大学生，我们到了某个寨门口，会有当地的老师校长来迎接我们，跟我们讨论说谁家的孩子需要怎样的帮助。就是这种被需求的感觉，成为激励我后来继续走下去的一个原因。让我感受到一个人的肩膀其实比脑袋更重要，因为只有有担当的人才有未来，聪明的人特别多，但我们更需要敢于为社会问题做出改变并且身体力行的人。

王文先生谈帮助苗族失学少女

公益的坚守——靠近灵魂，感悟幸福

在我进入大三之后，我其实一直在为我的考研而努力。在进入大四之后，我意外认识到了一位企业家，他创办了一家公司，希望我去当总经理，所以我在毕业前放弃了考研，去他的公司当了半年的总经理，并且继续着我的高校巡回演讲，希望能够呼吁更多的人去西部看看，去见识一下我们未知的世界，不仅为了帮助那些困苦地方的人们，也为了我们自己对这个社会有更加全面的认识。

当时也有越来越多的人开始关注公益慈善这个东西，我当时就想那为什么不把这么多人的力量聚集起来呢？一个人的力量也许微不足道，但一群人的力量肯定足够震撼人心，于是我就发起了一个春晖论坛，这个论坛现在也被称为是"青年达沃斯"。也因为这个论坛，华侨基金的总裁注意到了我，让我担任他们基金会的一个职位，并且当时被他们作为代表派出去与灵青慈善基金会接洽。我自然而然地又参加了灵青慈善基金会的工作。其实我认为这一切都是自然而然的事情，我也没有太大的目的性，我只是跟随着自己的心走，跟随着自己的感觉走。事实证明我是正确的，我现在做的这份工作给我带来了无比的幸福与成就感。很多人都会问我是怎么坚持下来的，还会坚持多久。其实在我眼中，这根本算不上坚持，只有在做让人难以忍受的事情的时候，才算坚持，而我是在享受我的事业，我乐在其中，因为做公益慈善也许是这个世界上最靠近灵魂、最具有幸福感的事情了。用阳明精神的"知行合一"来解释就是说，我是在不断实践，并且在实践中探索的最好例子。我从对公益不了解，到自己真正去做公益，并且在做公益慈善的过程中不断地完善这些项目，这就是"知行合一"。我认为"知行合一"就应该是在实践之后对其有一定的了解，再不断改变、不断升华的一个过程。

王文先生与团队成队合影

公益的传播——大国的担当

　　我最早接触到阳明文化是有一次去我国的宝岛台湾，大家都知道蒋介石先生是十分推崇阳明文化的，当地阳明山地区也有许多阳明先生的推崇者。我认为一种精神能够受到这么多人的推崇，肯定有它存在的意义，而"知行合一""致良知"

也是时常被社会上大部分人挂在嘴边的，说明它是有普遍意义的，然而从文化精神的角度对阳明文化进行传播还有许多的路要走。

　　我们在 2014 年开始在国外开展很多公益慈善项目，比如说给埃塞俄比亚的小孩儿供餐。并不是说为了显示我们中国现在有钱，而是为了说明中国在崛起、在发展的过程中，也是能够在国际上承担相应的大国责任的。而且其实国外落后地区不仅仅需要金钱上的支持，也有文化等一系列的需求。我们身体力行地做这些事情，在让他们中的一部分人解决温饱问题的同时，实现了阳明精神、阳明文化的海外传播。

　　我在做的这些事情让我感受到，人的一辈子如此短暂，也许只有短短几十年的时间，我在这么短的时间里能影响到其他人，甚至让他们有改变，这种成就感、幸福感真的什么都替代不了。这对我精神世界的影响真的非常大，也许我以后从事了政治或者是商业方面的工作，但这种潜移默化的行为是不会改变的，我还是会对这种社会问题时刻保持关注，我还是想用自己的力量去解决一些社会问题，无论通过什么方式。我的付出与收获一定是成正比的！我也希望未来能有越来越多的大学生多出去走走多出去感受一下这个社会，为这个社会做点什么，也收获些什么。希望你们让心灵去旅行，一直走在路上！

Doing Public Good Makes My Happy Soul

Narrator: Wang Wen

Compiled by: Sheng Jingyan

Supervised by: Ruan Zheng

The doctrine of the sage lies in the fact that my nature is sufficient. I was wrong in looking for principle in things and affairs.

—Wang Yangming

The Beginning of My Cause of Community Service: Broad Shoulders Are More Important than an Intelligent Mind

When I entered college in 2005, I did not have any idea about community service. I happened to get involved in working for the public good because I wanted to do something to prove my worth in the university. At that time, we students on campus showed little concern for the practice of public interest until we read about a survey report by a group of college students who brought a group of children from poor mountainous areas to our attention. They were a group of village girls of Miao nationality from Guizhou Province，most of whom couldn't continue their school education after finishing their primary school study at 15 years old because of their financial situation at home. Among them, there was a girl I was impressed with because she was lucky to have someone willing to financially support her study. While on the other hand, she was forced to give the chance up because it had been arranged by her parents that she marry a man early in her childhood. Such arranged marriages are very traditional and common in underdeveloped areas in China for families in poor financial situations because the appointments can bring them money in the form of bride dowries. This story really shocked me at the time and encouraged me to go into the mountains with the simple intention of helping the girls out of that kind of predestined life. However, when I really started my plan, I was faced with many difficulties. Firstly, I needed some volunteers to work with me as a team. Secondly, a plan with a series of activities was necessary to make it sustainable. Since I was a freshman, my proposal was laughed at by others. Actually, my proposal was not put into practice until the end of my first year at college.

In my second year, I started my practice with a group of like-minded friends. However, we still felt helpless for we failed to gain support from our college or society. To be frank, at that time, the reason why we insisted was no longer the hope of helping the Miao girls or our ambitious dreams, but it was about keeping a promise we had made public. Many teachers and seniors showed their interest and concern by asking about the project from time to time so that we couldn't give it up. Therefore, we raised money by collecting beverage bottles and discarded books on campus, during which period we became better bonded and stronger as a team. Actually, what we saw was different from our expectation when we finally met those girls. We were to a larger degree attracted to the beautiful scenery and the plain girls who were cheerful and active rather than desperate for our help. What we could do was getting to know more about them and their lives. It turned out that our action could not make a big difference to their lives in the long term. What was more important to us was that experiencing more was of great significance for the unknown difficulties and challenges we would face in the future. We could work together to learn more about the situation of people we met, the cases and even throughout the country. Therefore, we visited local families to ask more about their living conditions in the daytime and reviewed together each evening. Because we were the first group of college students to provide teaching assistance there, local teachers and even the headmaster came to meet us and introduced the detailed situation with great hospitality. We felt greatly satisfied because we were needed. It was this satisfaction that motivated us to go further along this road. It was also this experience that made me aware of the significance of broad shoulders rather than mere intelligence for a person's bright future. In other words, our social development needs people who are responsible and practical to effect change in our society.

Keep Going: My Happy Soul

When I was a junior student, I spent the whole year preparing for the postgraduate entrance exams. However, I changed my mind for I came across an entrepreneur who invited me to help manage his company. Finally, I gave up the chance to further my academic study and worked in his company for half a year. Meanwhile, I continued my tour of public speeches in many colleges and universities with the hope of attracting more and more participants to the development of poor rural areas in the West of China. At least, we could get to know more about real life there and we can also see a more complete picture of society.

At that time, more and more people began to pay close attention to public welfare. Learning this, I began to think about gathering these people's efforts together. An individual's power may not be influential enough, but our joint efforts may work wonders. Therefore, I started a bbs forum of public welfare named Spring Light, which is now also called as the "Youth Davos". It is also because of this forum that a CEO of an overseas Chinese Foundation contacted me and offered me a position in the foundation and I was on behalf of the foundation to consult with Shanghai Lingqing. That's why I am here now. Considering my experiences for these years, I believe I made these choices out of intuition and it proves that I made the right choices because my career has brought me happiness and a sense of achievement. Many people are amazed at my persistence in community service and wonder how long I can go on with it. I think they misunderstand me because people need a strong will to tolerate only when they do something boring. However, I enjoy my career because public welfare is the original pursuit in my heart, making me the happiest soul in the world. According to the philosophy of Wang Yangming, I think I am practicing "the unity of knowledge and action": I always practice based on what I have known to explore the unknown so that I can progress. What I do for the public now is the best lesson for me about public welfare and better project plans come to my mind. Therefore, my comprehension of "the unity of knowledge and action" is to progress through practice.

Spreading Over: Responsibility on Our Shoulders as a Powerful Nation

I first got acquainted with the philosophy of Wang Yangming because of a trip I made to Taiwan Island of China. As we all know, Mr. Chiang Kai-shek was an advocate of Wang Yangming. Besides, there are many others in the Yangming mountain area who support and spread Wang Yangming's philosophy. Therefore, I firmly believe that the thoughts that have received so much praise must be worthy of our learning and that "the unity of knowledge and action" and "realizing conscientious wisdom" known to the majority prove to have universal values. However, there is still a long way to go in order to spread the Yangming spirit.

Since 2014, we have started a lot of projects of public welfare all over the world. For example, we provided food to students in Ethiopia, not to prove our country's wealth and power but to undertake responsibility as a brother nation in this world. On the other hand, what the underdeveloped countries need is not only material supplies but also knowledge and culture. What we do for the public welfare is also the spreading of the philosophy of Wang Yangming overseas with personal practice.

By doing all this public good, I have realized the amazing value of my life with great satisfaction in that I can have a positive influence on other people and can even make them change for the better during my lifetime. The sense of achievement and happiness is one of the greatest things and is irreplaceable. Meanwhile, this has made a big difference to my spirits and my concern for public welfare never fades even if one day I am likely to be engaged in business or politics. No matter the means, I am glad to channel my personal efforts to solving social problems. I believe that my efforts pay off! I also call on more and more college students to participate in more social practice so that you know better about yourselves and the world as well. Best wishes to you on your way to a happy soul!

向善而行

盛晶艳

指导教师：阮　征

　　阳明文化是中华优秀传统文化的重要组成部分，是中华民族向心力、凝聚力的重要源泉。而宁波又是王阳明的故乡，王阳明先生"致良知"和"知行合一"的思想是宁波贡献给世界的价值观。2015年3月，习近平总书记在参加全国"两会"贵州代表团讨论时，提出了"王阳明的心学是中华传统文化中的精华"。我们作为王阳明的后代，为习近平总书记多次倡导"知行合一"而感到十分自豪，更应当主动承担起传播先贤思想的重大责任。所以，我们在2016年就投身到了探索阳明精神的传播者和实践者这一主题中。虽然我们对阳明精神的理解不够透彻，但我认为我们作为大学生能够在实践中感受阳明文化一定是对阳明文化最好的学习与传播。采访前我们也做了许多的准备工作，从寻找符合阳明精神的被采访者到后期的培训课程与采访大纲的撰写，都做出了充足的准备，并在暑假期间踏上了采访的征程！

　　这次采访过程中有几件事情对我的感触特别大。第一件是我们在采访前，王秘书长向我们询问了我们每个人对阳明精神的看法，同行的小伙伴也都说出了自己对于阳明精神的理解与看法，而我则表示阳明精神很深奥，不敢妄下定论。王秘书长也跟我们谈到了他对阳明精神的看法，他认为阳明精神是不断改变的，是先有的实践再有的认知，这一点让我们触动特别大。放在以往，我们都机械地认为"知行合一"一定是共同发生的，所以才称为"知行合一"。但是听了王秘书长的回答，我认为其实对阳明精神的看法并没有一个标准答案，每个人都可以有自己的想法，王秘书长的理解也是在他的实践中产生的，而我对回答这个问题的犹豫正是因为我怕自己的理解有误，说出来惹了笑话。但我回过头来想想，其实就算我自己的想法很浅显，也并不是错误的理解。因为我们作为大学生，没有很多的社会经验，在我们的认知世界里，阳明精神就只能够被理解到这个程度上。所以才说"知行合一"的重要性，我们只有不断地成长，不断地探索实践，才能对这个社会、对这个世界有更多的认知。以后要是有人问我对阳明精神的看法，我肯定当机立断说出心中所想！

　　还有就是王秘书长在大学期间走进大山寻找失学苗族女孩的事情令人印象深刻。就和他说的一样，在行动之前也许目的是帮助那些失学女孩能够重返校园，可是真的去实践之后发现事情并没有想象中的这么简单。获得更多的是对这个世界的重新看待，对社会问题的直面。大学生在这样的社会问题面前大多扮演的只是了解和宣传的角色，社会问题的解决还是要靠整个社会大家庭来一起想办法，所以更好地宣传这些社会问题，让大家都认识到这些问题才是大学生真正需要做的事情。而我们在做很多事情的时候也都是只知其所以然，以为自己想的就是真实的情况，实际上不然，很多时候因为我们社会经验的匮乏，我们看到的真的只是冰山一角。如果我们想了解这个世界的真实面貌，我们只有走出去，只有实践才能出真知。只有切身感受到了社会问题，我们才能更好地履行自己的社会责任，让更多的人知道问题所在并且一起努力解决它！其实这也符合阳明先生的"致良知"与"知行合一"，是在实践过程中对阳明先生理念的最好的传播。

在这次的采访行动中，王秘书长对阳明精神的了解、对公益慈善的看法都非常深入，这让我们很敬佩。作为大学生，我们就应该多做这样的社会实践，多接触形形色色的人与事，哪怕犯错，也有改正的机会，才会有深刻的认识。也许我们现在对阳明精神的了解只是最表层的，但只有当我们不断地去尝试，增长社会经验，我们才能不断地升级自己对阳明精神的理解，真正地理解阳明先生的良苦用心；才能更好地传播阳明文化，为阳明文化的传播做出自己的贡献！

团队成员：盛晶艳　章燕萍　高志海

Do for the Original Knowledge

Sheng Jingyan

Supervised by: Ruan Zheng

The philosophy of Wang Yangming is an important part of Chinese traditional culture, a source of cohesive force for our Chinese nation. Wang Yangming spread a philosophy of universal value—"realizing conscientious wisdom" and "the unity of knowledge and action"—from his hometown in Ningbo to the world. In March, 2015, when participating in the group discussions of the Guizhou delegation in the National People's Congress and Chinese People's Political Consultative Conference, General Secretary Xi Jinping pointed out that the philosophy of Wang Yangming is the essence of Chinese traditional culture. Proud of the philosophy which General Secretary Xi Jinping advocates, we, as the descendants, are supposed to take the initiative to assume responsibility for the spread of the great thought. Therefore, our theme for the year 2016, is the social practice of the spirit of Wang Yangming. What's more, our understanding of the philosophy of Wang Yangming can be improved and deepened through our interviews and social practice. Before the interviews, we have to do lots of preparation. All through this summer practice, we were surely prepared for every step, from identifying interviewees who spread and developed the philosophy of Wang Yangming, to participating in training classes and writing reports of interviews.

We have some impressive memories from the process. First of all, when we were asked about our understanding of the philosophy of Wang Yangming, I was hesitant, for I was afraid that I did not understand the ideas very well and so were other members. Mr. Wang, from his perspective of understanding, explained that how to comprehend the philosophy is as variable as a person's experiences and practices. I am convinced that it is reasonable to express our reflections on the philosophy in different stages based on our practices. Therefore, everyone has his own way to explain the philosophy of Wang Yangming. There is no absolute true or false way for it. Actually, we college students who are lacking in social experience should take this opportunity to learn from experienced practitioners like Wang Wen. When we don't have enough experience, we make mistakes and by correcting these mistakes we can be better armed with knowledge than before. This is maybe why "the unity of knowledge and action" is important. The next time I am asked about the philosophy of Wang Yangming, I will surely exchange my thoughts without any hesitation.

In addition, what impressed me much was his persistent effort to offer a helping hand to the Miao girls in the mountains. As he said, everything before the action was considered as pure and simple, while it turned out to be difficult in the real experience when he tried to help the Miao girls back to school. Beyond his expectation, he gained a more complete understanding of the society and new perceptions of the world. Facing many social problems, college students are supposed to raise social awareness and call on more social help for solutions. Most of the time, the truth is that college students take their partial perception of the world for granted, and it is something that can be improved. Therefore, if we want to see the true world, we must go out to practice so that we can come to know the social problems by ourselves and fulfill our responsibilities better. What's more, during our social practice, we are enabled to develop more contacts, to work together for a better social future. This is also in line with the philosophy of Wang Yangming and could be an effective approach to its spread in society.

To be honest, we extend our sincere admiration and respect to Mr. Wang Wen for his in-depth insights into the philosophy of Yangming and public welfare. At the same time, we are greatly encouraged by him to do more in social practice because meeting people in all walks of life provides different backgrounds and perspectives to know the world. Making mistakes is nothing horrible but is necessary for our students to learn from them. Mistakes and imperfection in practice help highlight the focus for improvement. This is the same with our understanding of the philosophy of Wang Yangming. So as college students, we may boost our spirits to spread the philosophy as far as we can because every bit of our effort is both a realization of the philosophy of Wang Yangming and the spread of it in society, as well as the benefits it offers to ourselves.

Team members: Sheng Jingyan, Zhang Yanping, Gao Zhihai

张建雷：益行阳明

Zhang Jianlei: Public Service with Goodwill

　　张建雷，宁波市鄞州区志愿者指导中心（区志愿者协会）、宁波市鄞州区青年志愿服务及公益性社会组织孵化中心主任。他曾于 2009 年、2013 年两度被评为宁波市志愿服务先进工作者。他的团队开发了众多志愿服务项目，如"快乐星期六"志愿服务日、"绿行"绿色出行古道环保项目、"一双红舞鞋"公益项目等。

Zhang Jianlei is the director of the Volunteers Guidance Center (Volunteers Association) in Yinzhou District, Ningbo as well as the director of the Youth Voluntary Service and Public Welfare Social Organization Incubation Center in Yinzhou District, Ningbo. He was awarded Ningbo Volunteer with Excellent Service in 2009 and 2013. His team developed a range of volunteer service projects, such as "Happy Saturday" as the volunteer service day, "Green Tours" to protect ancient roads from being destroyed, and "A Pair of Red Shoes" to enrich the free-time of children of migrant workers who come to help with the construction of Ningbo.

益行阳明

口述：张建雷
整理：单娇巧
指导教师：阮　征

引　子

知是行之始，行是知之成。

——王阳明

谈自我：正三观，暖暖心

我从学生时代起就开始从事志愿服务工作。我的志愿服务经历是从 2006 年 3 月开始的，这是我第一次自己策划、筹备、组织和实施的志愿活动，地点是在我们鄞州区的下应街道敬老院，服务的内容是亲情陪聊、打扫卫生等一些慰问活动。我在学校里面也是学生干部，这次活动充分体现了我的价值观，不管是同学、敬老院还是学校，都对这次活动非常认可，我的信心也逐步树立起来。

2008 年 8 月，我到了宁波鄞州区志愿者指导中心工作，成为一名全职的志愿工作者。当时，我的主要工作是筹备鄞州区志愿者协会的成立。

采访张建雷

到了 2009 年的 4 月，我和我的领导、同事们一起筹备正式成立志工委和志愿者协会，并投入了大量的时间、精力和感情做相关的准备工作。同时到了这一步，我觉得自己从事公益的信念也更加强烈。当时的想法也很简单，就是为了帮助更多需要帮助的人。

接着我继续投入到工作中，2012 年成立鄞州区志愿者协会和青年志愿服务及公益性社会组织孵化中心，这些都是由我的领导和自己一手努力推动发展的。

2014 年 4 月，我和朋友们创建了鄞州区梦想公益发展中心，以自己的小团体去开展一些更有意义的公益活动。

如今想来我为什么要从事公益行业，原因有三个。首先公益活动实现了自己的正确的人生观、世界观和价值观；其次，每一个梦想都有前行的力量，公益是我为之坚持不懈的事业；最后，生活在有爱的圈子里，让自己的生活充满爱，让自己的生活更有意义。

谈阳明：知行合一

如今，公益事业蓬勃发展，就我在工作中接触到的人来说，经常从事志愿公益服务的有三大类人群，他们分别是成功人士、社区志愿者和高校大学生。成功人士包括企业家、政府人员、社会爱心人士等。社区志愿者包括家庭主妇、青少年等。相比前两者，高校大学生服务周期比较短，对公益的奉献力度相对较弱。虽然部分人参加公益，只是为了完成任务，但同时他们对缓解社会矛盾有着积极作用，并且实现了个人价值。在我看来，有热心、有信心、有恒心的人才会把公益做得更好。

王阳明先生在心学体系中强调"知行合一、力行实践"的精神，他说："知是行的主意，行是知的功夫。知是行之始，行是知之成。"意思是说，道德是人行为的指导思想，按照道德的要求去行动是达到"良知"的功夫，在道德指导下产生的意念活动是行为的开始，符合道德规范要求的行为是"良知"的完成。我很赞同这句话，在公益活动中必须要坚持"知行合一"的精神。公益活动中贵在行，行大于知。只有行动，才有结果；有结果，才有感受；有感受，才能从浅知变成真知。同时在公益活动中，不能舍去"良知"。

谈公益：目标、使命和愿景

志愿服务工作是一项与时俱进的工作，当今志愿服务工作已经走向项目化、社会化、专业化和常态化的道路。项目化是指具有定时、定期、定量的特点，即活动的开展有专门人员负责，有特定的活动计划和活动目的，在特定的时间，由特定的人群，完成特定的活动。社会化是指公益活动的可持续发展，吸引广大群众的参与。专业化是指一群具有专业知识、专业设备的社会公益群体正逐渐崛起。

常态化是指志愿服务融入我们的日常生活，而不是"雷锋叔叔没户口，三月来了四月走"。

一个公益项目想要获得成功必须要有正确的公益三要素，即目标、使命和愿景。例如我们自己开展的"绿行计划"，这是一个环保志愿项目，是在古道上拾荒的活动。它的目标是建立民间环保草根志愿服务公益团队，通过志愿＋环保、生活＋自然、古道＋净滩的服务模式，实现全民志愿服务活动。它的使命是让生活回归自然。它的愿景是通过"绿行计划"志愿服务活动，呼吁全民参与，让人与自然和谐相处的意识深入人心。只有确定了目标、使命和愿景，一个公益项目才能顺利地开展，这就是"知是行的主意"。

此外，公益事业的长久发展离不开公益创业。经过多年发展，中国志愿服务事业已经达到了从搞活动到创事业的阶段。公益创业是志愿服务专业化、常态化发展的必然结果。公益创业可以培育公益组织，激发社会活力，对促进社会创新、引领公益风尚具有重要意义。

我觉得公益事业的发展还是要以项目为本，确定核心的目标、使命和愿景。通过采购志愿服务行动、承接企业社会责任、公益创投、政府支持等途径，获得人力、物力、财力的支持，开展多方合作模式。采购志愿服务行动实质是承接政府职能，比如五水共治、垃圾分类等。公益创投是近几年从国外传入我国的一个新名词，其运作模式是为初创期和中小型的公益组织提供"种子资金"。

我所在的鄞州区青年志愿服务及公益性社会组织孵化中心，为初创期的公益性社会组织和志愿服务团队提供关键性的支持。我们的目标是吹响公益集结号角，汇聚各类优质资源，为青年性公益组织打造有形、创新的支持平台。使命是充分调动社会各界参与青年性公益事业的积极性，为处于初创期的青年社会组织，尤其是青年公益性组织提供关键性支持。愿景是打造宁波城市文明地标，构建可持续发展的公益生态集群。

我们中心集公共咨询、重点培育、团队孵化、项目研发、成果展示、综合服务等六大功能，通过律师、会计师等五大专业团队为初创期公益性社会组织和志愿服务团队提供优质服务，并以科学化管理模式，对入孵组织以及团队进行孵化培育。

在公益的宣传上，我们协会工作以大力弘扬团结友爱互助的精神为核心要素，让更多的人认可和参与志愿服务。此外，我们每年3月举办一系列大型志愿活动，搭建平台，弘扬公益。对于孵化中心里的公益组织，我们借助孵化中心品牌形象形成"打包式"宣传，提升孵化团队及项目品牌的影响力。

谈未来

最后，我认为，不管是我们从事志愿工作的专职人员还是志愿者都应该始终保持热心、恒心、信心，去奉献自己的爱心，做到阳明先生的"致良知"。此外，学历、身份、地位在这些领域里不是最重要的。态度决定一切，你可以慢慢培养经验。

张建雷与采访团队成员合影

在未来公益的道路上，我会在志愿活动中坚持力行"知行合一"的理念，益行阳明，积极发扬社会主义核心价值观，将公益事业发展地更好。在自身方面，需要不断加强专业水平。此外，我将坚持项目为本，抱团取暖，集约各个资源，开展特色模式的公益项目。

Public Service with Goodwill

Narrator: Zhang Jianlei

Compiled by: Shan Jiaoqiao

Supervised by: Ruan Zheng

Knowledge is the direction for action and action is the effort of knowledge.

—Wang Yangming

About Self: Positive Views and a Warm Heart

I began my volunteer service when I was a student in March 2006. It was the first volunteer activity in which I myself oversaw all steps from planning, preparation and organization, to the final practice. Volunteers were organized for the nursing home in Xiaying Street, Yinzhou District, accompanying the senior citizens there by chatting with them and cleaning their rooms etc. As a student leader in school, my views on value were fully reflected in my action, which was spoken highly of not only by the nursing home but also by my schoolmates and teachers. Therefore, my confidence in public service has been boosted.

In August 2008, I was employed in the Volunteers Guidance Center in Yinzhou District, Ningbo as a full-time member of staff. My main task at the time was to prepare for the establishment of the Volunteers Association in Yinzhou District.

Until April 2009, my seniors, colleagues and I channeled our joint efforts and a great deal of time into the formal procedures to establish the working committee and volunteers association. After these experiences, I felt a strong belief in public welfare with a simple good will to help more people in need.

With persistent efforts in public welfare all through these years, in 2012, we succeeded in establishing the Volunteers Association and the Youth Voluntary Service and Public Welfare Social Organization Incubation Center in Yinzhou District.

In April 2014, my friends and I established the Public Service Dream Center in Yinzhou District, which helped carry out some more meaningful activities.

In my opinion, the following three reasons account for why I engage in public welfare. Firstly, public welfare activities help me achieve my world view and my sense of worth. Secondly, every dream is like an engine to help move forward and public welfare is my dream, the cause of my own perseverance. Finally, engaging in public welfare is living with love around, which will make your life shine with love and meaning.

About Wang Yangming: "The Unity of Knowledge and Action"

Nowadays, public welfare is flourishing. As far as I know, there are three major groups of people who are engaged in voluntary service: successful career people, community volunteers and college students. Successful people include entrepreneurs, government officials, caring public figures etc. Community volunteers are usually housewives and teenagers. Comparatively speaking, college students' service lasts for a relatively short period. Moreover, their dedication to public service is weaker. Although some people participate in public welfare to complete some assigned tasks, they play a positive role in alleviating social problems and also realize their value to some extent. In my opinion, people with enthusiasm, confidence and perseverance will do better in public welfare.

Wang Yangming stressed "the unity of knowledge and action" in his philosophy. In his opinion, the original knowledge guides people's action, while action promotes a higher level of conscience. Knowledge starts one's action while action reviews one's knowledge. I quite agree with this point. In public welfare activities, we must adhere to the spirit of "the unity of knowledge and action". To express one's original knowledge in action is critical in public welfare because only practical action brings out achievements. With practice we can feel pros and cons, and thus these judgments can help turn our rudimentary knowledge into genuine knowledge. It is most fundamental that we do not drive away from the original knowledge while participating in public welfare activities.

About Public Welfare: Goal, Mission and Vision

Volunteer service work is changing with the times and thus it has been on the way of project organization, socialization, professionalization and normalization. Project organization means quantified organization at a regular time periodically. That is, with a systematic and comprehensive plan, activities will be carried out by professional personnel for a specific purpose each time at a set time targeted at a specific group of people. Socialization refers to the sustainable development of the public welfare activities aiming to attract participation of the masses. Professionalization means that facilitated service groups with professional knowledge and training are gradually rising.

Normalization refers to the voluntary service integrated into our daily lives rather than concentrated in a short period of time along a year, such as March each year in China, which is publicized as Leifeng Month in order to call on people's care for others in need of help.

A successful public welfare project is supposed to have three elements: goal, mission and vision. Taking our project Green Tours as an example, volunteers are organized to pick up waste along ancient roads as an environmental protection project. Its goal is to build a folk environmental protection volunteer service team, which aims at public service in a mode of voluntary environmental protection and of natural life with clean ancient roads and coasts. Its mission is to help human life return to nature. Its vision is an involvement of the public community under the influence of the Green Tours program and the increasing awareness of harmony between man and nature. Only with clear and firm objectives, mission and vision can a public project be successfully carried out, which is known as the original knowledge guiding our action.

In addition, public welfare entrepreneurship is also critical to the long-term development of public welfare. After years of development, the voluntary service in China has been transformed from simple service activities to entrepreneurship development, which is the inevitable consequence of professionalization and normalization of public service. Public welfare entrepreneurship can foster public welfare organizations, stimulate the vitality of social community, which is of great significance to promote social innovation and to advance public welfare.

I think that the development of public welfare should be based on specific projects with determined core objectives, mission and vision. By making public service deals, undertaking corporate social responsibility, venture philanthropy and governmental support, we have gained human, material and financial resources to carry out multi-cooperation. Making public service deals is actually undertaking government functions, such as water treatment and garbage classification in Ningbo. Venture capital is a new term introduced into China in the past few years, which means seed funding for the start-up period of the small- and medium-sized public welfare organizations.

The organization where I work, the Youth Voluntary Service and Public Welfare Social Organization Incubation Center in Yinzhou District, provides essential support to the start-up of the public welfare social organizations and volunteer service teams. Our goal is to gather all the excellent resources for the youth public welfare organizations in order to establish tangible, innovative and supportive platforms. Our mission is to boost the passion of the community to participate in the youth public welfare to the best degree so that the community may provide key support in the early stage of youth social organizations, especially of young public welfare organizations. Our vision is to realize the sustainable development of the public welfare ecological cluster, which can be viewed as a landmark of Ningbo civilization development.

Our center serves functions such as consulting, team cultivating, organization incubation, project research and development, achievement display, comprehensive services by five professional teams like lawyers, accountants and so on. High-quality services with the scientific management mode for the public welfare organization and volunteer service team incubation are offered here.

In terms of publicity of public service, our center calls for more people to recognize and participate in voluntary service on the basis of solidarity and mutual assistance as the core elements. In addition, we hold a series of large-scale voluntary activities each year in March to build a platform to promote public welfare. The incubation center develops a "packaged" publicity to enhance the incubator team and project brand influence.

About the Future

Finally, I think that whether we do volunteer work full-time or part-time, we should always maintain enthusiasm, perseverance, confidence and thus benevolence and it is the way in which we realize what Wang Yangming refers to as the conscience. What's more, a person's education, identity, or status is not the most important thing for public service. Attitude decides the future and practice makes a person experienced.

In the future path of public service, I will stick to "the unity of knowledge and action", practice the philosophy of Wang Yangming, and thus actively promote the socialist core values in order to develop public welfare better. As for myself, I ought to keep strengthening my professional knowledge. In addition, I will go on developing projects of great meaning and features by integrating various resources.

公益与良知共舞——访张建雷有感

单娇巧

指导教师：阮　征

阳明文化是中华优秀传统文化的重要组成部分，是中华民族向心力、凝聚力的重要源泉。宁波是王阳明的故乡，王阳明先生"致良知"和"知行合一"的思想是宁波贡献给世界的价值观。本次"用声音叙事"活动主题为"我是阳明青年"，目的是寻找阳明文化的践行者和传播者。我很荣幸鄞州区志愿者指导中心、青年志愿服务及公益性社会组织孵化中心的主任张建雷老师接受了我的采访。

在去采访的路上我一直在思考公益家的办公室会是怎样的。进入张老师的办公室，我就被墙上的两幅书法所吸引——"创益人"和"宁静致远"。两幅书法字体浑圆、平实中寓有姿态，洋溢着深厚的文化内涵。我的思维像一只小船随着他思想的高度悠悠荡荡，时而停泊，时而前行。

采访中，张老师向我们谈了他对公益与阳明文化的看法。2006 年，从他第一次自己组织策划公益活动到 2008 年在区志愿者协会担任全职工作，再到如今，他和他的团队开发了许多志愿服务项目，展开过众多志愿服务工作，培养以目标、使命和愿景为要素的正确公益理念，让群众更好地参与公益，让志愿成为一种生活方式。

王阳明先生在心学体系中强调"知行合一、力行实践"的精神，他说："知是行的主意，行是知的功夫。知是行之始，行是知之成。"意思是说，道德是人行为的指导思想，按照道德的要求去行动是达到"良知"的功夫。在道德指导下产生的意念活动是行为的开始，符合道德规范要求的行为是"良知"的完成。王阳明先生认为，只有通过同步行动，才能获得知识，并拒绝以所有其他方式获得它。对他来说，获得它是没有办法只用知识的，因为他相信知识和行动是统一的。付诸行动之前已获得的任何知识，都是错觉或虚假的。我很赞同这句话，在公益活动中必须要坚持"知行合一"的精神。公益活动中行大于知。只有行动，才有结果；有结果，才有感受；有感受，才能从浅知变成真知。同时在公益活动中，不能舍去"良知"。他强调阳明的"知行合一"和"致良知"思想，对当代人的心灵塑造、人格培养也有非常重要的现实意义。知与行就是要求人心动时自然知善知恶，并依善而行。

"良知"思想是王阳明心学体系的理论核心。正如乌云虽然能遮住太阳，但并不能完全遮住太阳的光线，私欲习气也不能完全遮蔽良知本体的光辉。从私欲的乌云中透露出来的这一丝光辉，就是知是知非、知善知恶之心。是非之心、善恶之心是每个人都能感觉到的，即便一个十足的恶棍也会不时感觉到是非之心对他的谴责，这就是我们说的"良心"。

五百年前，心学宗师王阳明在龙场悟道，"圣人之道，吾性自足，向之求理于事物者误也"，世界是一个心的世界，一切从心开始。公益，是社会公众的福祉和利益，围绕大众的所需所求，尽展内心世界的纯真与舍给。

当你递给焦渴的路人一杯凉茶，公益就在你殷殷的双手上；当你帮助残疾人推动轮椅艰难上坡，公益就在你掌心微沁的汗水里；当你在敬老院里真诚地陪着孤寂的老人聊天解闷，公益就在你善良虔诚的亲情里。一杯凉茶、一滴汗水便能刻画一个动人的画面，物质往往充当了公益的媒介，但同时诠释了公益的感人内涵与人文情怀。公益传承演绎的往往是一个壮举，亦是一个很平凡的给予。彼此帮扶，相互跟进，既是公益范畴的细化内容，亦是公益新常态赋予的新内容。

公益事业是关乎人类福祉的事业，如何正确有效地组织和参与公益活动很重要。就像张老师所强调的益行阳明，知行合一，正确的公益理念和社会责任意识，这是"知"；乐于奉献，凝聚众人力量，这是"行"。每一个人，不管他的身份、地位、学历，只要他有热心、恒心和信心，他便能奉献自己的爱心。

与爱同行，公益事业离不开有着公益爱心的公益人。但愿在以习总书记倡导的新常态、新思路、新领域的公益文化体系中，国人与良知共舞，在善举中升华。

团队成员：盛晶艳　贺　芸　高梦婷　单娇巧

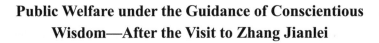

Public Welfare under the Guidance of Conscientious Wisdom—After the Visit to Zhang Jianlei

Shan Jiaoqiao

Supervised by: Ruan Zheng

The philosophy of Wang Yangming is an important part of Chinese traditional culture, a source of cohesive force for our Chinese nation. Wang Yangming's philosophy of universal value, "realizing conscientious wisdom" and "the unity of knowledge and action", is being spread from his hometown, Ningbo, to the world. The theme of this social practice of "Beyond the Voices" is "I'm a Young Practitioner of Yangming Philosophy". Its purpose is to seek out the practitioner and disseminator of Yangming culture. I was honored to interview Zhang Jianlei, the director of the Volunteers Guidance Center, the Youth Voluntary Service and Public Welfare Social Organization Incubation Center in Yinzhou District.

On the way to the interview, I was all the time anxious about what the public welfare volunteer's office would be like. Entering Mr. Zhang's office, I was attracted by the two calligraphy scrolls on the wall—"创益人" and "宁静致远". The two calligraphy scrolls fully reflect the strength, attitude and culture. My mind was like a small boat which berthed and moved forward with his flow of thoughts.

During the interview, Mr. Zhang shared with us his views on public welfare and Yangming culture. From 2006 when he first prepared, organized and put into effect a volunteer activity to 2008 when he went to the Volunteers Guidance Center in Yinzhou District to work as a full-time staff, till now, he and his team have launched a number of voluntary service projects, promoting the public welfare with goal, mission and vision as essential elements so that the social public welfare develops better and to be volunteers becomes a part of people's lives.

Wang Yangming stressed "the unity of knowledge and action" in his philosophy. In his opinion, the original knowledge guides people's action, while action promotes a higher level of conscience. Knowledge starts one's action while action reviews one's knowledge. Wang believed that knowledge is simultaneously acquired in action. For him, there was no way to use knowledge gained ahead of time because he believed that knowledge and action were unified as one. It is false that any theoretical knowledge is gained first and then put into action. I quite agree to this point. In public welfare activities, we must adhere to the spirit of "the unity of knowledge and action". To express one's original knowledge in action is critical in public welfare because only practical action brings out achievements. With practice we can feel pros and cons, and thus these judgments can help turn our rudimentary knowledge into genuine knowledge. It is most fundamental that we do not move away from the conscience while participating in public welfare activities. It also has very important realistic meaning to the contemporary people's mind and personality cultivation. Knowing and acting is asking people to tell what the good is from the evil and acting according to the good.

The conscience is the core of Wang Yangming's theory of an ideological system. Clouds can cover the sun, but they do not completely cover the rays of the sun. Likewise, desire also cannot cover the glory of conscience. The glory is the human original judgment of what is right and wrong, of what is good and evil. Everyone has this judgment including a villain who may feel the guilt against his behavior. This is what we refer to as the conscience.

Five hundred years ago, the master in the Philosophy of Mind, Wang Yangming attained enlightenment in Longchang. He believed that each person, in the process of becoming a saint, should turn to his own heart and mind for genuine knowledge without external demand. It is wrong to seek genuine knowledge from the outside world. The world is a mind world, where everything starts from the mind. Public welfare is social welfare and interests, while engaging in public welfare means meeting public needs and showing innocence and benevolence of the inner world.

When you are handing out a cup of tea to thirsty passers-by, public welfare is in your hands. When you are pushing the disabled uphill in a wheelchair, public welfare is the sweat in your palms. When you are sincerely accompanying the old at a nursing home, public welfare is in your kind words and sincere affection. Since either a cup of tea or a drop of sweat can portray a moving picture, material often acts as a medium of public welfare and as a window of the meaning and humanity of public welfare. Therefore, efforts for public welfare are both ordinary and extraordinary. Mutual help and follow-up contacts are now details of public welfare and also the new content of the present normalization.

Public welfare is the cause of human welfare, so it is very important to organize and participate in public welfare activities effectively. Just as Mr. Zhang stressed, in terms of "the unity of knowledge and action", the correct concept of public service and social responsibility is "knowledge", while willingness to sacrifice and enhance collective power is "action". Each person is able to devote his benevolence with enthusiasm, perseverance and confidence, regardless of his identity, status and education.

Public welfare is moving forward with love, with people full of benevolence. I hope under the guidance of General Secretary Xi Jinping in terms of the new normalization, new ideas and new fields in the public welfare culture system, we Chinese people do advance ourselves in kindness and in pursuit of genuine knowledge.

Team members: Sheng Jingyan, He Yun, Gao Mengting, Shan Jiaoqiao

后 记

Postscript

"知行合一"就是成就可能

"The Unity of Knowledge and Action" Makes It Possible

王洁心

Wang Jiexin

　　总说人生是无数段际遇的叠加，遇到一些人，经历一些事，然后再奔赴新的旅程。在匆匆来去的间隙，偶尔停下脚步去整理记忆的库存，我们会惊喜地发现那些还在散发着温度的片段构成了我们对生命意义的探询。我相信"用声音叙事"实践经历会在每位队员的成长记忆里闪烁着光芒，对于我而言，这更是一段妙不可言的奇遇。

　　因为2016—2017年度"用声音叙事"的调研主题是探访阳明文化的传承者和践行者，国内一位学术涵养深厚又德高望重的学者最早进入我们的视野，他就是吴光先生。吴光教授对包括阳明学在内的儒学、浙学不遗余力地挖掘、推广和实践，先后主持完成《王阳明全集》《刘宗周全集》《黄宗羲全集》《马一浮全集》的整理、编辑和点校工作，出版《黄老之学通论》《黄宗羲传》《儒家哲学片论》等著作。在阳明学思想传播领域，他先后主编《阳明学研究丛书》《阳明学研究》《阳明学综论》等丛书；实践中，早在20世纪，他就与冈田武彦等中日学者一起发起阳明行迹探索活动，并以学者的执着积极投入江西赣州大余县落星亭、浙江绍兴阳明墓的恢复和修缮工作。此外，在传播实践方面，除了身体力行地在国内外举办了百余场阳明学术讲座，他还对浙江、江西、贵州、广州等地的阳明学研究团队给以持续的学术指导和帮助。吴光先生的威望和学识得到国内外众多学者的高度认可，他倡导以"惟求其是"的精神探索阳明文化，主张挖掘阳明文化的现当代意义，是国内践行和传播阳明文化的一面旗帜。

我和吴光先生的相遇是由一个个"不可能完成的任务"构成的。我知道学术差距的"不可能",但是还是选择吴光老师作我的采访对象;我知道人情世故的"不可能",但还是接受了蔡亮老师要求挑战自我的任务。抛却一切不可能的想法,经过无数次兜转曲折,终于听到电话那头传来一个亲切的声音:"喂!你好,我是吴光。"就这样,奇迹真真切切地发生了。当吴光先生爽快地答应接受我们的采访时,我心中的感动和紧张多于惊喜。虽然蔡亮老师、王碧颖老师和我一起做了非常充分的准备,我还是担心生疏的沟通技巧和不全面的采访大纲会让吴光先生嫌弃和不悦。然而当我们见到吴光先生的时候,他的慈眉善目、温和敦厚彻底缓解了我和小组成员的焦虑。在采访过程中,吴光先生不厌其烦地解答我的问题,不断地为我们讲解阳明文化,给出传播阳明精神的宝贵建议,也尽可能为我这样一个非专业的学生提供专业性的帮助。令我更加意外的是,在采访的最后,教授将他珍藏的为数不多的阳明思想书籍赠予我们。在我心里,他不再是想象中一位孤傲自许、目无下尘的大家,而是一位"黑发积霜织日月,粉笔无言写春秋"的榜样和良师。此后的故事随之一切都显得那么自然,2016 年 12 月吴光先生接受邀请来访我校阳明学堂,并与师生一起共话阳明文化的传播和现当代意义,一段"知行合一"成就的阳明文化传播的佳话就此流传。

　　感谢"用声音叙事"实践中相识相知的每一个人,我们因阳明文化走到了一起,也因阳明文化而在彼此的心中留下难忘的回忆。"知行合一"的精神对于我已经不仅仅是将思想付诸实践,更是成就可能性的最佳路径,厚谊常存魂梦里,深恩永志我心中。

附 录
Appendix

第一章　科学精神

1. 君子之学，岂有心乎同异？惟其是而已。——摘自《王阳明全集》

Let Plato be your friend, and Aristotle, but more let your friend be Truth.（哈佛校训英文版）

2. 大人者，以天地万物为一体者也，其视天下如一家，中国犹一人焉。——摘自《传习录》

The great man regards Heaven, Earth, and the myriad things as one body. He regards the world as one family and the country as one person.（陈荣捷译）

3. 志不立，天下无可成之事。——摘自《传习录》

That nothing reaches completion is all an outcome of the fact that the determination has not been fixed. (Frederick Goodrich Henke)

4. 知行合一，明德亲民。

The unity of knowledge and action, the remolding of people with illustrious virtue.

5. 学术乃天下之公器。

Academia is the public skill for all the people.

6. 身之主宰便是心。

The master of the body is the heart.

7. 民之所好好之，民之所恶恶之，此之谓民之父母。

"Love what the people love and hate what the people hate" implies that the superior men are as parents to the people. (Frederick Goodrich Henke)

8. 知者行之始，行者知之成。

Knowledge is the beginning of the action, and action is the completion of knowledge.

9. 格物致知。

Study things to acquire knowledge.

第二章　工匠精神

1. 惟一是惟精主意，惟精是惟一功夫，非惟精之外复有惟一也。——摘自《传习录》

Singleness is the goal of refinement and refinement is the effort to achieve singleness. It is not that outside of refinement there is another thing called singleness. (陈荣捷译)

2. 虽百工技艺，未有不本于志者。——摘自《王阳明全集》

Though there are a hundred different professionals, there is not a single one but depends upon the determination. (Frederick Goodrich Henke)

3. 要得此米纯然洁白，便是惟一意。然非加舂簸筛拣惟精之工，则不能纯然洁白也。——摘自《传习录》

Singleness means having the rice absolutely pure and white. However, this state cannot be achieved without the work of refining, such as winnowing, sifting, and grinding. These are the work of refining, but their purpose is no more than to make rice absolutely pure and white, that is all. (陈荣捷译)

4. 知之真切笃实处即是行，行之明觉精察处即是知。——摘自《传习录》

When knowledge is genuine and sincere, practice is included; when practice is clear and minutely adjusted, knowledge is present. / Action can truly reflect knowledge, while observations in action reflect knowledge.

5. 身是菩提树，心如明镜台，时时勤拂拭，莫使惹尘埃。（神秀大师）

The body is a Bodhi tree, the mind a bright standing mirror. At all times polish it diligently, and let no dust alight.

6. 菩提本无树，明镜亦非台，本来无一物，何处惹尘埃。（慧能大师）

Bodhi is fundamentally without any tree, and the bright mirror is also not a stand. Fundamentally there is not a single thing, where could any dust be attracted?

7. 十年磨一剑。

It takes ten years to grind a sword.

8. 志不立，天下无可成之事。

People will never be successful unless they possess a strong will and firm resolution.

9. 良知在人心，良知即准则。

Conscience lies in people's heart and mind, and conscience is people's guideline.

10. 三天打鱼，两天晒网。

Go fishing for three days and dry the nets for two.

11. 此心光明，亦复何言？

Being conscientious the whole life, what else can I say?

第三章　企业家精神

1. 人须在事上磨，方能立得住，方能静亦定、动亦定。——摘自《传习录》

One must be trained and polished in the actual affairs of life. Only then can one stand firm and remain calm whether in activity or in tranquility. （陈荣捷译）

2. 尽心知性知天，是生知安行事。——摘自《传习录》

As to exerting one's mind to the utmost, knowing one's nature, and knowing Heaven, these are the acts of those who are born with such knowledge and practice it naturally and easily. （陈荣捷译）

3. 你看到满大街都是圣人，满大街的人看你也是圣人。——摘自《传习录》

In your view the people filling the street are all sages, but in their view, you are a sage, too. （陈荣捷译）

4. 人胸中各有个圣人，只自信不及，都自埋倒了。——摘自《传习录》

There is a sage in everyone. Only one has not enough self-confidence buries his own chance. （陈荣捷译）

5. 知交尽四海，万里有亲朋。

Make friends all over the world.

6. 人之初，性本善。

All people are born kind.

7. 我心光明，惟致良知。

My heart is righteous, and the only thing I need to do is to realize conscientious wisdom.

8. 得民心者得天下。

If you win all people's heart, then you win the whole world.

9. 吾心光明，亦复何言。

My heart is righteous, so I don't have to say anything anymore.

10. 吾心，良知也。光明，已致良知也。

My heart, means the inceptive insights of moral mind. Righteous, means he has already realized his conscientious wisdom.

11. 只在此心去人欲，存天理上用功便是。

The only thing we need to do is to remove selfish desires from our heart and keep justice.

12. 今人乍见孺子将入于井，皆有怵惕恻隐之心。

All people will show their sympathy when they suddenly see a child falling into a well.

13. 个个人心有仲尼。

All people have original good will.

14. 知是行之始，行是知之成。

Knowledge is the beginning of action, and action is the result of knowledge.

第四章　学人精神

1. 致吾心良知之天理于事事物物，则事事物物皆得其理矣。——摘自《传习录》

When the Principle of Nature in the innate knowledge of my mind is extended to all things, all things will attain their principle. （陈荣捷译）

2. 此心无私欲之蔽，即是天理。——摘自《传习录》

Now as selfish human desires are gradually removed, the mind will be increasingly harmonious with moral principles. （陈荣捷译）

3. 知者行之始，行者知之成：圣学只一个功夫，知行不可分作两事。——摘自《传习录》

Knowledge is the beginning of action and action is the completion of knowledge. Learning to be a sage involves only one effort. Knowledge and action should not be separated. （陈荣捷译）

4. 仁人者，正其谊不谋其利，明其道不计其功。——摘自《传习录》

The man of the highest virtue confines himself to what is right and proper, and does not plan for his own advantage; he exhibits the truth of the doctrine, and does not devise schemes for acquiring fame and merit. (Frederick Goodrich Henke)

5. 博学之，审问之，慎思之，明辨之，笃行之。——摘自《传习录》

Studying extensively, inquiring accurately, thinking carefully, sifting clearly, practicing earnestly. （陈荣捷译）

6. 良知之说，从百死千难中得来。

The theory of conscience comes from countless difficulties and sufferings.

7. 人人都有良知，人人都是圣人。

Everyone has conscience; everyone can be a saint.

8. 路漫漫其修远兮，吾将上下而求索。

The way stretches endlessly ahead. I shall search heaven and earth.

9. 圣人之道，吾性自足。

The principles of the sages lie in their self-satisfaction.

10. 心外无物，心外无理。

Nothing in the universe exists independent of the mind; no law is apart from the mind. (Frederick Goodrich Henke)

11. 心外无佛，即心是佛。

Buddha exists nowhere but in your heart.

12. 存天理，去人欲。

Keeping the natural law and abolishing the selfishness.

13. 饮食者，天理也；要求美味，人欲也。

Diet, heavenly principle; delicious food, human desire.

第五章　公益精神

1. 须先有根然后有枝叶，不是先寻了枝叶，然后去种根。——摘自《传习录》

There must first be roots before there can be leaves and branches. One does not seek to find leaves and branches and then cultivate the root. （陈荣捷译）

2. 真知即所以为行，不行不足谓之知。——摘自《传习录》

Knowledge is what constitutes action and unless it is acted on, it cannot be called knowledge. （陈荣捷译）

3. 圣人之道，吾性自足。向之求理于事物者误也。——摘自《传习录》

The doctrine of the sage lies in the fact that my nature is sufficient. I was wrong in looking for principle in things and affairs. (Frederick Goodrich Henke)

4. 三人行，必有我师。

We can always find something to learn from people who keep us company.

5. 不忘初心，方得始终。

Only when you bear your aspirations in mind can you achieve your goal.

6. 人胜我，勿生嫉妒。人弱我，勿生鄙吝。

I'm neither jealous of whoever is better than me nor stingy to whoever is weaker than me.

7. 心外无理，心外无物。

Everything in the universe is in one's mind and under human control.

8. 廪实而知礼节，衣食足而知荣辱。

Well fed, well bred.

9. 路漫漫其修远兮，吾将上下而求索。

The way ahead is long; I see no ending, yet high and low I will search with my will unbending.

10. 知是行的主意，行是知的功夫。知是行之始，行是知之成。

The original knowledge guides people's action, while action promotes a higher level of conscience.

图书在版编目（CIP）数据

我是阳明青年：汉英对照 / 蔡亮主编. —杭州：
浙江大学出版社，2019.6
（用声音叙事）
ISBN 978-7-308-18457-1

Ⅰ.①我… Ⅱ.①蔡… Ⅲ.①王守仁(1472—1528)—
哲学思想—研究—汉、英 Ⅳ.①B248.25

中国版本图书馆 CIP 数据核字(2018)第 170703 号

用声音叙事：我是阳明青年
主　编　蔡　亮

策划编辑	张　琛
责任编辑	诸葛勤
责任校对	董齐琪　杨利军
封面设计	周　灵
出版发行	浙江大学出版社
	（杭州市天目山路 148 号　邮政编码 310007）
	（网址：http://www.zjupress.com）
排　版	浙江时代出版服务有限公司
印　刷	浙江省良渚印刷厂
开　本	710mm×1000mm　1/16
印　张	18.5
字　数	429 千
版 印 次	2019 年 6 月第 1 版　2019 年 6 月第 1 次印刷
书　号	ISBN 978-7-308-18457-1
定　价	68.00 元